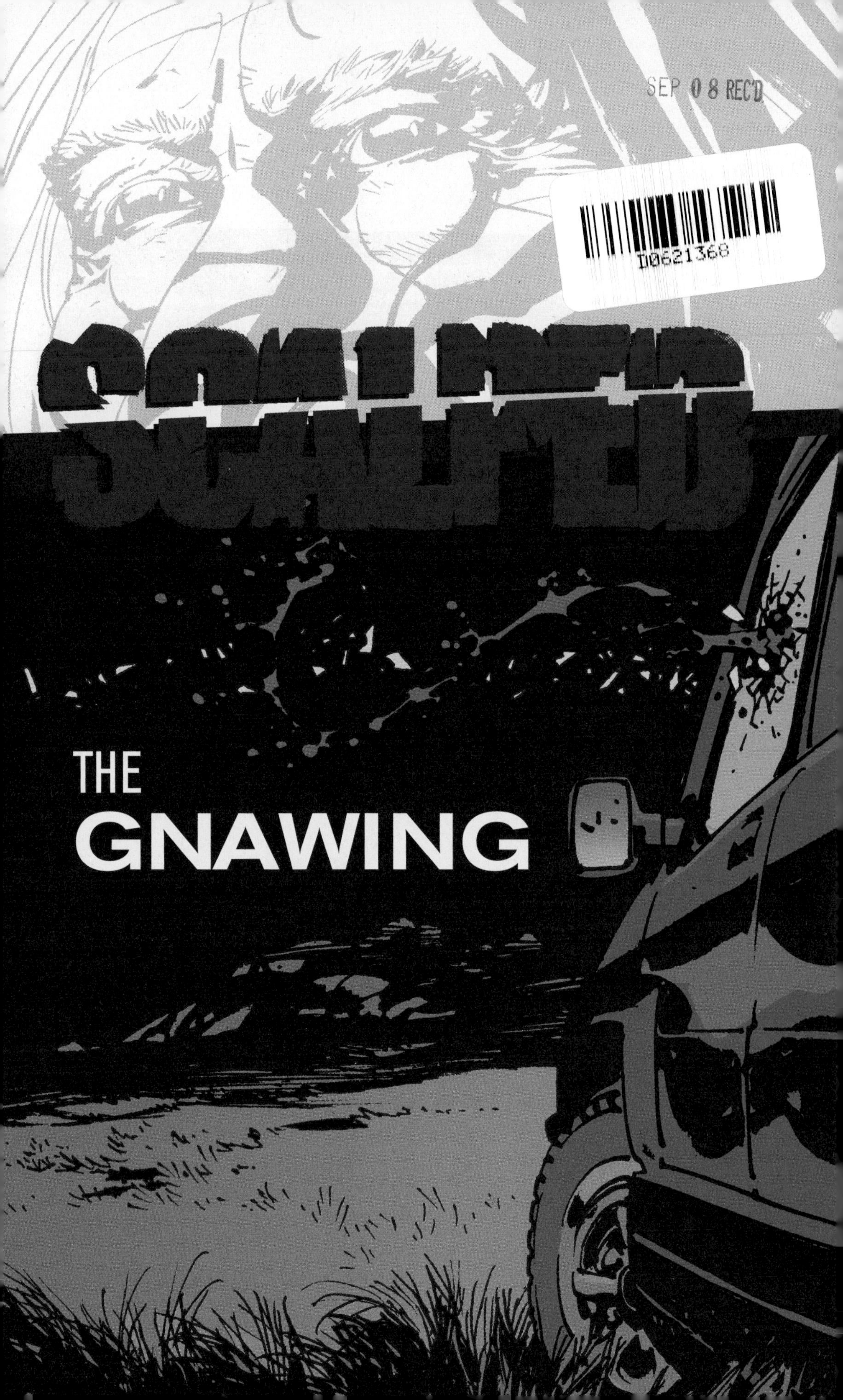
SCALPED
THE GNAWING

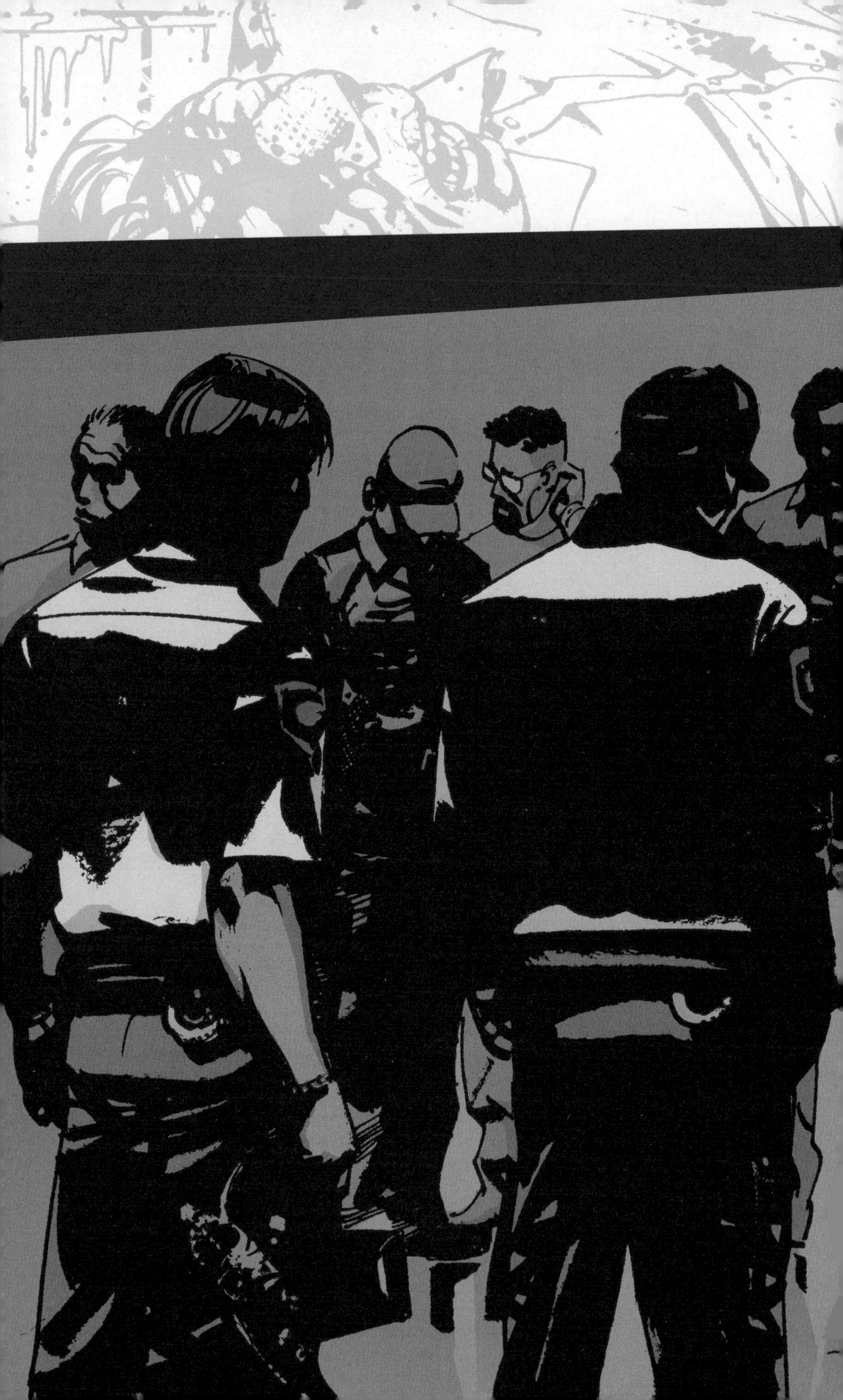

SCALPED

JASON AARON
WRITER

R.M. GUÉRA
ARTIST

THE GNAWING

GIULIA BRUSCO
WITH TRISH MULVIHILL
(CHAPTER 2)
COLORISTS

STEVE WANDS
LETTERER

JOCK
ORIGINAL SERIES COVERS

MATT FRACTION
INTRODUCTION

SCALPED created by
JASON AARON and R.M. GUÉRA

WILL DENNIS
Editor – Original Series

MARK DOYLE
Associate Editor – Original Series

ROBBIN BROSTERMAN
Design Director – Books

SHELLY BOND
Executive Editor – Vertigo

HANK KANALZ
Senior VP – Vertigo and Integrated Publishing

DIANE NELSON
President

DAN DIDIO and JIM LEE
Co-Publishers

GEOFF JOHNS
Chief Creative Officer

JOHN ROOD
Executive VP – Sales, Marketing and Business Development

AMY GENKINS
Senior VP – Business and Legal Affairs

NAIRI GARDINER
Senior VP – Finance

JEFF BOISON
VP – Publishing Planning

MARK CHIARELLO
VP – Art Direction and Design

JOHN CUNNINGHAM
VP – Marketing

TERRI CUNNINGHAM
VP – Editorial Administration

ALISON GILL
Senior VP – Manufacturing and Operations

JAY KOGAN
VP – Business and Legal Affairs, Publishing

JACK MAHAN
VP – Business Affairs, Talent

NICK NAPOLITANO
VP – Manufacturing Administration

SUE POHJA
VP – Book Sales

COURTNEY SIMMONS
Senior VP – Publicity

BOB WAYNE
Senior VP – Sales

Cover illustration and logo design by JOCK

SCALPED: THE GNAWING

DC Comics, 1700 Broadway, New York, NY 10019
A Warner Bros. Entertainment Company.
Printed in the USA. Fifth Printing.
ISBN: 978-1-4012-2717-3

SUSTAINABLE FORESTRY INITIATIVE **Certified Sourcing**
www.sfiprogram.org
SFI-01042
APPLIES TO TEXT STOCK ONLY

THE GNAWING, OR,
THE LEGEND OF THE ALABAMA CORN SNAKE

Do you know the story of the Alabama Corn Snake? I swear I'll never let it be forgotten and I'll never let those words slip too far from my tongue. I'll tell you, too, just after I tell you why I love SCALPED:

My favorite comics make me marvel over their construction. They look and feel and read like little watchworks, with points of view and perspectives so alien that the experience of engaging with them, of reading them and getting lost in their stories, feels like taking a trip somewhere in a new suit of skin. I read them again and again, and each time is a joy because at no point does the writer in me pipe up to say anything more than, "Man... how did they do that?" I have no notes, I don't see where it's coming or going; I don't think about how I would write them any differently. My favorite comics are so good I can actually read them and not just size 'em up.

I'm not sure if you realize how much that little voice ruins stuff for people like me all the time, but it happens ALL THE TIME.

So I was going to talk about SCALPED through that lens – that it's one of my favorite comics going, if not my very favorite, because, month in and month out I fall in love with the thing all over again. I've read the entire run a good half-dozen times now and reread the run every time a new collection like this comes out. What Jason Aaron and R. M. Guéra have here deepens and strengthens the longer it goes; it both remains great and becomes greater as it gains in size and sweep. I love this book. I love it, I love it, I love it.

Then I realized, well, hell – this is the sixth fucking collection. What kind of introductory expectations does anyone rightfully have for book SIX of... howevermany it'll be? If you're reading this, you are, like me, on Team SCALPED and don't need convincing to buy or read the thing. So rather than tell you what you already know – that this book beats the fucking band like it's owed money – let me maybe tell you something you DON'T know, and at least, this way, if I'm lucky, you won't feel like this is ripping you off.

And what you don't know, I am sure of in my very bones, is the legend of the Alabama Corn Snake. It's a story that mommas tell their babies and daddies ruminate over way down in Shelby County, Alabama.

Came a time when life in Shelby Co. wasn't what it is today, and guys you'd not necessarily want hanging around were, in fact, hanging around. I'm talking of course about Methodists, but you can fill that blank in with whatever undesirables you like. Down in the SC it was the Methodists, and that was what it was. It was a different time.

Gangs of Methodist toughs would cajole and threaten, would bend and break the law. They'd hiss at young mothers and cuss at grandmothers; they threw rocks at the men and chased down the boys with switches. The county was under siege until one man fought back.

And they called him the Alabama Corn Snake. I think because he'd run out of cornfields and beat the hell out of everybody then go running away again, I'm not sure of the etymology of the thing.

I do know this: Brandishing a sock-full of nickels and a long steel-handled flashlight (his "Methodist Masher," he called it), the Alabama Corn Snake took back the night, one skull fracture at a time. He made those Methodists renounce their heathen Methodist god or suffer even greater pummeling.

The Alabama Corn Snake saved my life from a wilding pack of Methodists one brutal August night as I stopped for gas, heading up I-65 from Montgomery to Huntsville where I was attending Space Camp for a record tenth time.

I stood, frozen in fear, as he mashed Methodist after Methodist, sock to flashlight and back again, spattering blood and shattering faith as easily as you or I would wipe bug guts from a windshield.

And when he was done we stared at each other, I in my sky-blue jumpsuit and he in his ROLL TIDE T-shirt and Adidas track-shorts. The Methodists coughed and wheezed and prayed for a god who would not come and I asked him, "Alabama Corn Snake! What happens when there aren't no more Methodists to punish? How on earth will you occupy this monster that lives inside of you and clearly cries out for bloodshed and vengeance?"

"It's okay," said the Alabama Corn Snake. "I'm going to write comic books."

Jason Aaron IS the Alabama Corn Snake. I know because I saw it with my own eyes. Next time you see him, say it to him. Alabama Corn Snake. And watch the devils and wolves that run wild inside the man and gnaw on his very bones come to the surface once more.

Matt Fraction
Portland, OR

Matt Fraction is an Eisner Award-winning writer whose works include THE FIVE FISTS OF SCIENCE, CASANOVA, THE INVINCIBLE IRON MAN *and* UNCANNY X-MEN.

WHO'S WHO

SPECIAL AGENT DASHIELL BAD HORSE

As a teenager, Dash left the Prairie Rose Reservation and never looked back. Years later, after stints as everything from an underground fighter to a soldier in Kosovo, circumstances—and the FBI—forced him to return on a mission to bring down the Rez's corrupt crimelord, Chief Lincoln Red Crow, by posing as Red Crow's enforcer in the local police department.

CHIEF LINCOLN RED CROW

A former protestor and radical turned powerful gangster and political figure, Red Crow is overseeing the opening of a casino he hopes to see restore glory to his people and cash to his wallet—and he'll take out anyone who stands in his way, by any means necessary.

GINA BAD HORSE

Dash's estranged mother and Red Crow's former comrade (and lover), Gina had stayed true to her activist roots, earning her many enemies both inside and outside the Rez. Involved in a shooting that left two FBI agents dead during her radical days, she had recently been desperately trying to reconnect with her prodigal son—until she herself ended up murdered.

AGENT BAYLIS NITZ

Dash's ruthless FBI supervisor has held a grudge against Red Crow and Gina ever since their involvement with the murder of two of his fellow agents decades ago. He's forced Dash to pin a murder, any murder, on his archnemesis Red Crow...and if the victim happens to be Dash himself, Nitz won't lose any sleep.

DIESEL

A white wannabe brave, Diesel claims to be 1/16th Kickapoo, and he's psychotic enough to force everyone to go along. His criminal enterprises have put him at murderous odds with Red Crow's drive to clean up whatever crime he himself can't monopolize. His secret status as FBI Special Agent Brett Fillenworth is known to Dash, but that won't stop Dash from seeking revenge over the death of a young boy Diesel gunned down—a boy Dash had taken under his wing.

CAROL ELLROY

As distant from her dad the Chief as Dash was from his mother, Carol's sexually self-destructive, and she's been pushing her illicit, torrid affair with Dash to the limit.

SHUNKA

Red Crow's right hand man and most loyal enforcer, Shunka is suspicious of Dash — and wary of his boss's sentimentality.

CATCHER

One of Red Crow and Gina's former radical running buddies, this Rhodes scholar turned hopeless alcoholic claims that his people's revered Thunder Beings have been sending him visions of impending doom—all centered on Dash.

OFFICER FRANKLIN FALLS DOWN

The only honest cop on the Rez, Officer Falls Down was assigned to investigate Gina Bad Horse's murder and he may be getting closer to the truth than anyone wants.

THE HMONGS

An Asian-American organized crime outfit with a vested interest in Red Crow's dealings, the Hmongs have offered to send in an "expert" named Mr. Brass to help ensure Red Crow's success—and Red Crow returned the favor by sending Brass to jail.

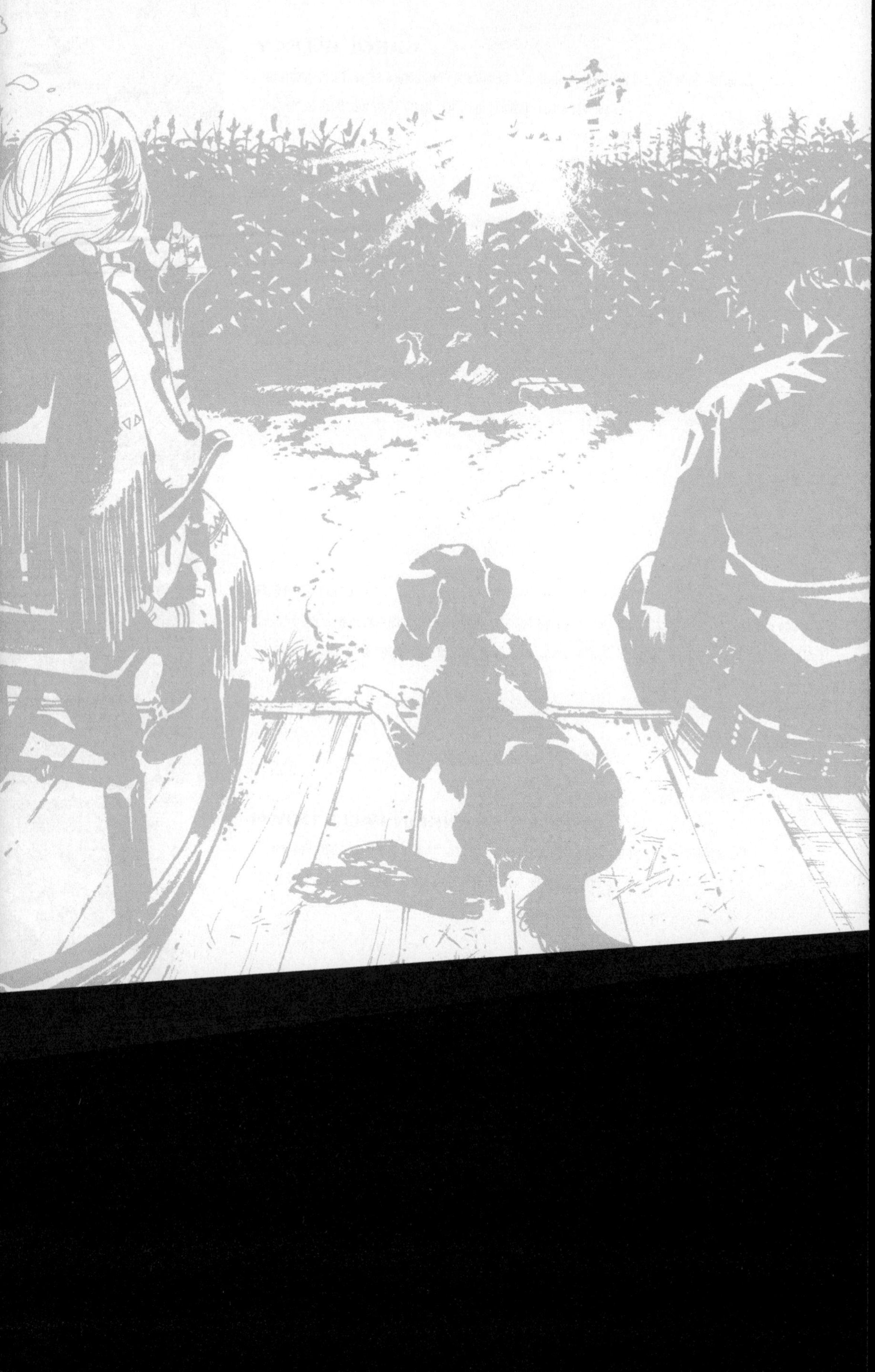

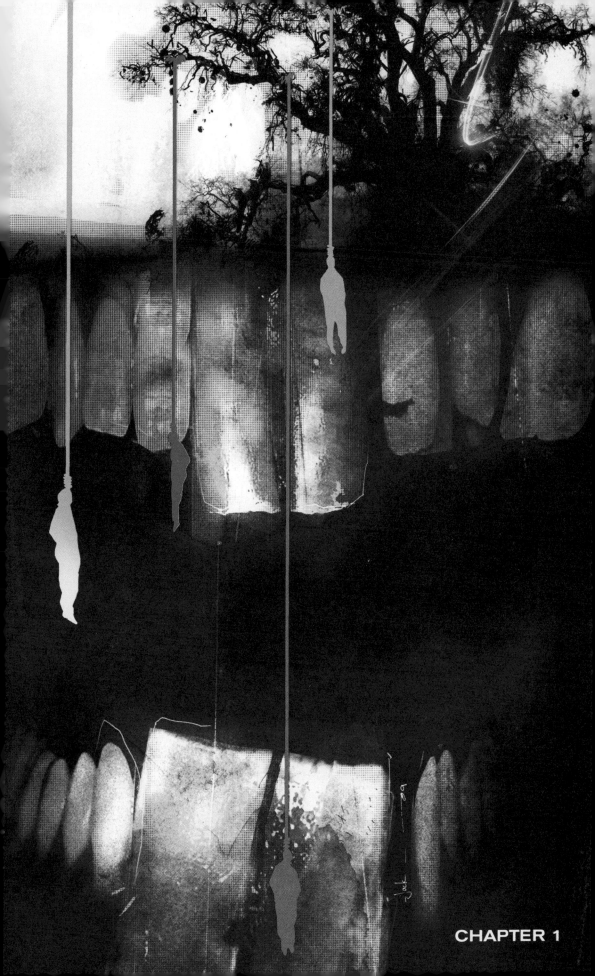

CHAPTER 1

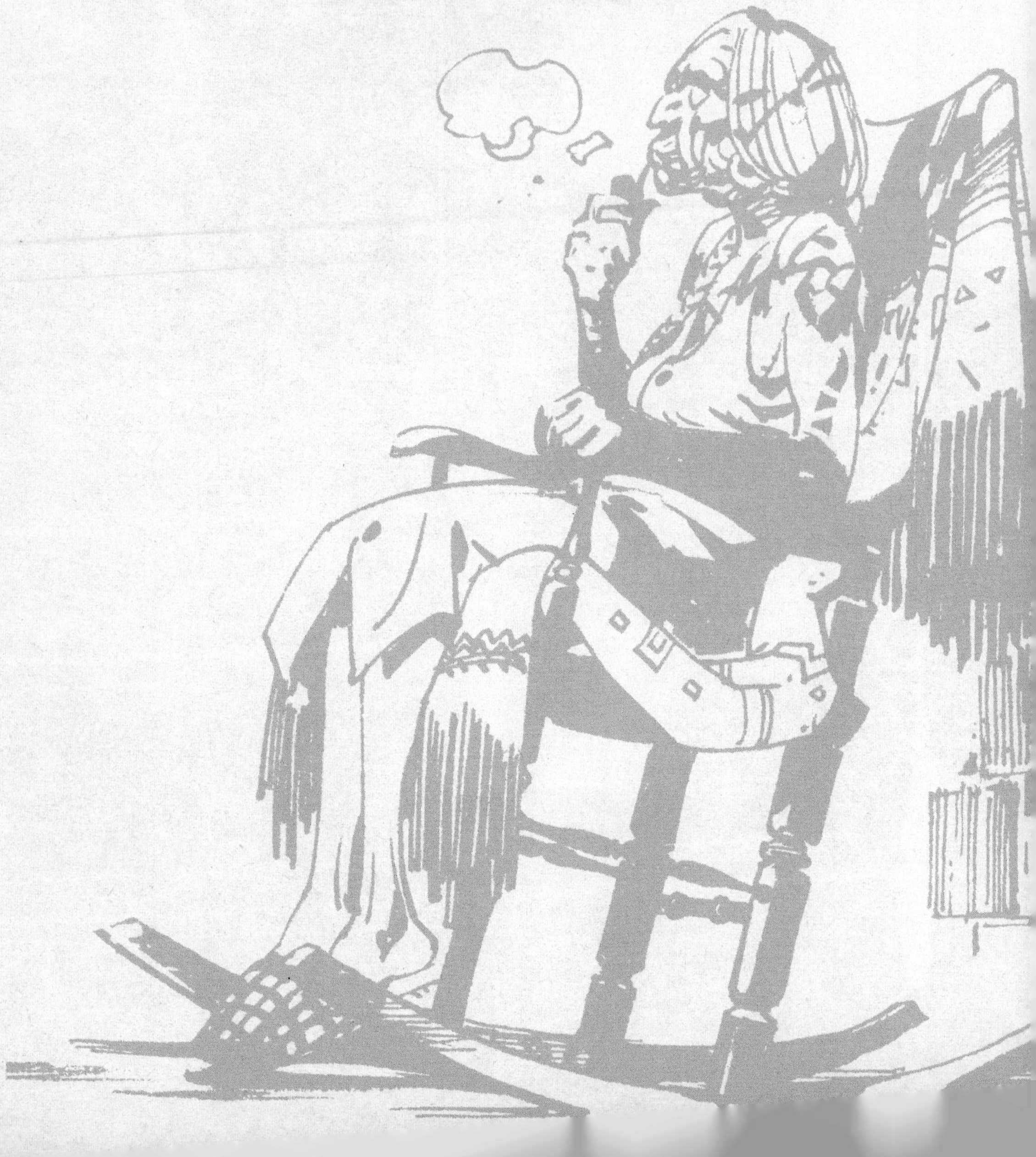

I HAD A *DREAM* LAST NIGHT.

I WAS FALLING. AND THE WHOLE WORLD WAS FALLING WITH ME.

GINA WAS THERE. SHE WAS FALLING TOO. I TRIED TO GRAB HER HAND, BUT I COULDN'T REACH IT. SHE FELL ON PAST ME.

WHAT YOU THINK IT *MEANS?*

MEANS YOU STILL GOT A LOTTA *WORK* TO DO.

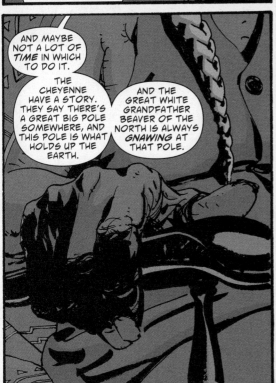

AND MAYBE NOT A LOT OF *TIME* IN WHICH TO DO IT.

THE CHEYENNE HAVE A STORY. THEY SAY THERE'S A GREAT BIG POLE SOMEWHERE, AND THIS POLE IS WHAT HOLDS UP THE EARTH.

AND THE GREAT WHITE GRANDFATHER BEAVER OF THE NORTH IS ALWAYS *GNAWING* AT THAT POLE.

HE'S BEEN GNAWING AT IT FOR A LONG, LONG TIME, AND IT'S ALREADY HALF CHEWED UP.

WHEN THE PEOPLE DO SOMETHING TO MAKE HIM ANGRY, THE OLD GRANDFATHER BEAVER GETS TO GNAWIN' FASTER.

PRETTY SOON, HE'LL HAVE GNAWED ALL THE WAY THROUGH.

AND THEN THAT POLE WILL TOPPLE AND THE WHOLE WORLD WILL CRASH INTO BOTTOMLESS NOTHING.

AND THAT WILL BE THE END OF EVERYTHING. THE END OF ALL ENDS.

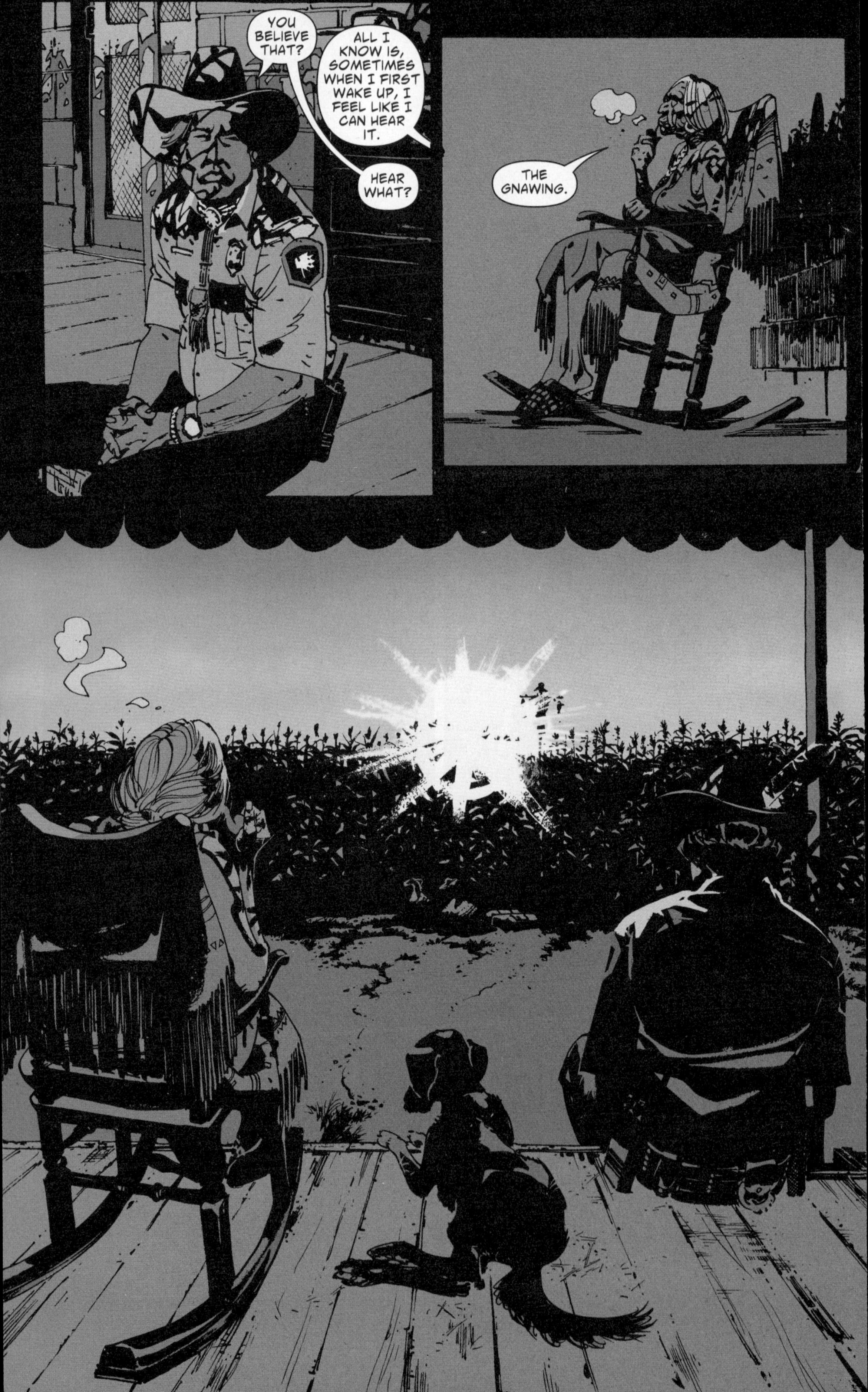
YOU BELIEVE THAT?
ALL I KNOW IS, SOMETIMES WHEN I FIRST WAKE UP, I FEEL LIKE I CAN HEAR IT.
HEAR WHAT?
THE GNAWING.

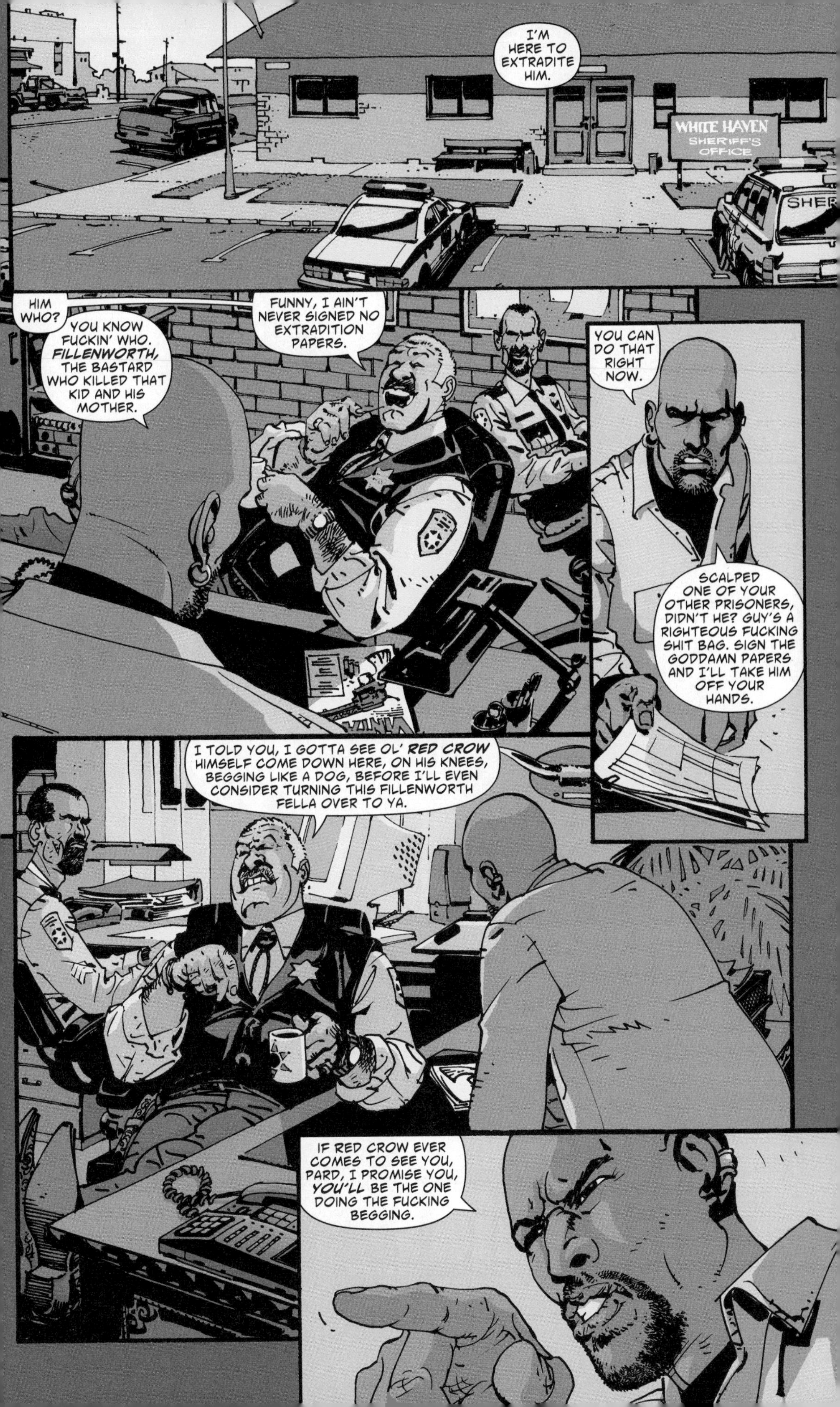
I'M HERE TO EXTRADITE HIM.
WHITE HAVEN SHERIFF'S OFFICE
SHER
HIM WHO?
YOU KNOW FUCKIN' WHO. FILLENWORTH, THE BASTARD WHO KILLED THAT KID AND HIS MOTHER.
FUNNY, I AIN'T NEVER SIGNED NO EXTRADITION PAPERS.
YOU CAN DO THAT RIGHT NOW.
SCALPED ONE OF YOUR OTHER PRISONERS, DIDN'T HE? GUY'S A RIGHTEOUS FUCKING SHIT BAG. SIGN THE GODDAMN PAPERS AND I'LL TAKE HIM OFF YOUR HANDS.
I TOLD YOU, I GOTTA SEE OL' RED CROW HIMSELF COME DOWN HERE, ON HIS KNEES, BEGGING LIKE A DOG, BEFORE I'LL EVEN CONSIDER TURNING THIS FILLENWORTH FELLA OVER TO YA.
IF RED CROW EVER COMES TO SEE YOU, PARD, I PROMISE YOU, YOU'LL BE THE ONE DOING THE FUCKING BEGGING.

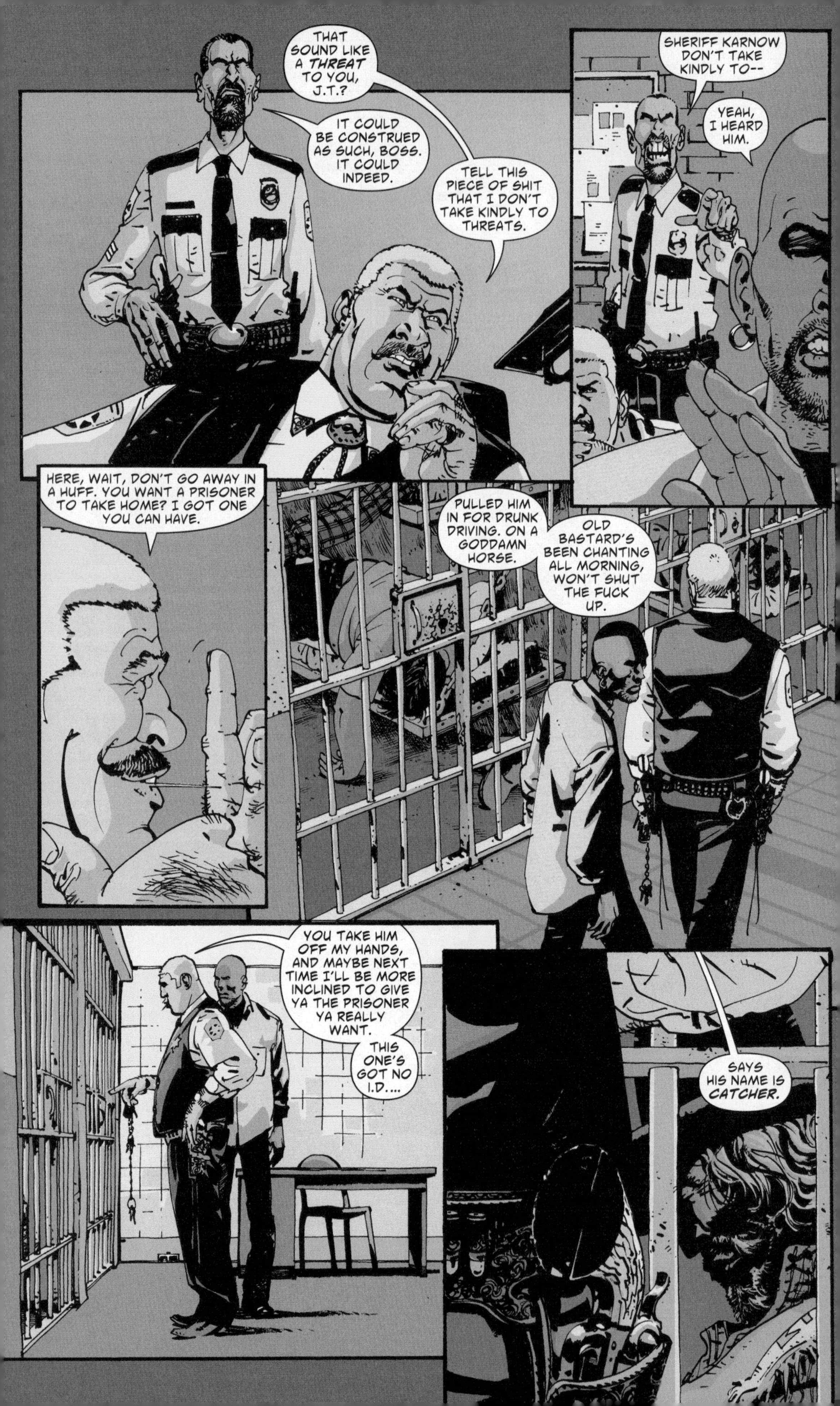
THAT SOUND LIKE A *THREAT* TO YOU, J.T.?
IT COULD BE CONSTRUED AS SUCH, BOSS. IT COULD INDEED.
TELL THIS PIECE OF SHIT THAT I DON'T TAKE KINDLY TO THREATS.
SHERIFF KARNOW DON'T TAKE KINDLY TO--
YEAH, I HEARD HIM.
HERE, WAIT, DON'T GO AWAY IN A HUFF. YOU WANT A PRISONER TO TAKE HOME? I GOT ONE YOU CAN HAVE.
PULLED HIM IN FOR DRUNK DRIVING. ON A GODDAMN HORSE.
OLD BASTARD'S BEEN CHANTING ALL MORNING, WON'T SHUT THE FUCK UP.
YOU TAKE HIM OFF MY HANDS, AND MAYBE NEXT TIME I'LL BE MORE INCLINED TO GIVE YA THE PRISONER YA REALLY WANT.
THIS ONE'S GOT NO I.D....
SAYS HIS NAME IS *CATCHER*.

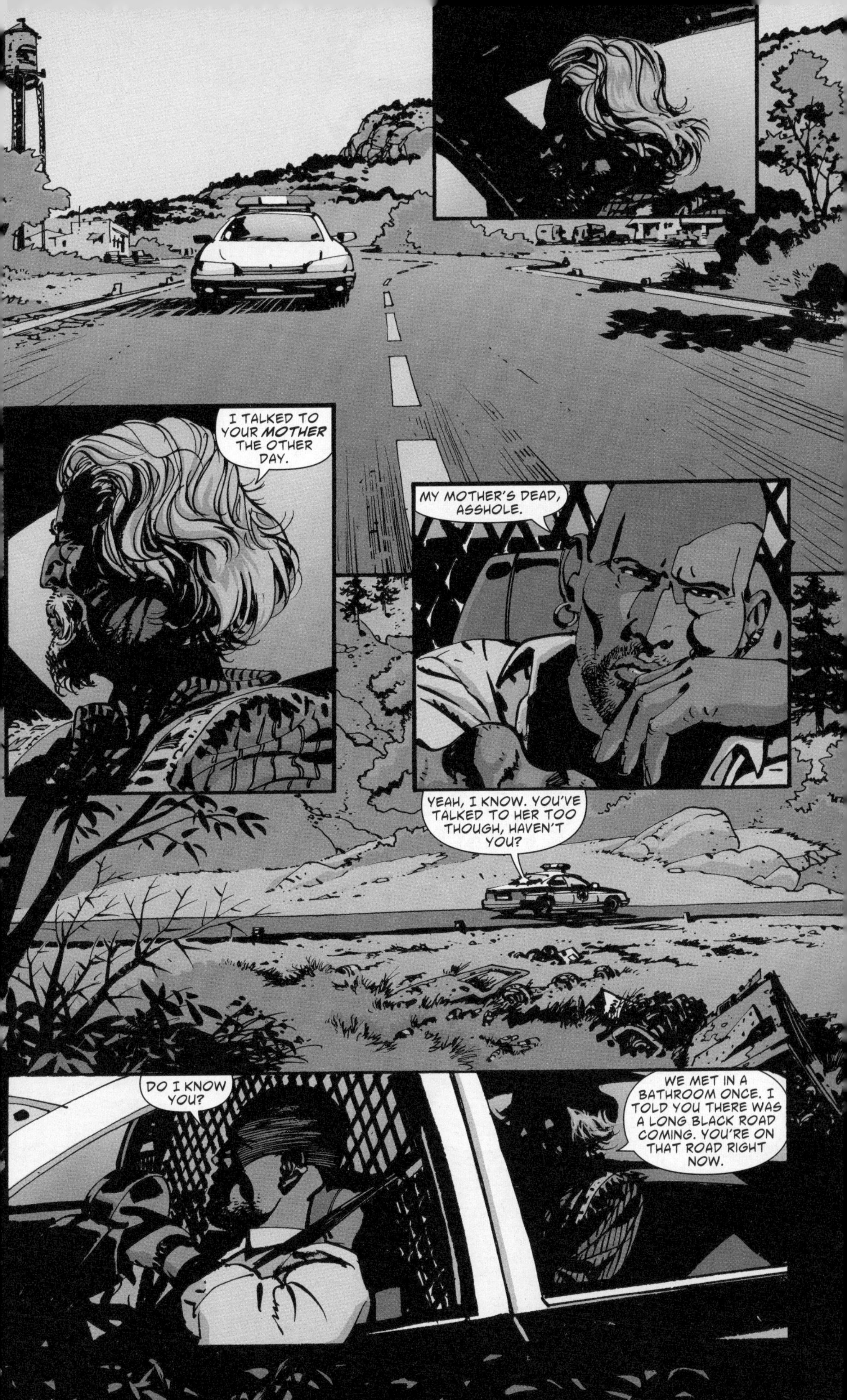
I TALKED TO YOUR MOTHER THE OTHER DAY.
MY MOTHER'S DEAD, ASSHOLE.
YEAH, I KNOW. YOU'VE TALKED TO HER TOO THOUGH, HAVEN'T YOU?
DO I KNOW YOU?
WE MET IN A BATHROOM ONCE. I TOLD YOU THERE WAS A LONG BLACK ROAD COMING. YOU'RE ON THAT ROAD RIGHT NOW.

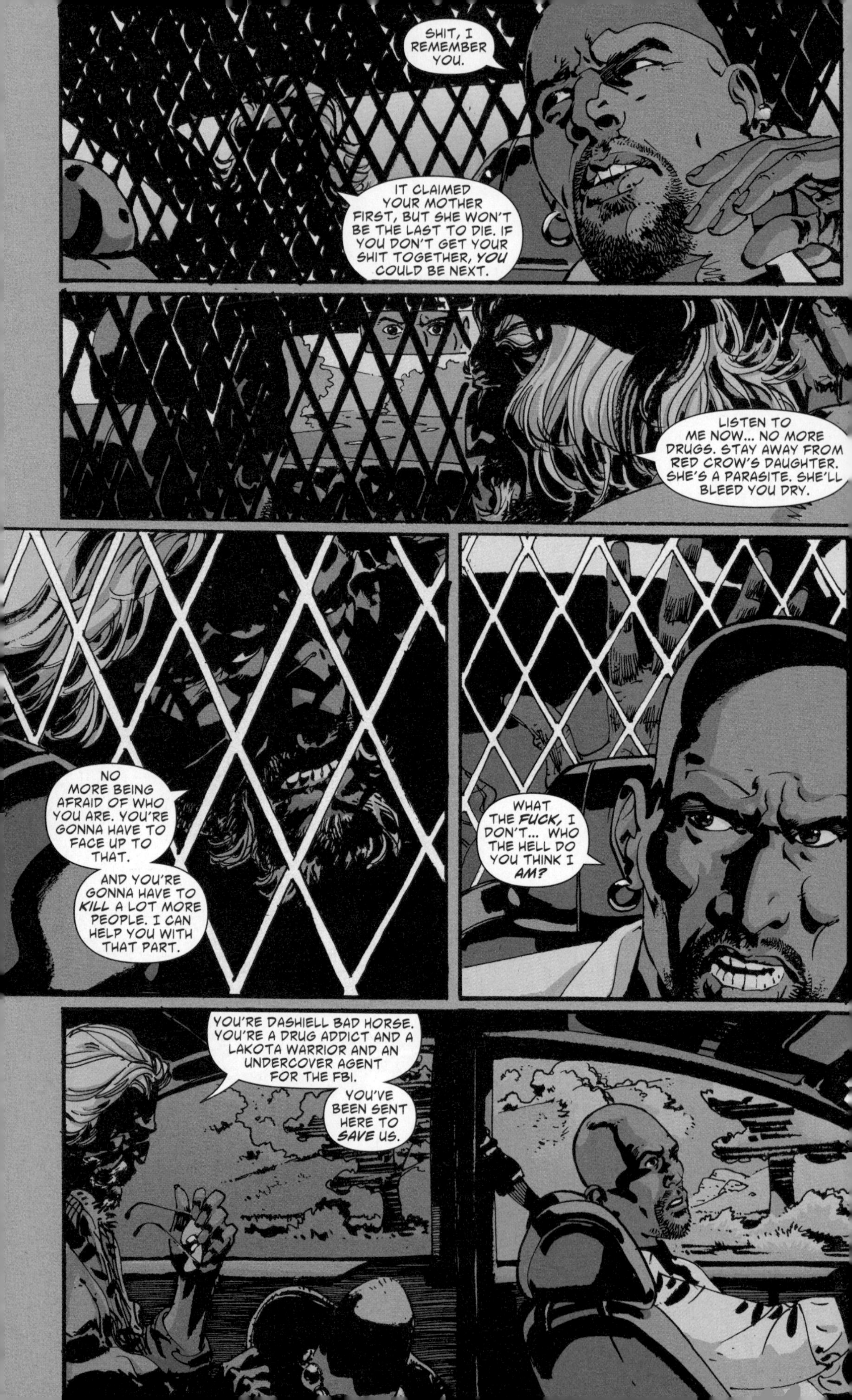
SHIT, I REMEMBER YOU.
IT CLAIMED YOUR MOTHER FIRST, BUT SHE WON'T BE THE LAST TO DIE. IF YOU DON'T GET YOUR SHIT TOGETHER, YOU COULD BE NEXT.
LISTEN TO ME NOW... NO MORE DRUGS. STAY AWAY FROM RED CROW'S DAUGHTER. SHE'S A PARASITE. SHE'LL BLEED YOU DRY.
NO MORE BEING AFRAID OF WHO YOU ARE. YOU'RE GONNA HAVE TO FACE UP TO THAT.
AND YOU'RE GONNA HAVE TO KILL A LOT MORE PEOPLE. I CAN HELP YOU WITH THAT PART.
WHAT THE FUCK, I DON'T... WHO THE HELL DO YOU THINK I AM?
YOU'RE DASHIELL BAD HORSE. YOU'RE A DRUG ADDICT AND A LAKOTA WARRIOR AND AN UNDERCOVER AGENT FOR THE FBI.
YOU'VE BEEN SENT HERE TO SAVE US.

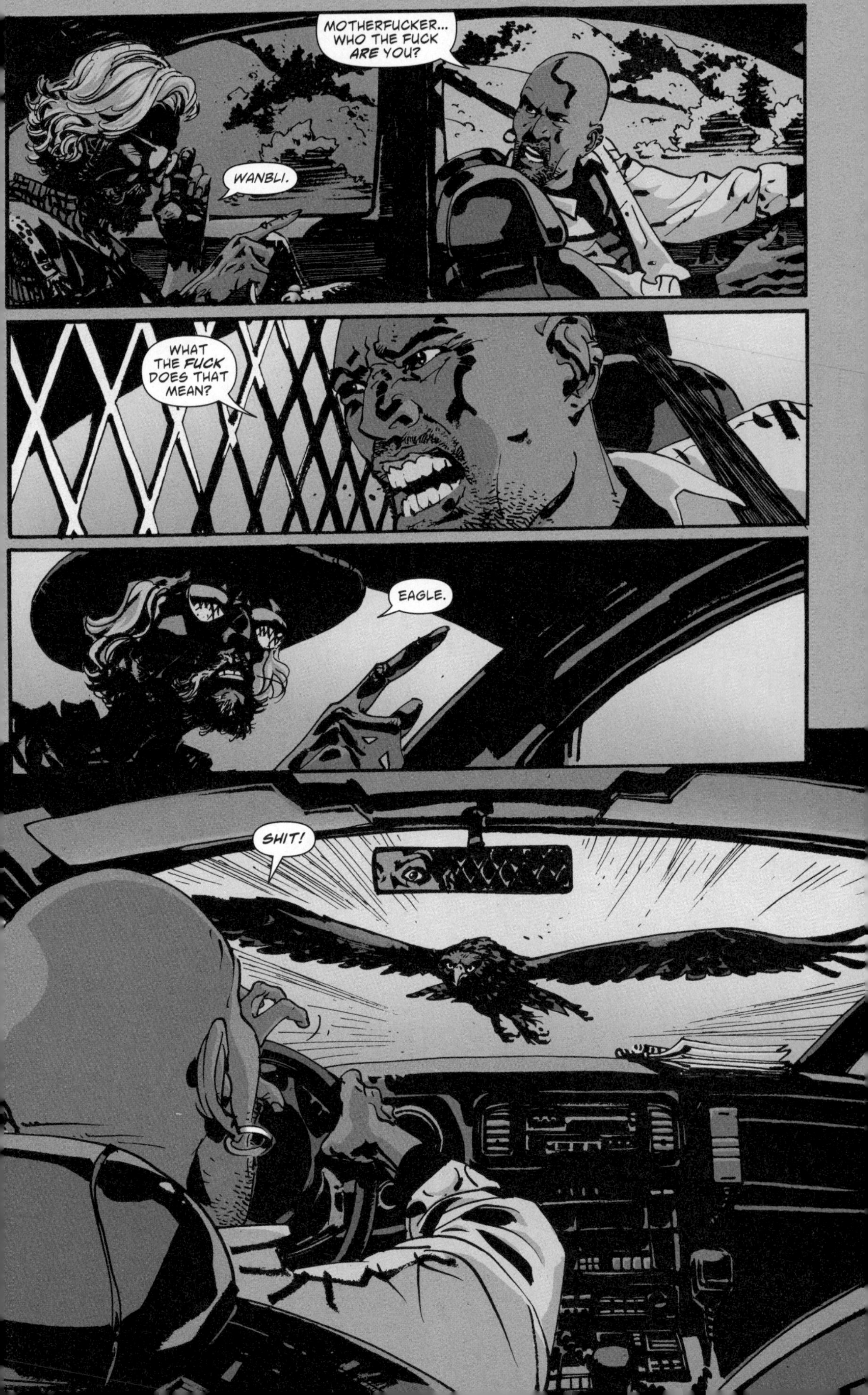
MOTHERFUCKER... WHO THE FUCK ARE YOU?
WANBLI.
WHAT THE FUCK DOES THAT MEAN?
EAGLE.
SHIT!

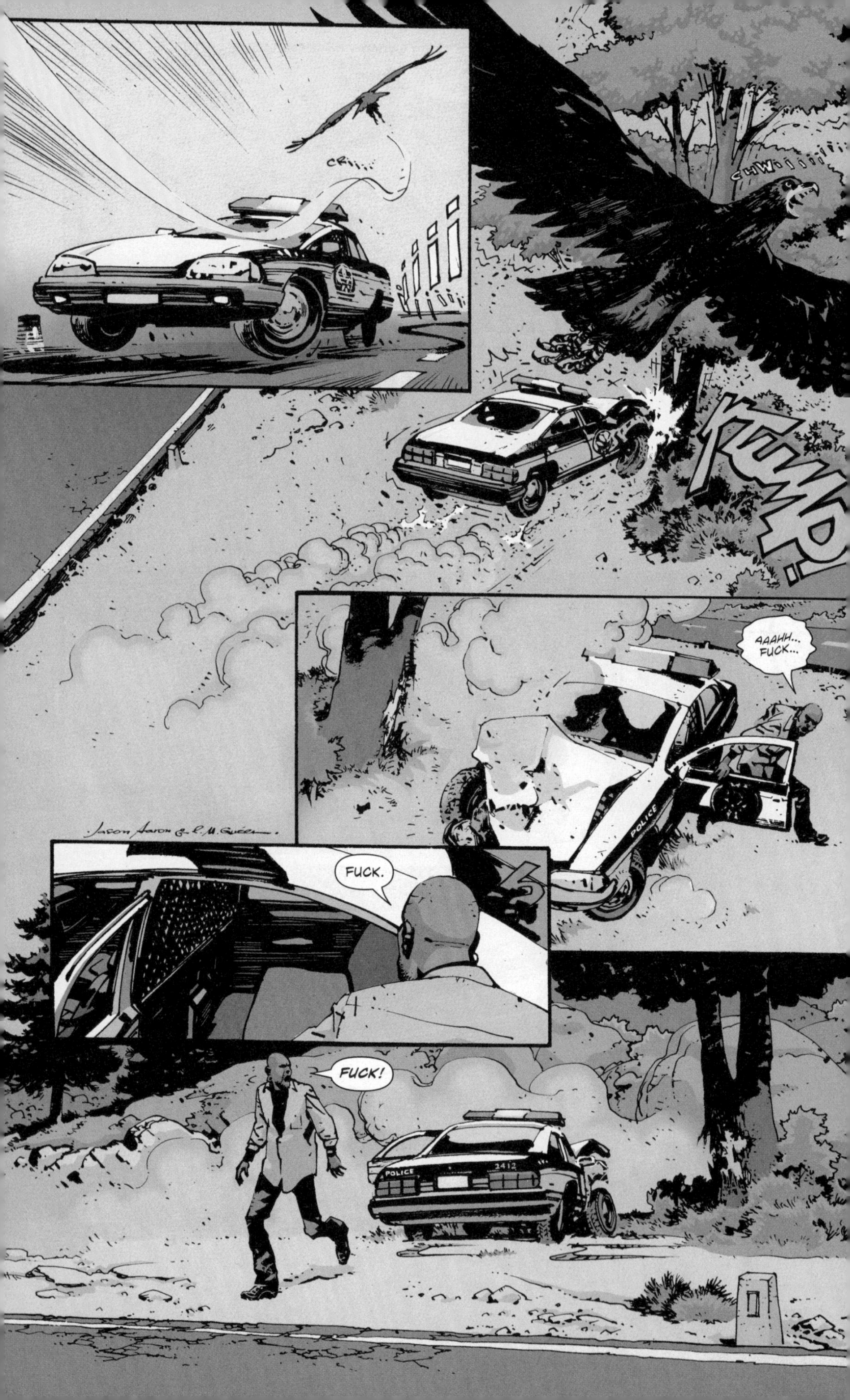
CRIIII...
CHWIIII...
KTHUMP!
AAAHH... FUCK...
FUCK.
FUCK!

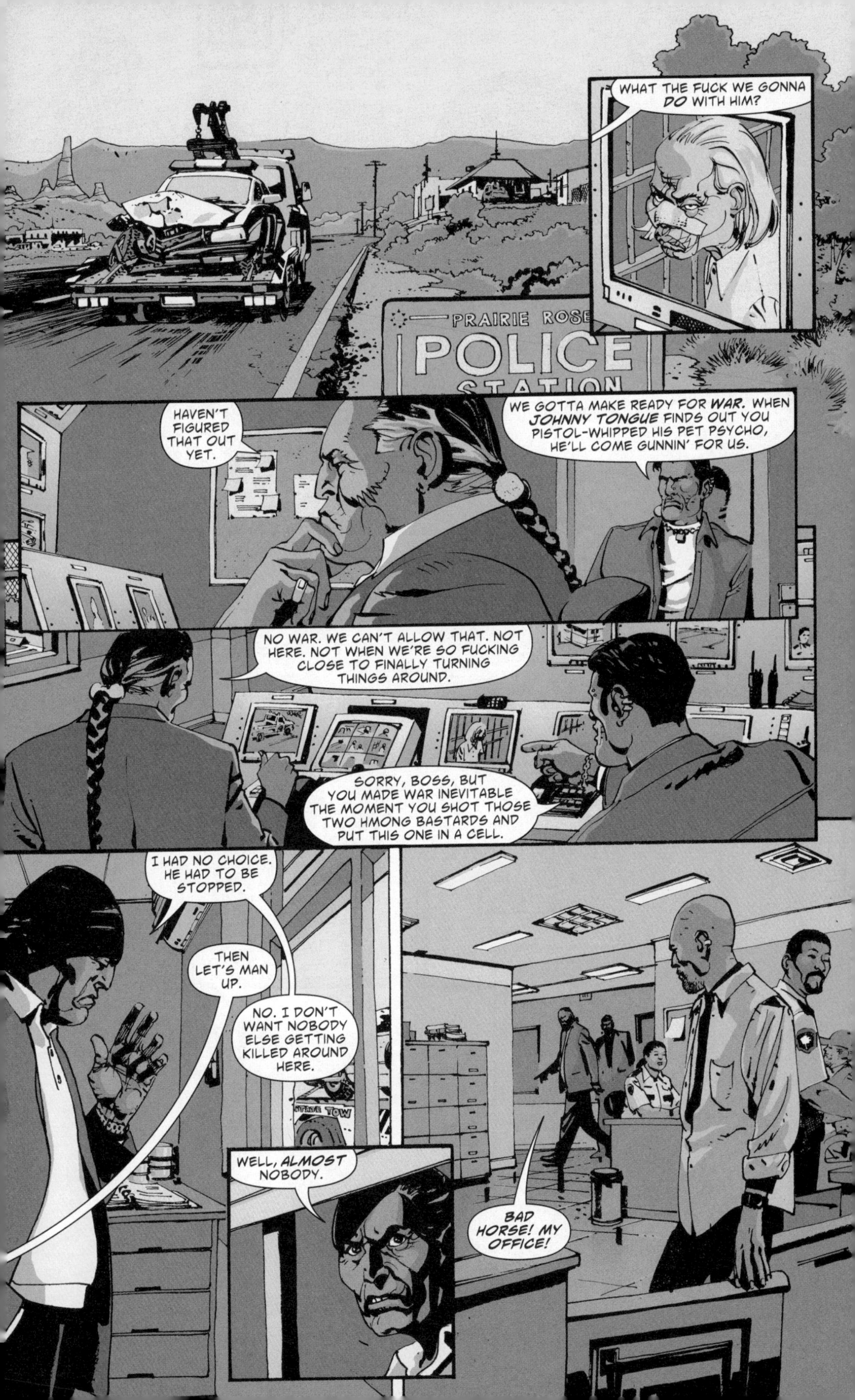
PRAIRIE ROSE
POLICE
STATION
WHAT THE FUCK WE GONNA DO WITH HIM?
HAVEN'T FIGURED THAT OUT YET.
WE GOTTA MAKE READY FOR WAR. WHEN JOHNNY TONGUE FINDS OUT YOU PISTOL-WHIPPED HIS PET PSYCHO, HE'LL COME GUNNIN' FOR US.
NO WAR. WE CAN'T ALLOW THAT. NOT HERE. NOT WHEN WE'RE SO FUCKING CLOSE TO FINALLY TURNING THINGS AROUND.
SORRY, BOSS, BUT YOU MADE WAR INEVITABLE THE MOMENT YOU SHOT THOSE TWO HMONG BASTARDS AND PUT THIS ONE IN A CELL.
I HAD NO CHOICE. HE HAD TO BE STOPPED.
THEN LET'S MAN UP.
NO. I DON'T WANT NOBODY ELSE GETTING KILLED AROUND HERE.
WELL, ALMOST NOBODY.
BAD HORSE! MY OFFICE!

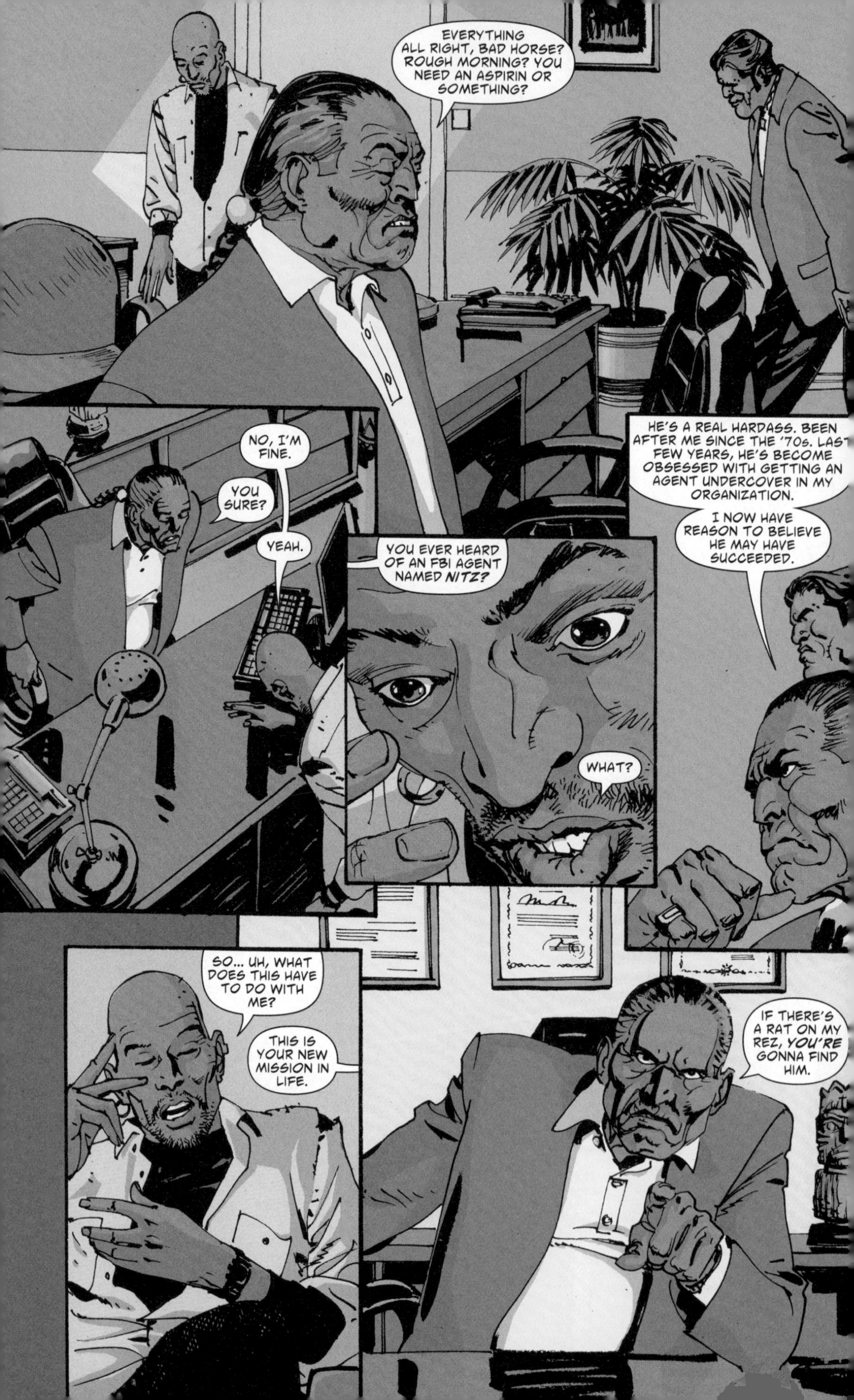
EVERYTHING ALL RIGHT, BAD HORSE? ROUGH MORNING? YOU NEED AN ASPIRIN OR SOMETHING?
NO, I'M FINE.
YOU SURE?
YEAH.
YOU EVER HEARD OF AN FBI AGENT NAMED NITZ?
WHAT?
HE'S A REAL HARDASS. BEEN AFTER ME SINCE THE '70s. LAST FEW YEARS, HE'S BECOME OBSESSED WITH GETTING AN AGENT UNDERCOVER IN MY ORGANIZATION.
I NOW HAVE REASON TO BELIEVE HE MAY HAVE SUCCEEDED.
SO... UH, WHAT DOES THIS HAVE TO DO WITH ME?
THIS IS YOUR NEW MISSION IN LIFE.
IF THERE'S A RAT ON MY REZ, YOU'RE GONNA FIND HIM.

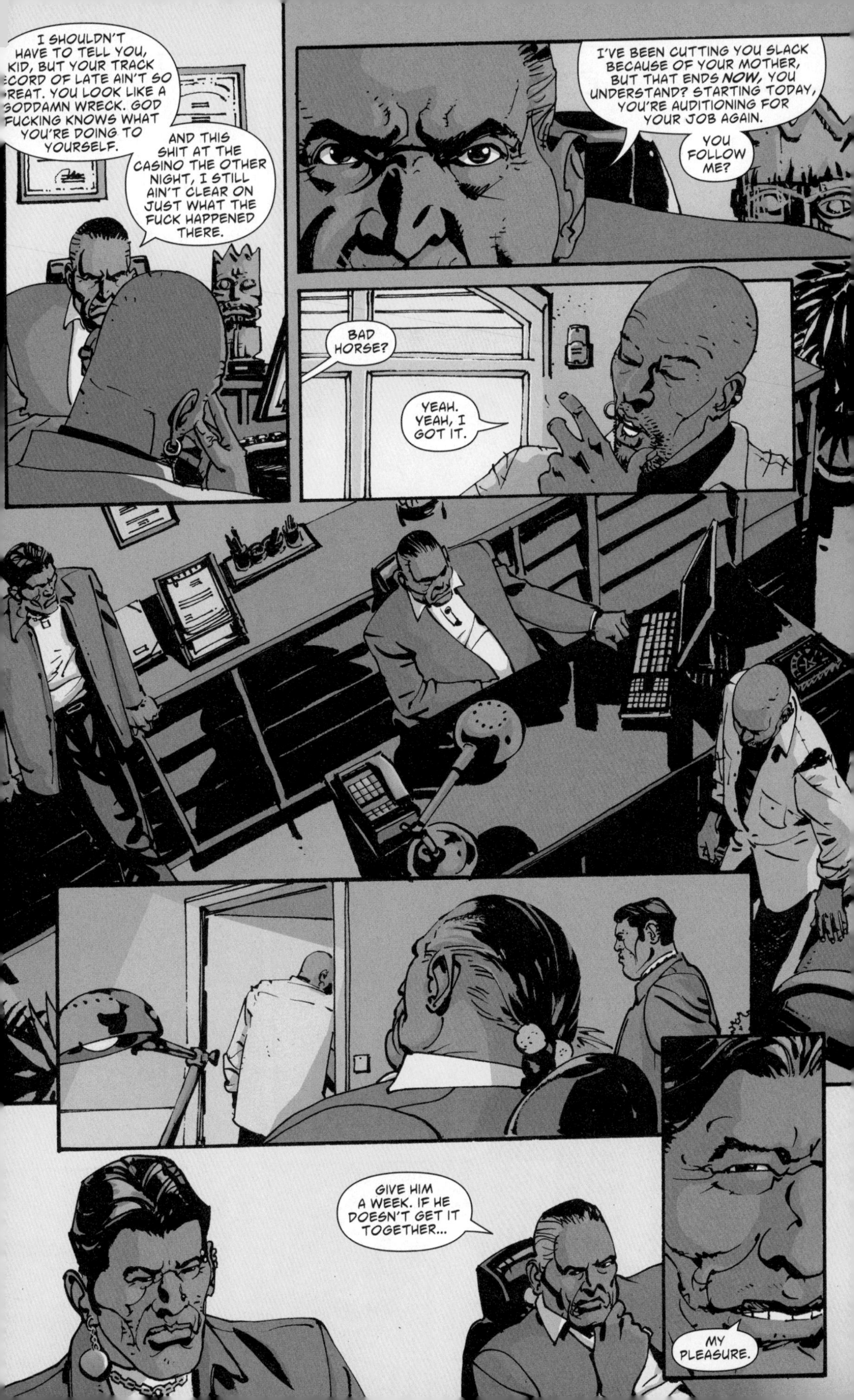
I SHOULDN'T HAVE TO TELL YOU, KID, BUT YOUR TRACK RECORD OF LATE AIN'T SO GREAT. YOU LOOK LIKE A GODDAMN WRECK. GOD FUCKING KNOWS WHAT YOU'RE DOING TO YOURSELF.
AND THIS SHIT AT THE CASINO THE OTHER NIGHT, I STILL AIN'T CLEAR ON JUST WHAT THE FUCK HAPPENED THERE.
I'VE BEEN CUTTING YOU SLACK BECAUSE OF YOUR MOTHER, BUT THAT ENDS NOW, YOU UNDERSTAND? STARTING TODAY, YOU'RE AUDITIONING FOR YOUR JOB AGAIN.
YOU FOLLOW ME?
BAD HORSE?
YEAH. YEAH, I GOT IT.
GIVE HIM A WEEK. IF HE DOESN'T GET IT TOGETHER...
MY PLEASURE.

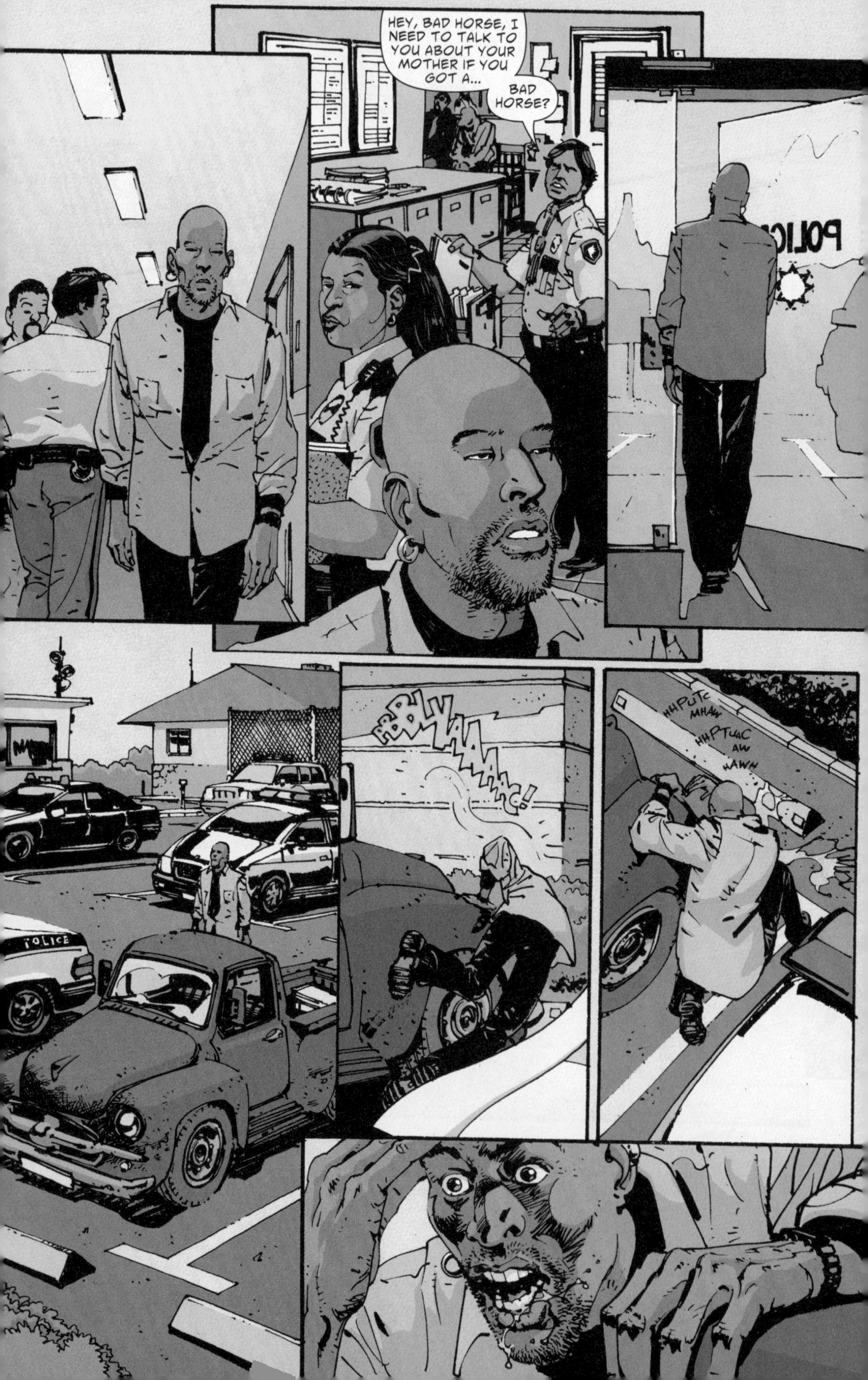
HEY, BAD HORSE, I NEED TO TALK TO YOU ABOUT YOUR MOTHER IF YOU GOT A...
BAD HORSE?
POLICE
POLICE
BBBLVAAAAC!
HHPUTC MHAW
HHPTUAC AW
HAWH

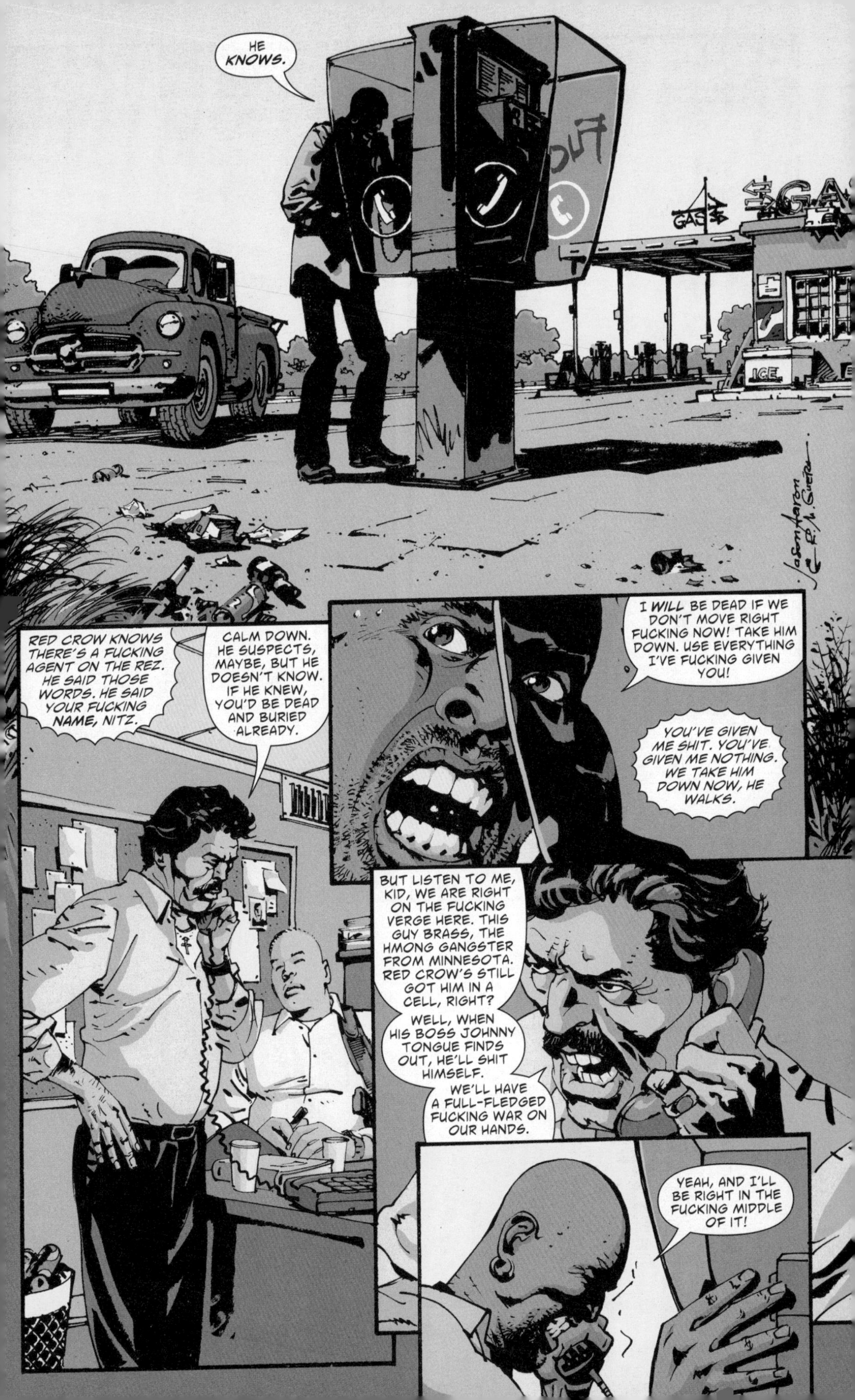
HE KNOWS.
GAS
GAS
ICE
Jason Aaron
R.M. Guera
RED CROW KNOWS THERE'S A FUCKING AGENT ON THE REZ. HE SAID THOSE WORDS. HE SAID YOUR FUCKING NAME, NITZ.
CALM DOWN. HE SUSPECTS, MAYBE, BUT HE DOESN'T KNOW. IF HE KNEW, YOU'D BE DEAD AND BURIED ALREADY.
I WILL BE DEAD IF WE DON'T MOVE RIGHT FUCKING NOW! TAKE HIM DOWN. USE EVERYTHING I'VE FUCKING GIVEN YOU!
YOU'VE GIVEN ME SHIT. YOU'VE GIVEN ME NOTHING. WE TAKE HIM DOWN NOW, HE WALKS.
BUT LISTEN TO ME, KID, WE ARE RIGHT ON THE FUCKING VERGE HERE. THIS GUY BRASS, THE HMONG GANGSTER FROM MINNESOTA. RED CROW'S STILL GOT HIM IN A CELL, RIGHT?
WELL, WHEN HIS BOSS JOHNNY TONGUE FINDS OUT, HE'LL SHIT HIMSELF.
WE'LL HAVE A FULL-FLEDGED FUCKING WAR ON OUR HANDS.
YEAH, AND I'LL BE RIGHT IN THE FUCKING MIDDLE OF IT!

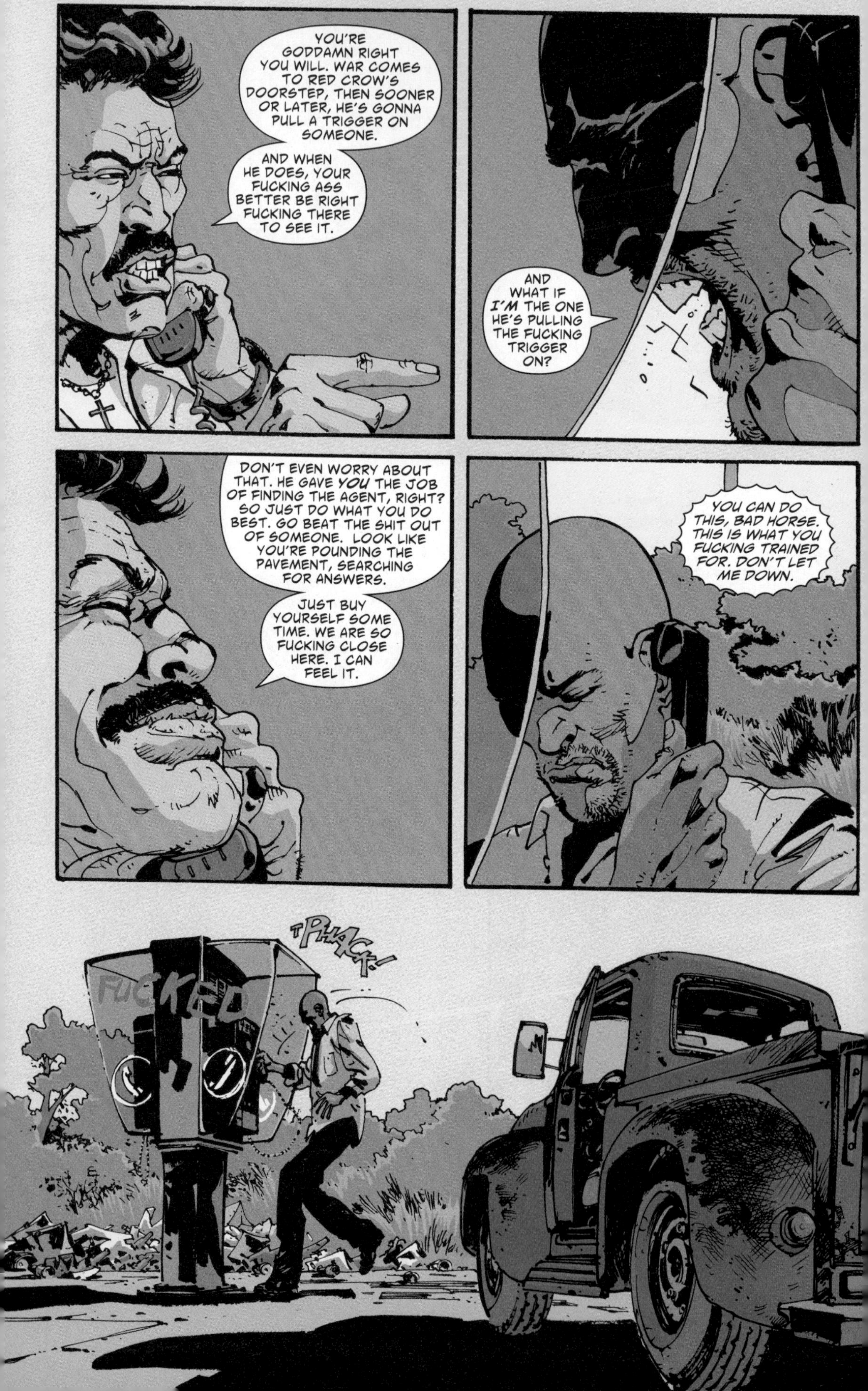
YOU'RE GODDAMN RIGHT YOU WILL. WAR COMES TO RED CROW'S DOORSTEP, THEN SOONER OR LATER, HE'S GONNA PULL A TRIGGER ON SOMEONE.
AND WHEN HE DOES, YOUR FUCKING ASS BETTER BE RIGHT FUCKING THERE TO SEE IT.
AND WHAT IF I'M THE ONE HE'S PULLING THE FUCKING TRIGGER ON?
DON'T EVEN WORRY ABOUT THAT. HE GAVE YOU THE JOB OF FINDING THE AGENT, RIGHT? SO JUST DO WHAT YOU DO BEST. GO BEAT THE SHIT OUT OF SOMEONE. LOOK LIKE YOU'RE POUNDING THE PAVEMENT, SEARCHING FOR ANSWERS.
JUST BUY YOURSELF SOME TIME. WE ARE SO FUCKING CLOSE HERE. I CAN FEEL IT.
YOU CAN DO THIS, BAD HORSE. THIS IS WHAT YOU FUCKING TRAINED FOR. DON'T LET ME DOWN.
TPHACK!
FUCKED

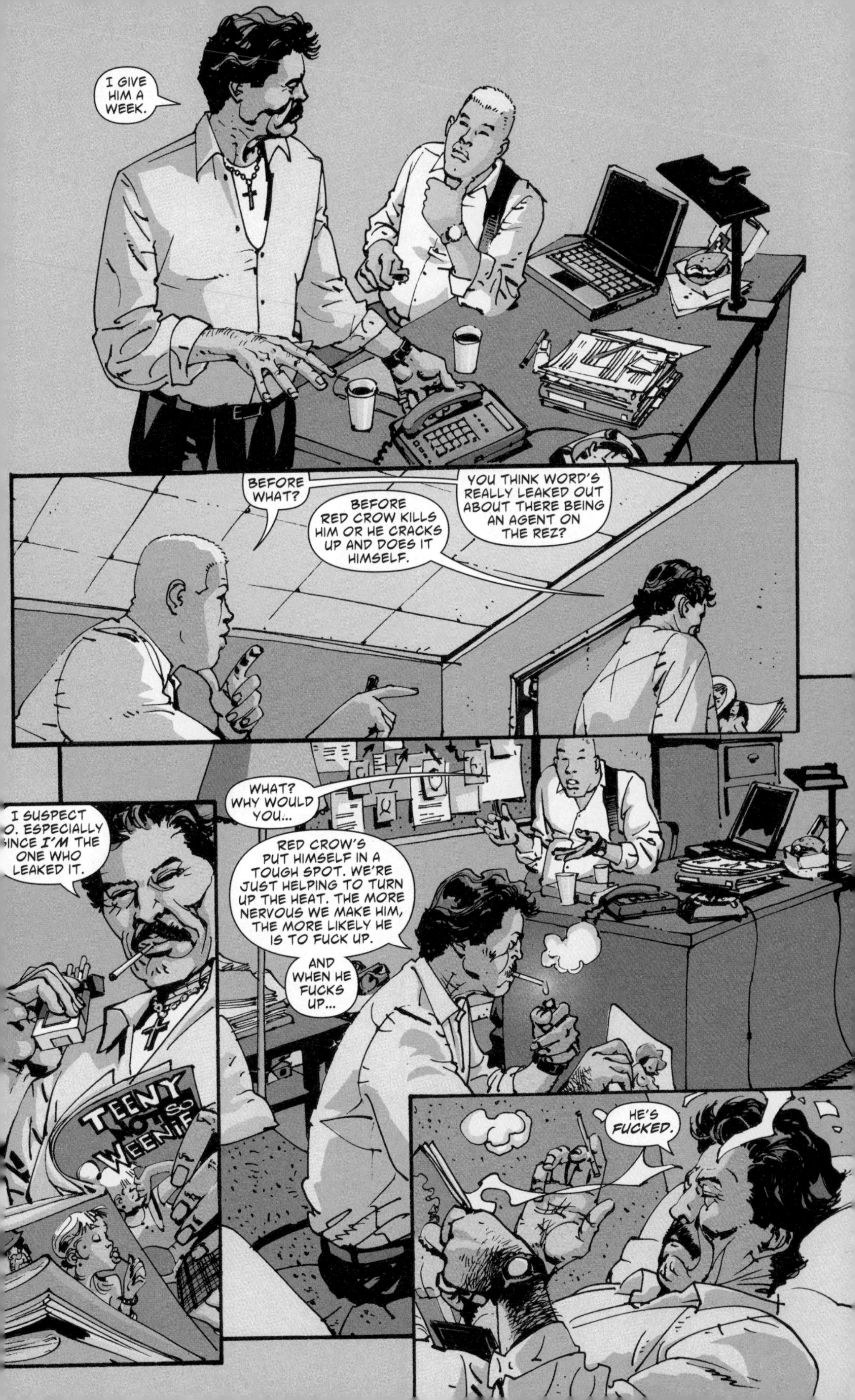
I GIVE HIM A WEEK.
BEFORE WHAT?
YOU THINK WORD'S REALLY LEAKED OUT ABOUT THERE BEING AN AGENT ON THE REZ?
BEFORE RED CROW KILLS HIM OR HE CRACKS UP AND DOES IT HIMSELF.
I SUSPECT SO. ESPECIALLY SINCE I'M THE ONE WHO LEAKED IT.
WHAT? WHY WOULD YOU...
RED CROW'S PUT HIMSELF IN A TOUGH SPOT. WE'RE JUST HELPING TO TURN UP THE HEAT. THE MORE NERVOUS WE MAKE HIM, THE MORE LIKELY HE IS TO FUCK UP.
AND WHEN HE FUCKS UP...
TEENY NOT SO WEENIE
HE'S FUCKED.

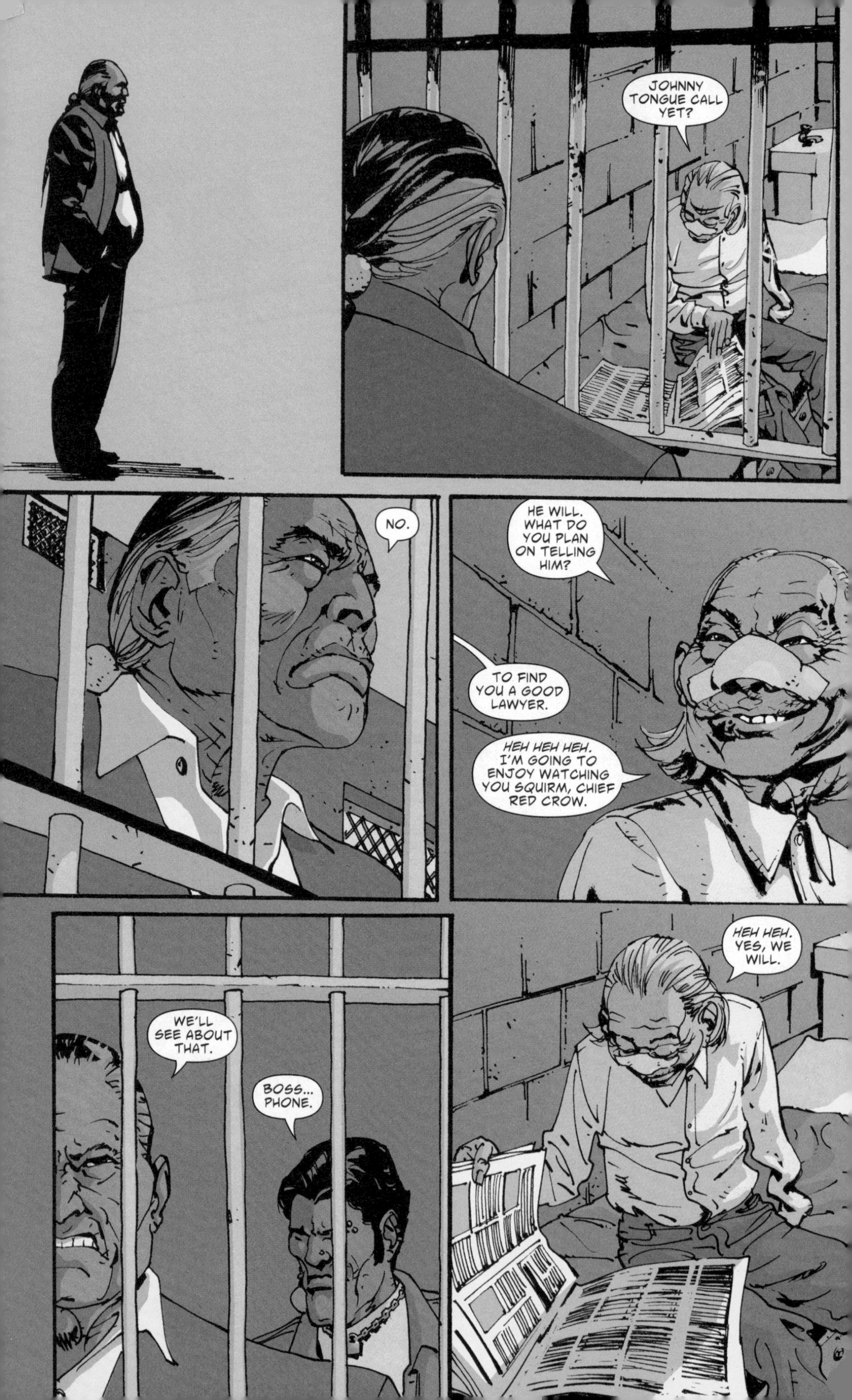
JOHNNY TONGUE CALL YET?
NO.
HE WILL. WHAT DO YOU PLAN ON TELLING HIM?
TO FIND YOU A GOOD LAWYER.
HEH HEH HEH. I'M GOING TO ENJOY WATCHING YOU SQUIRM, CHIEF RED CROW.
WE'LL SEE ABOUT THAT.
BOSS... PHONE.
HEH HEH. YES, WE WILL.

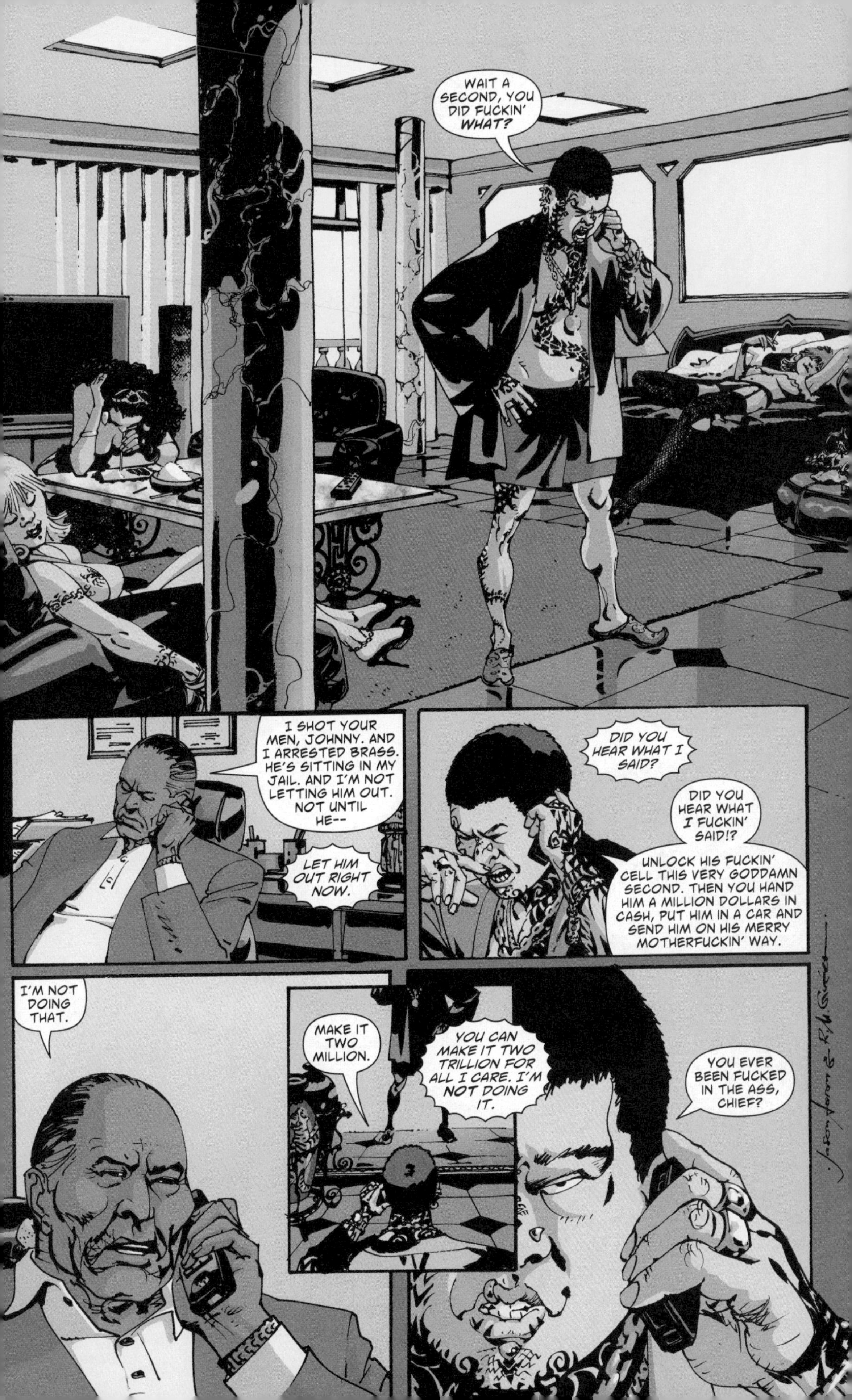
WAIT A SECOND, YOU DID FUCKIN' WHAT?
I SHOT YOUR MEN, JOHNNY. AND I ARRESTED BRASS. HE'S SITTING IN MY JAIL. AND I'M NOT LETTING HIM OUT. NOT UNTIL HE--
LET HIM OUT RIGHT NOW.
DID YOU HEAR WHAT I SAID?
DID YOU HEAR WHAT I FUCKIN' SAID!?
UNLOCK HIS FUCKIN' CELL THIS VERY GODDAMN SECOND. THEN YOU HAND HIM A MILLION DOLLARS IN CASH, PUT HIM IN A CAR AND SEND HIM ON HIS MERRY MOTHERFUCKIN' WAY.
I'M NOT DOING THAT.
MAKE IT TWO MILLION.
YOU CAN MAKE IT TWO TRILLION FOR ALL I CARE. I'M NOT DOING IT.
YOU EVER BEEN FUCKED IN THE ASS, CHIEF?

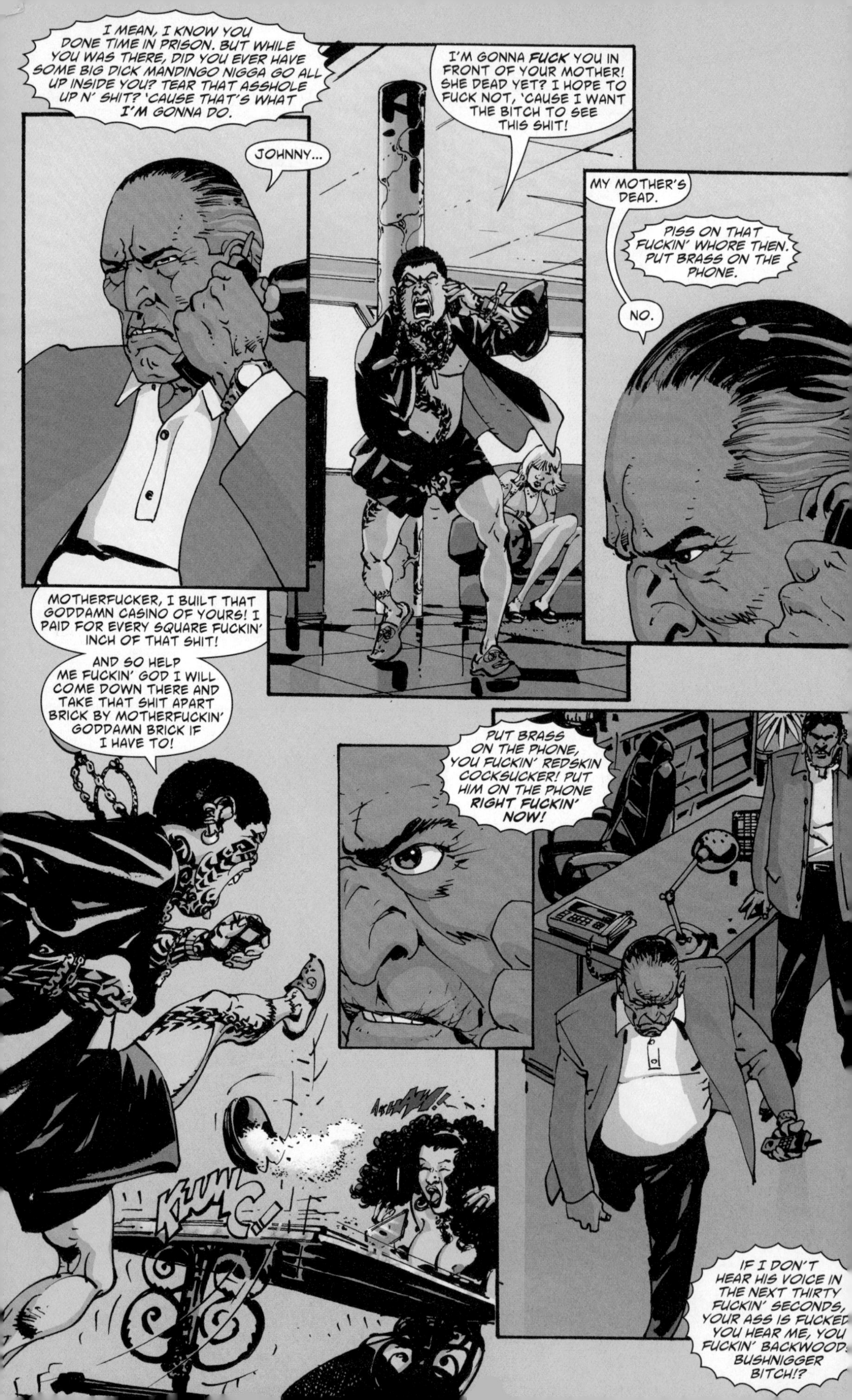

I MEAN, I KNOW YOU DONE TIME IN PRISON. BUT WHILE YOU WAS THERE, DID YOU EVER HAVE SOME BIG DICK MANDINGO NIGGA GO ALL UP INSIDE YOU? TEAR THAT ASSHOLE UP N' SHIT? 'CAUSE THAT'S WHAT I'M GONNA DO.
JOHNNY...
I'M GONNA FUCK YOU IN FRONT OF YOUR MOTHER! SHE DEAD YET? I HOPE TO FUCK NOT, 'CAUSE I WANT THE BITCH TO SEE THIS SHIT!
MY MOTHER'S DEAD.
PISS ON THAT FUCKIN' WHORE THEN. PUT BRASS ON THE PHONE.
NO.
MOTHERFUCKER, I BUILT THAT GODDAMN CASINO OF YOURS! I PAID FOR EVERY SQUARE FUCKIN' INCH OF THAT SHIT!
AND SO HELP ME FUCKIN' GOD I WILL COME DOWN THERE AND TAKE THAT SHIT APART BRICK BY MOTHERFUCKIN' GODDAMN BRICK IF I HAVE TO!
PUT BRASS ON THE PHONE, YOU FUCKIN' REDSKIN COCKSUCKER! PUT HIM ON THE PHONE RIGHT FUCKIN' NOW!
KLUNK
IF I DON'T HEAR HIS VOICE IN THE NEXT THIRTY FUCKIN' SECONDS, YOUR ASS IS FUCKED. YOU HEAR ME, YOU FUCKIN' BACKWOODS BUSHNIGGER BITCH!?

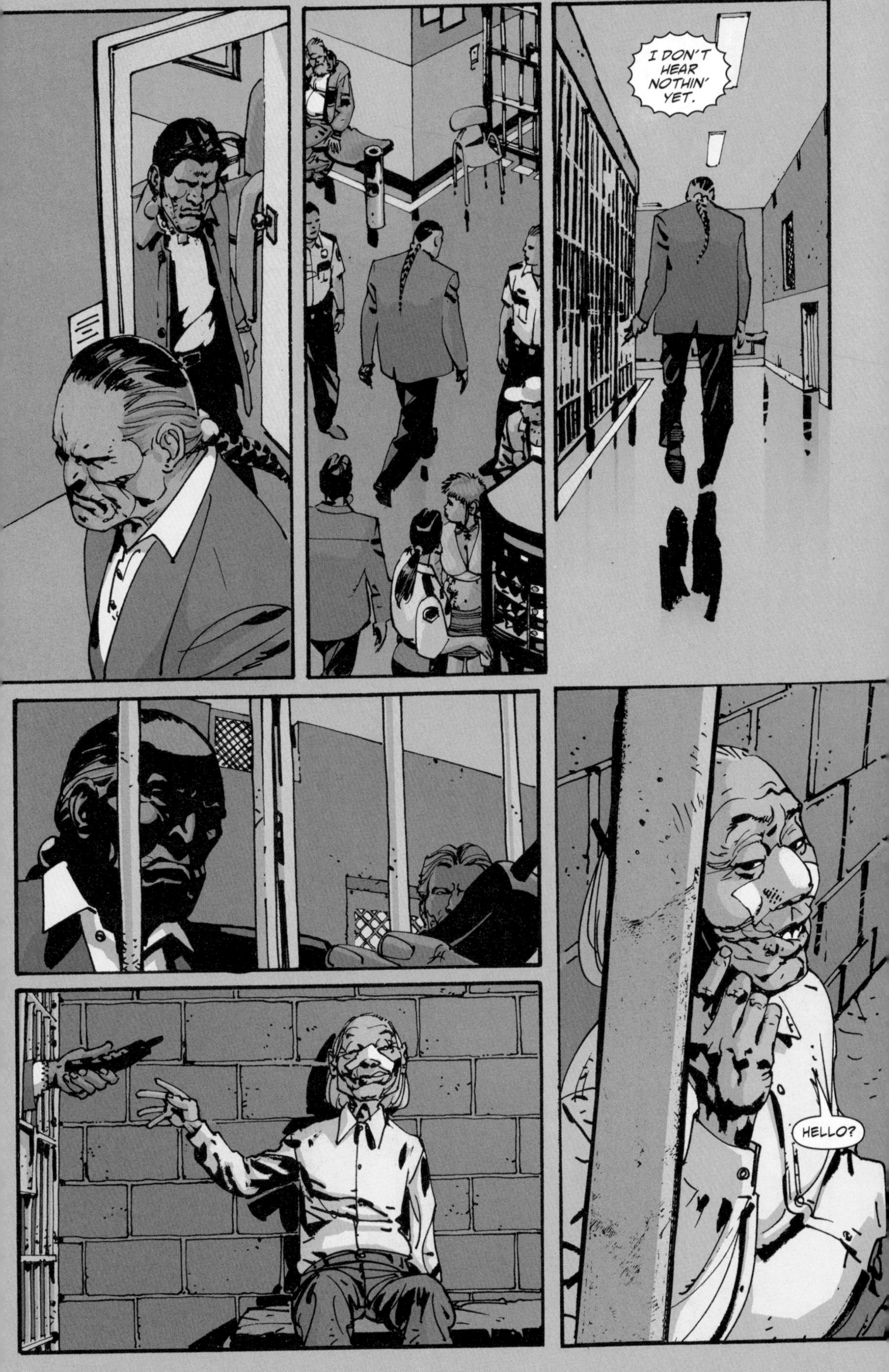
I DON'T HEAR NOTHIN' YET.
HELLO?

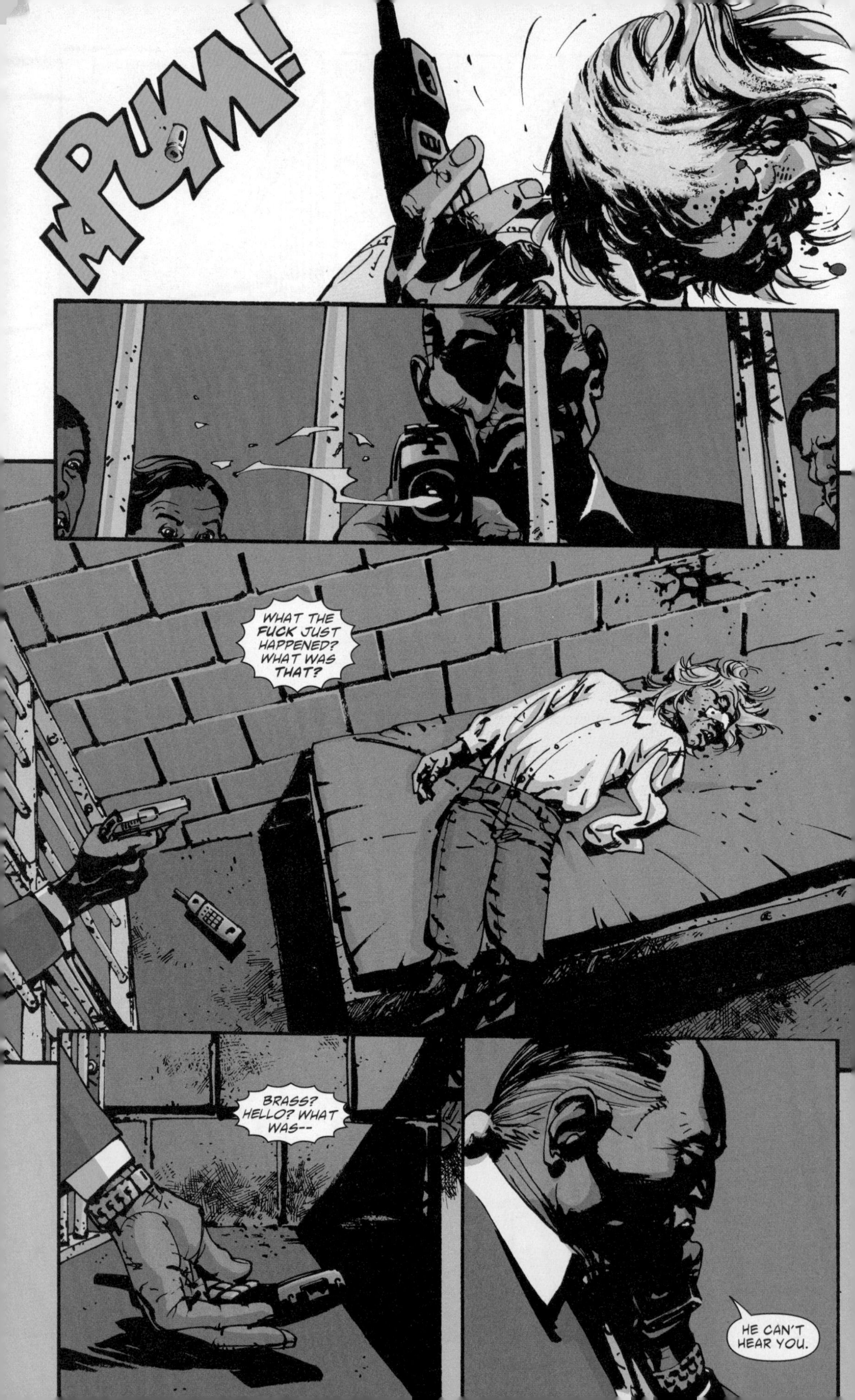

KAPUM!
WHAT THE FUCK JUST HAPPENED? WHAT WAS THAT?
BRASS? HELLO? WHAT WAS--
HE CAN'T HEAR YOU.

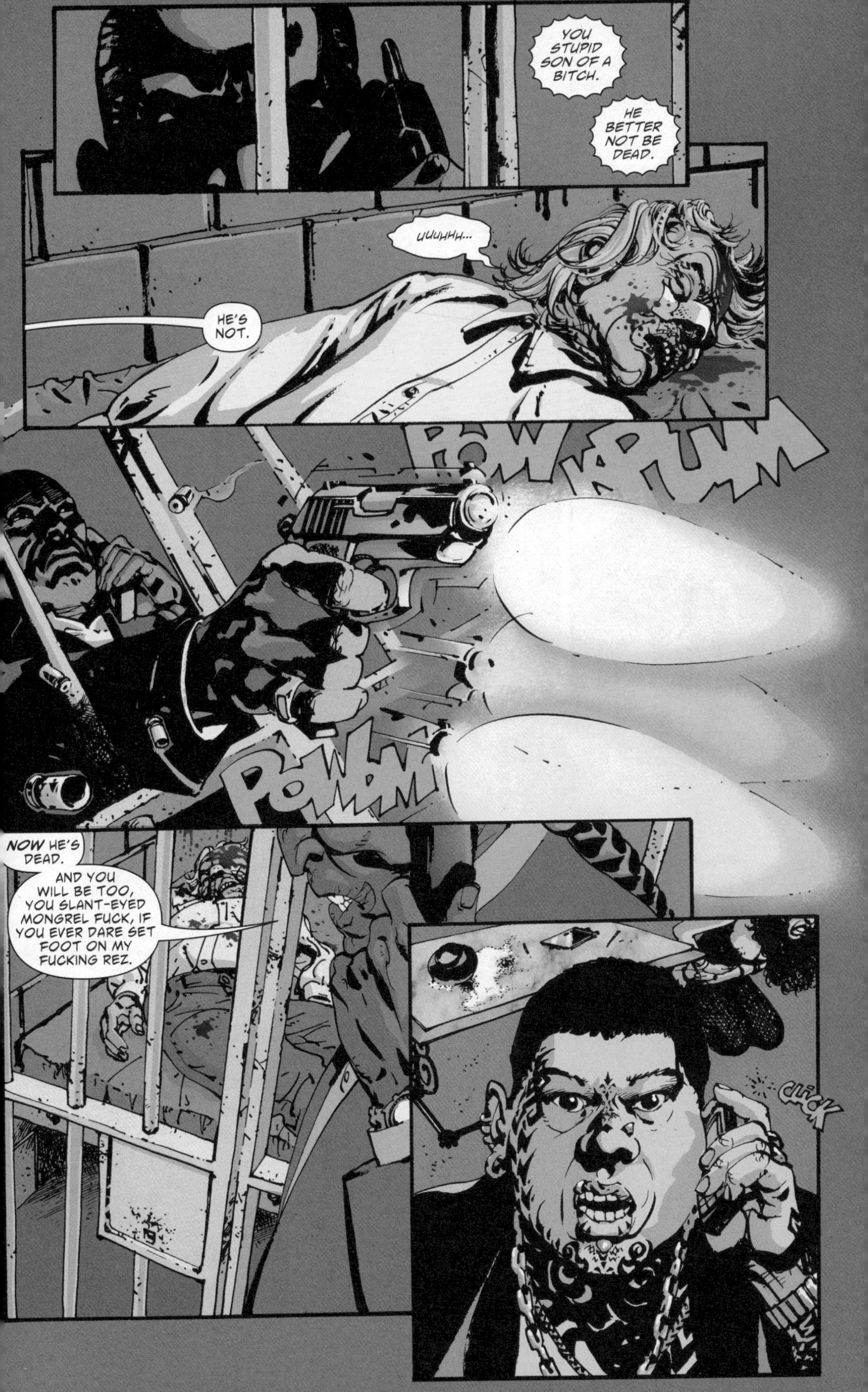
YOU STUPID SON OF A BITCH.
HE BETTER NOT BE DEAD.
UUUHHH...
HE'S NOT.
POWKAPTUM
POWM
NOW HE'S DEAD.
AND YOU WILL BE TOO, YOU SLANT-EYED MONGREL FUCK, IF YOU EVER DARE SET FOOT ON MY FUCKING REZ.
CLICK

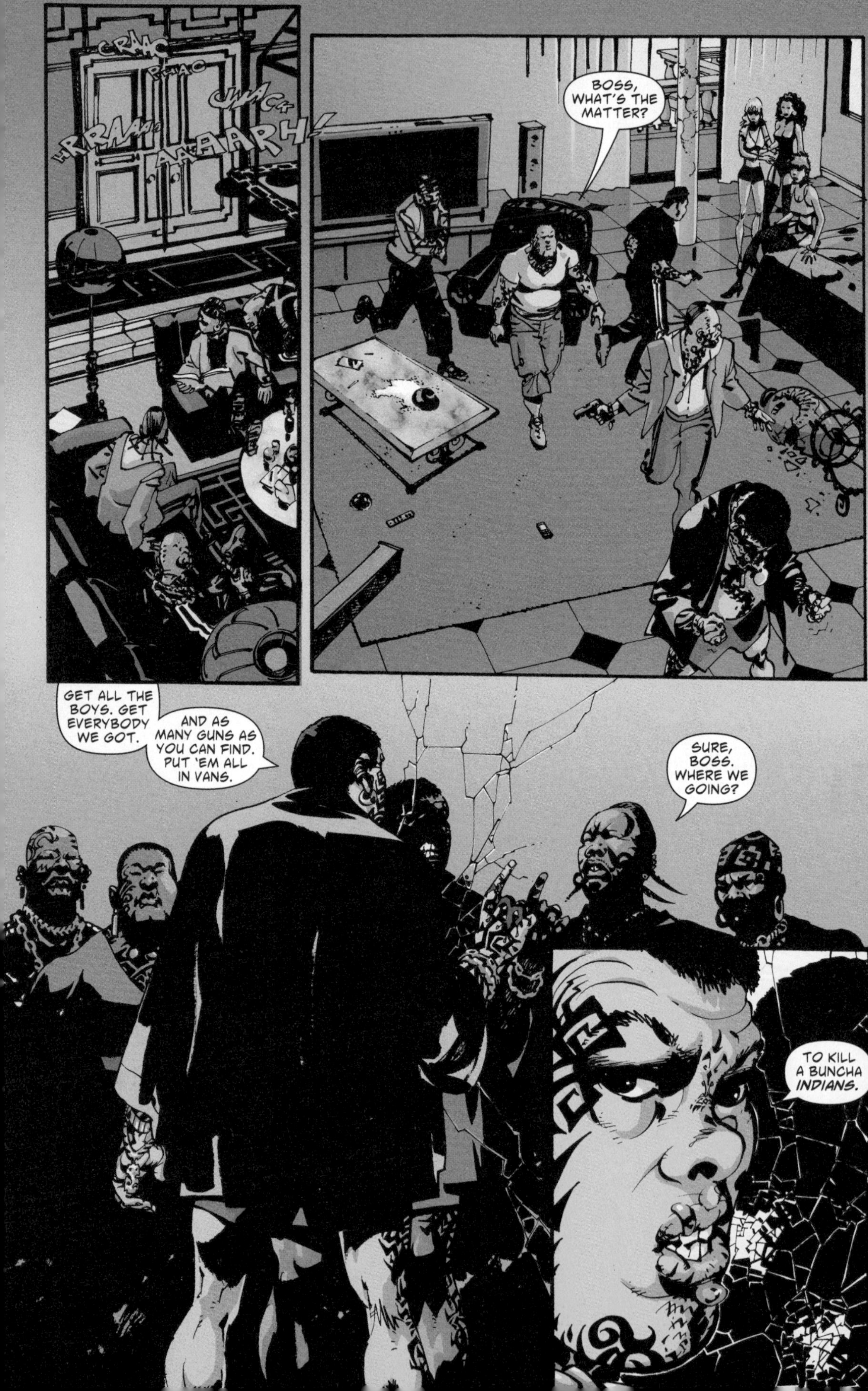
CRAAC
PHAC
CWACK
HRRAAA
AAAAARH!
BOSS, WHAT'S THE MATTER?
GET ALL THE BOYS. GET EVERYBODY WE GOT.
AND AS MANY GUNS AS YOU CAN FIND. PUT 'EM ALL IN VANS.
SURE, BOSS. WHERE WE GOING?
TO KILL A BUNCHA *INDIANS.*

CHAPTER 2

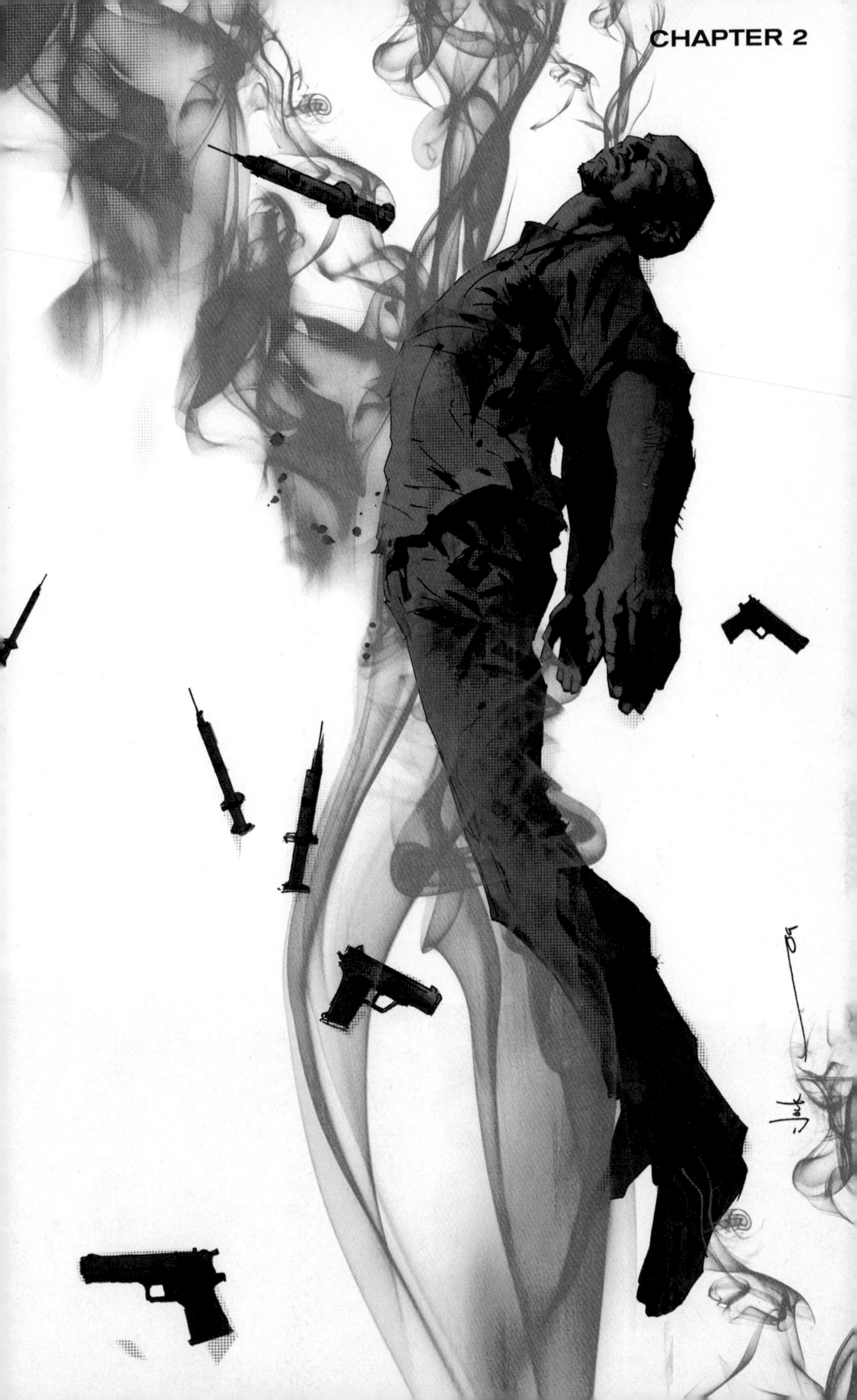

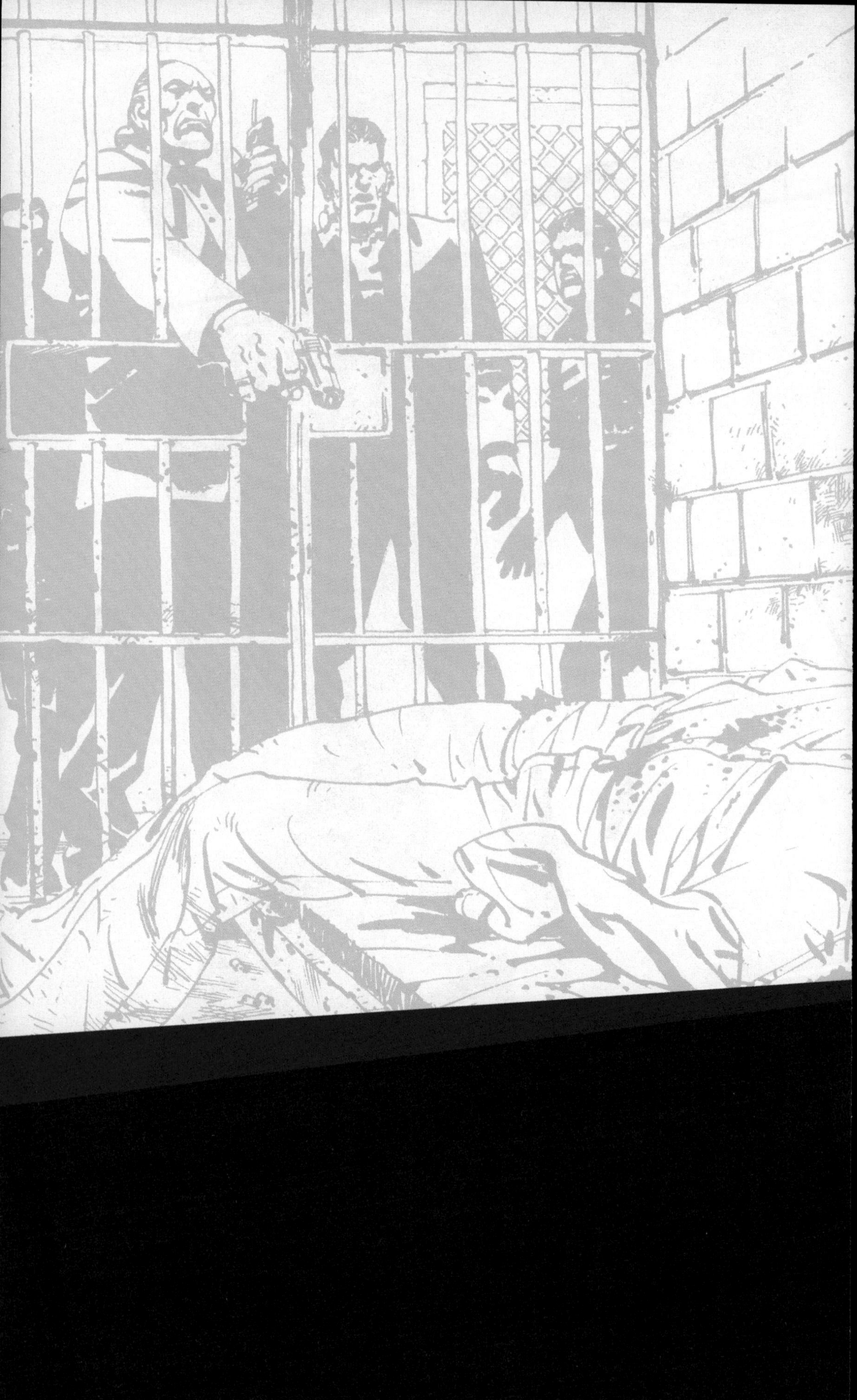

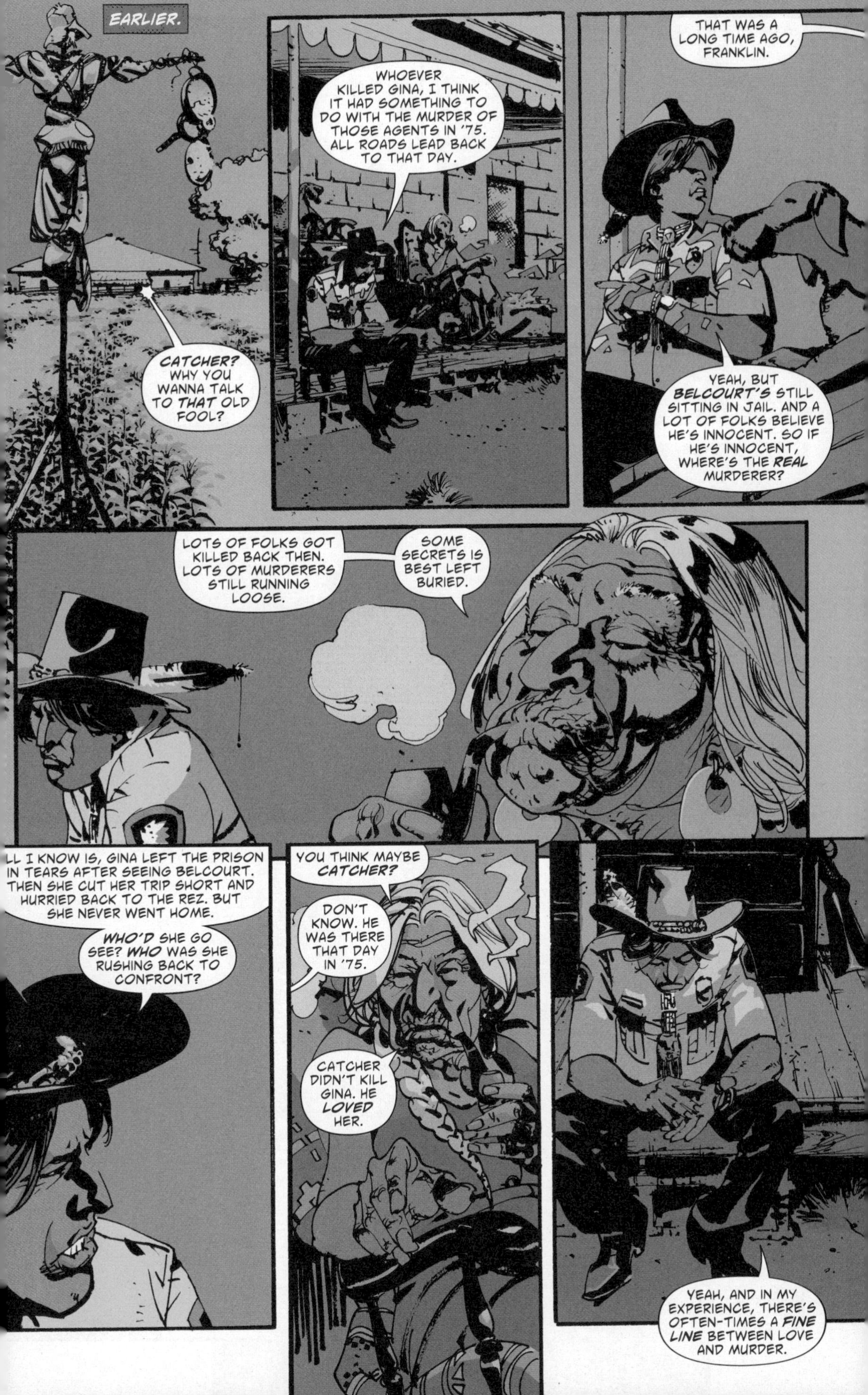
EARLIER.
CATCHER? WHY YOU WANNA TALK TO THAT OLD FOOL?
WHOEVER KILLED GINA, I THINK IT HAD SOMETHING TO DO WITH THE MURDER OF THOSE AGENTS IN '75. ALL ROADS LEAD BACK TO THAT DAY.
THAT WAS A LONG TIME AGO, FRANKLIN.
YEAH, BUT BELCOURT'S STILL SITTING IN JAIL. AND A LOT OF FOLKS BELIEVE HE'S INNOCENT. SO IF HE'S INNOCENT, WHERE'S THE REAL MURDERER?
LOTS OF FOLKS GOT KILLED BACK THEN. LOTS OF MURDERERS STILL RUNNING LOOSE.
SOME SECRETS IS BEST LEFT BURIED.
LL I KNOW IS, GINA LEFT THE PRISON IN TEARS AFTER SEEING BELCOURT. THEN SHE CUT HER TRIP SHORT AND HURRIED BACK TO THE REZ. BUT SHE NEVER WENT HOME.
WHO'D SHE GO SEE? WHO WAS SHE RUSHING BACK TO CONFRONT?
YOU THINK MAYBE CATCHER?
DON'T KNOW. HE WAS THERE THAT DAY IN '75.
CATCHER DIDN'T KILL GINA. HE LOVED HER.
YEAH, AND IN MY EXPERIENCE, THERE'S OFTEN-TIMES A FINE LINE BETWEEN LOVE AND MURDER.

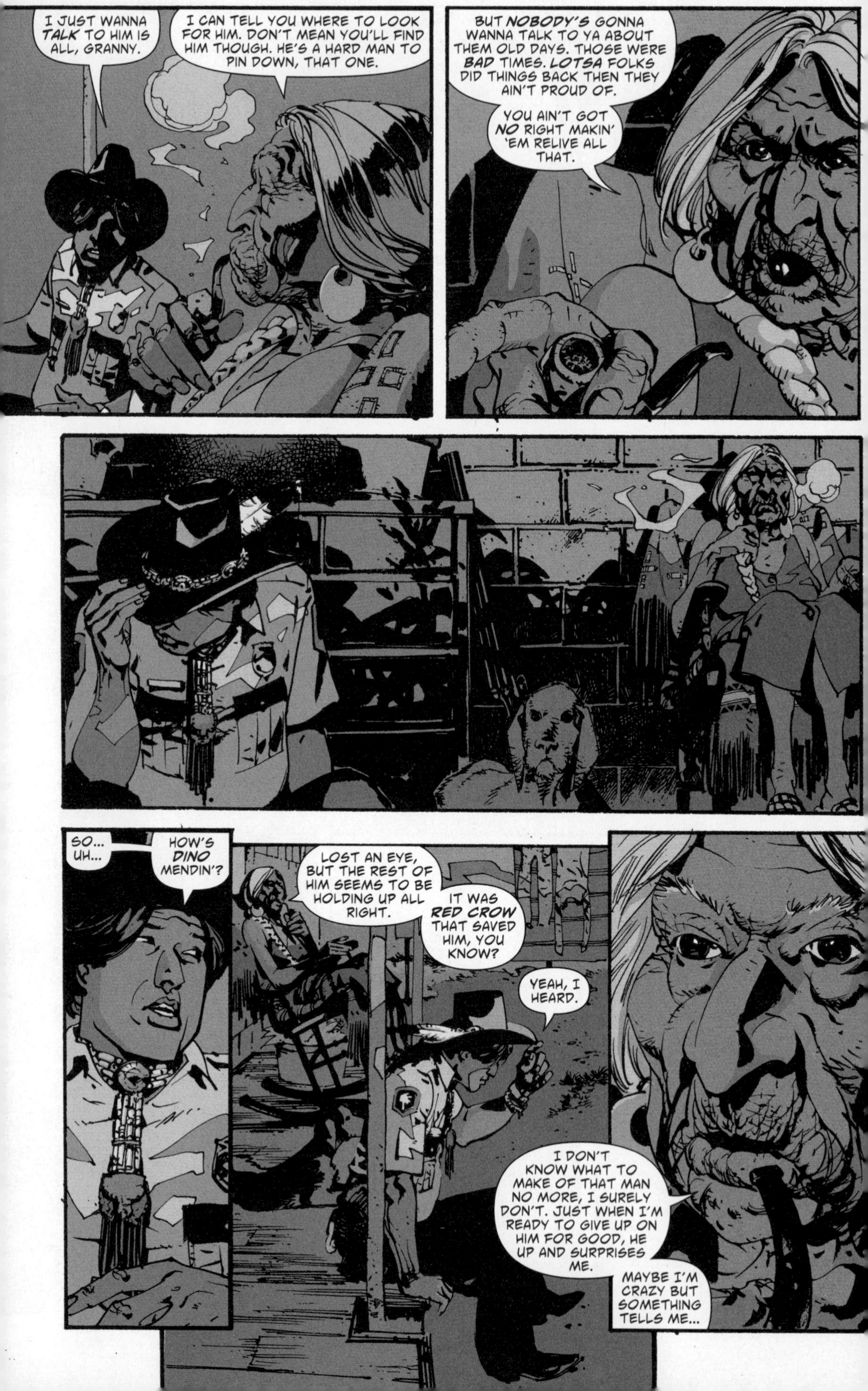
I JUST WANNA TALK TO HIM IS ALL, GRANNY.
I CAN TELL YOU WHERE TO LOOK FOR HIM. DON'T MEAN YOU'LL FIND HIM THOUGH. HE'S A HARD MAN TO PIN DOWN, THAT ONE.
BUT NOBODY'S GONNA WANNA TALK TO YA ABOUT THEM OLD DAYS. THOSE WERE BAD TIMES. LOTSA FOLKS DID THINGS BACK THEN THEY AIN'T PROUD OF.
YOU AIN'T GOT NO RIGHT MAKIN' 'EM RELIVE ALL THAT.
SO... UH...
HOW'S DINO MENDIN'?
LOST AN EYE, BUT THE REST OF HIM SEEMS TO BE HOLDING UP ALL RIGHT.
IT WAS RED CROW THAT SAVED HIM, YOU KNOW?
YEAH, I HEARD.
I DON'T KNOW WHAT TO MAKE OF THAT MAN NO MORE, I SURELY DON'T. JUST WHEN I'M READY TO GIVE UP ON HIM FOR GOOD, HE UP AND SURPRISES ME.
MAYBE I'M CRAZY BUT SOMETHING TELLS ME...

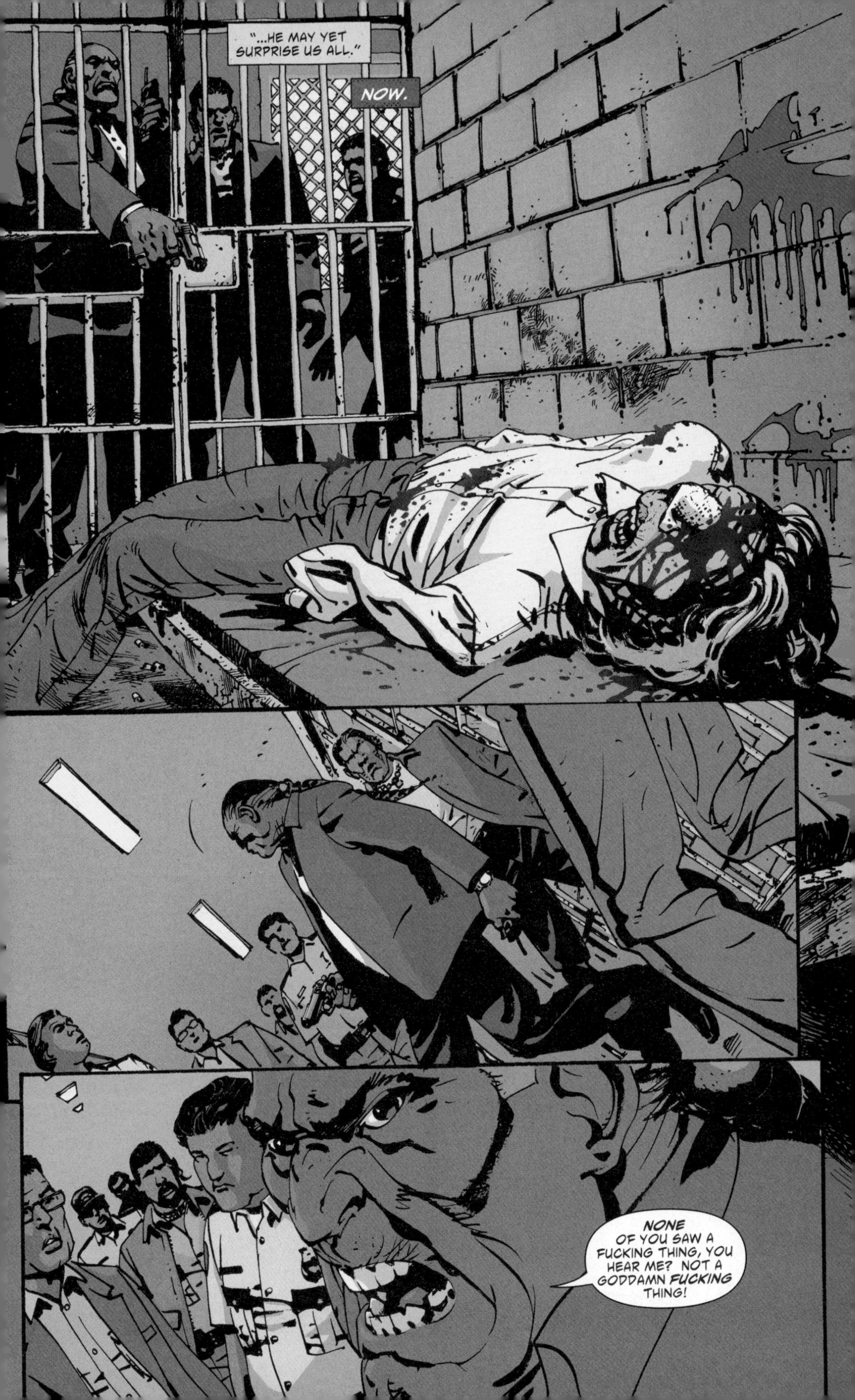
"...HE MAY YET SURPRISE US ALL."
NOW.
NONE OF YOU SAW A FUCKING THING, YOU HEAR ME? NOT A GODDAMN FUCKING THING!

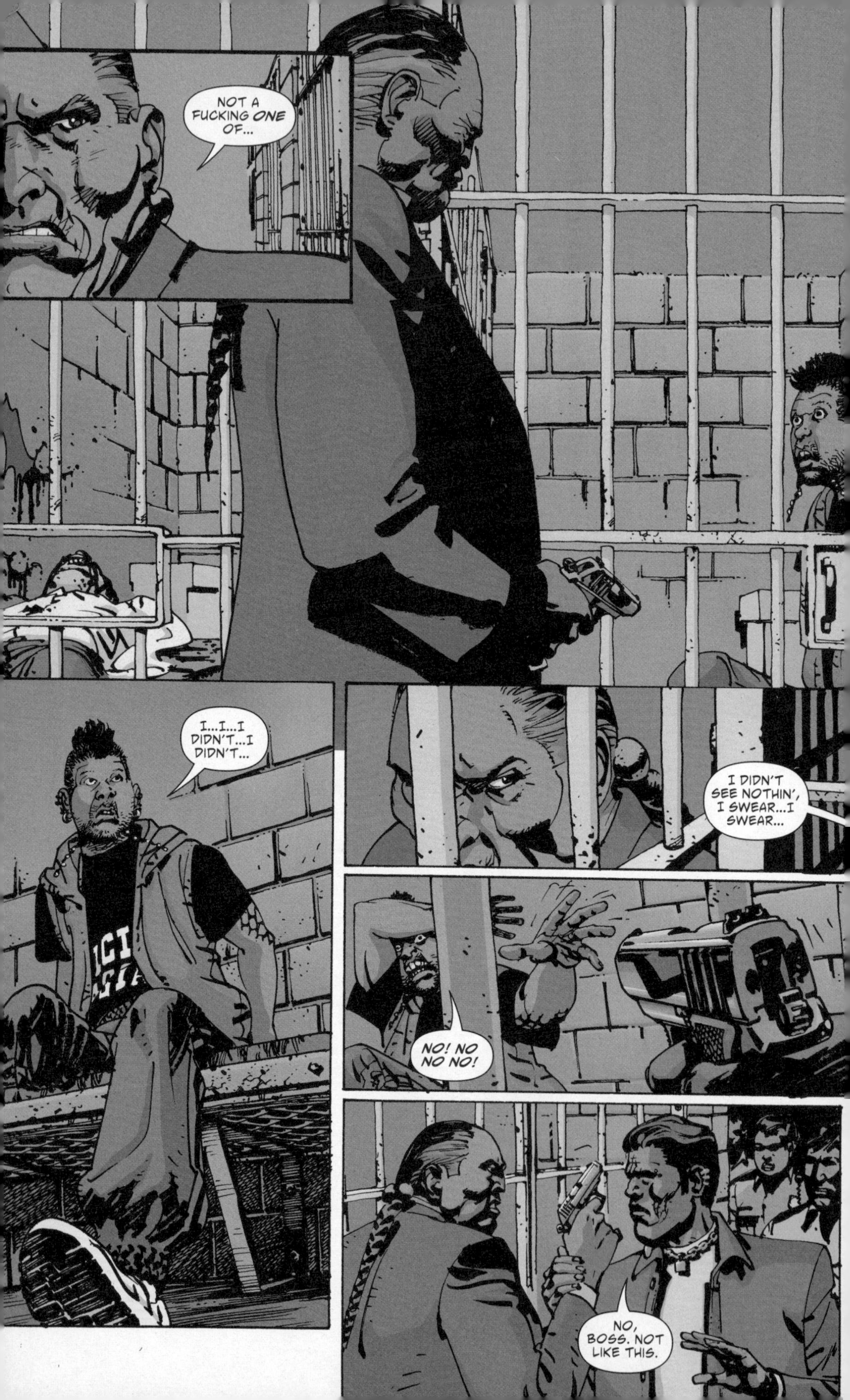
NOT A FUCKING ONE OF...
I...I...I DIDN'T...I DIDN'T...
I DIDN'T SEE NOTHIN', I SWEAR...I SWEAR...
NO! NO NO NO!
NO, BOSS. NOT LIKE THIS.

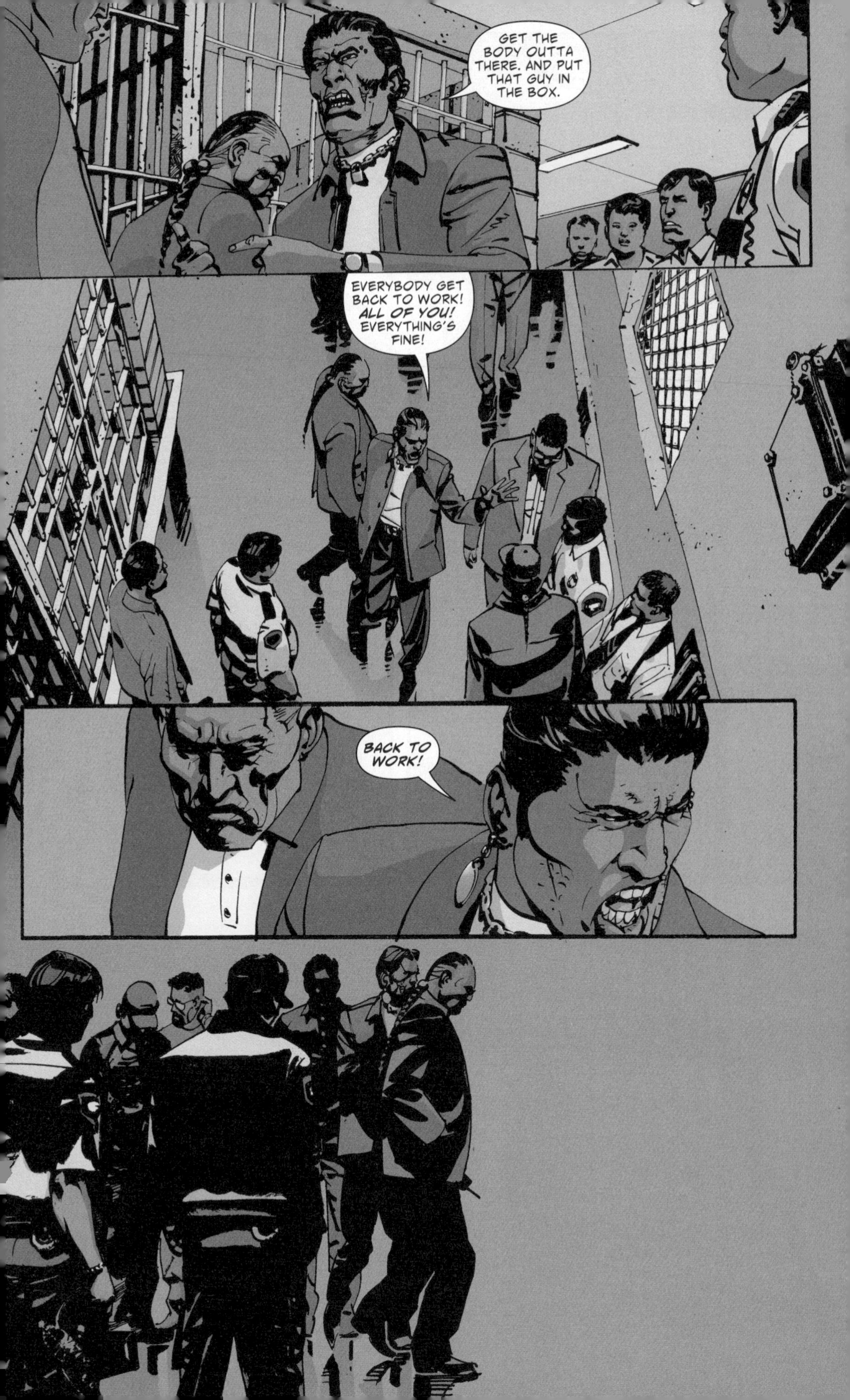
GET THE BODY OUTTA THERE. AND PUT THAT GUY IN THE BOX.
EVERYBODY GET BACK TO WORK! *ALL OF YOU!* EVERYTHING'S FINE!
BACK TO WORK!

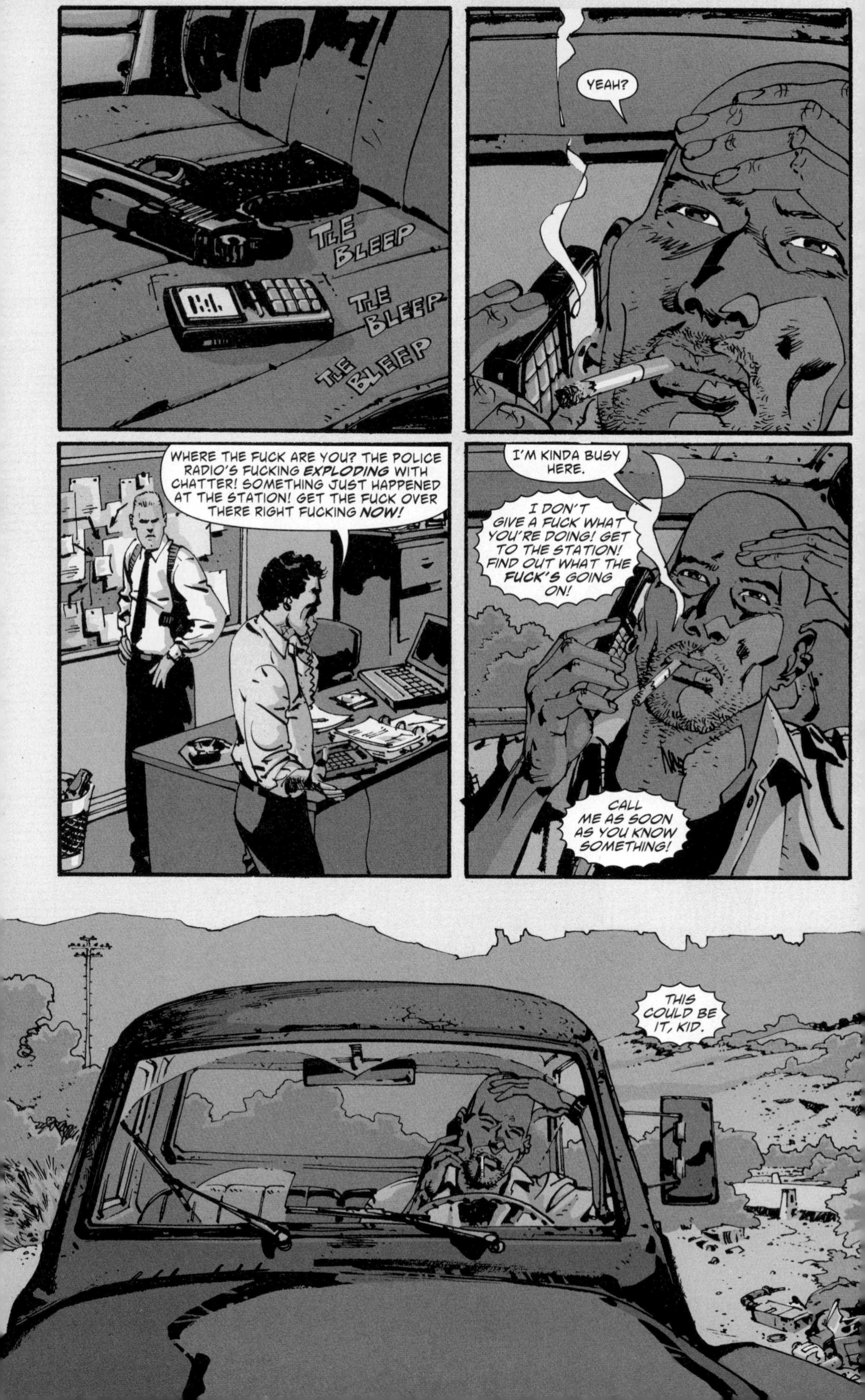
TLE BLEEP
TLE BLEEP
TLE BLEEP
YEAH?
WHERE THE FUCK ARE YOU? THE POLICE RADIO'S FUCKING EXPLODING WITH CHATTER! SOMETHING JUST HAPPENED AT THE STATION! GET THE FUCK OVER THERE RIGHT FUCKING NOW!
I'M KINDA BUSY HERE.
I DON'T GIVE A FUCK WHAT YOU'RE DOING! GET TO THE STATION! FIND OUT WHAT THE FUCK'S GOING ON!
CALL ME AS SOON AS YOU KNOW SOMETHING!
THIS COULD BE IT, KID.

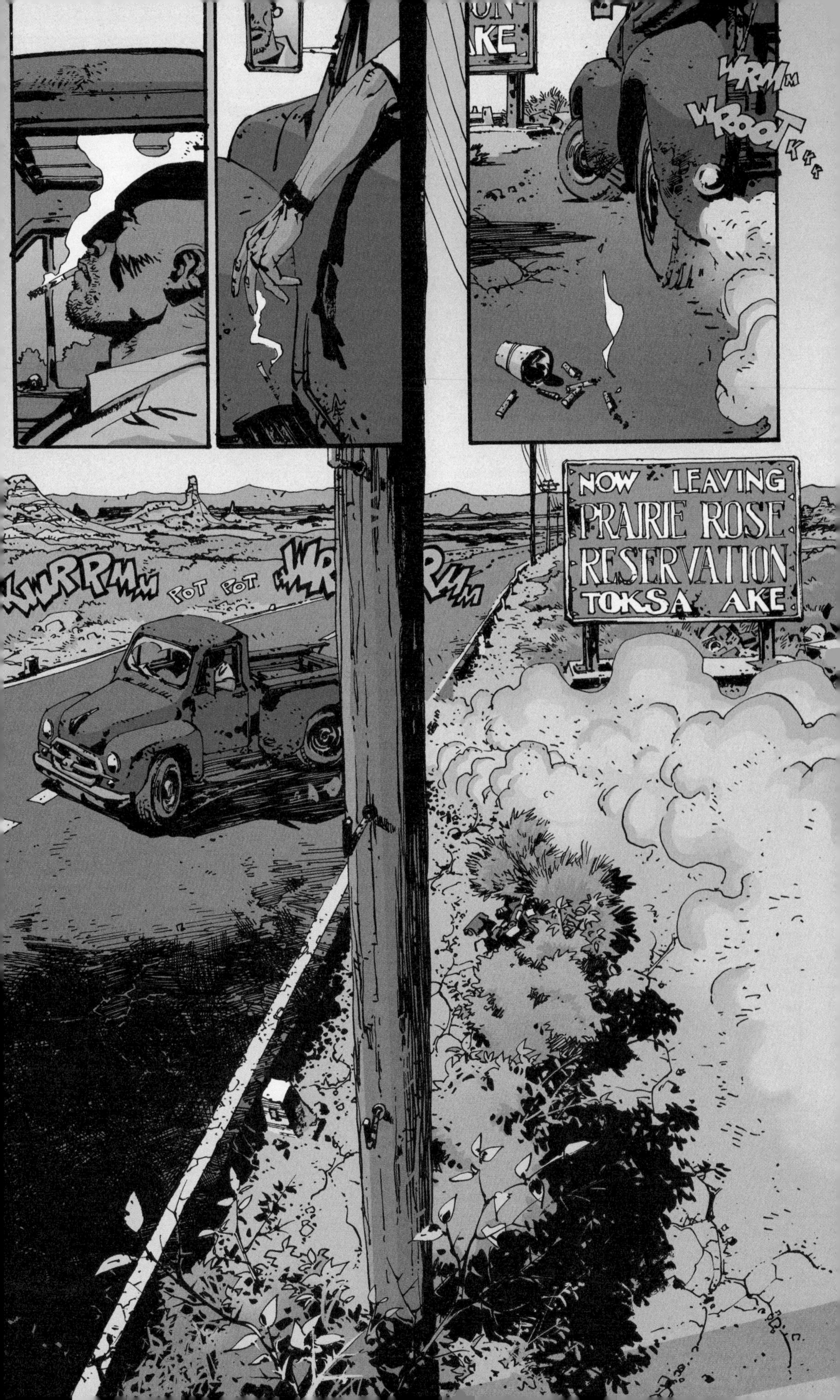

POT POT
NOW LEAVING
PRAIRIE ROSE
RESERVATION
TOKSA AKE

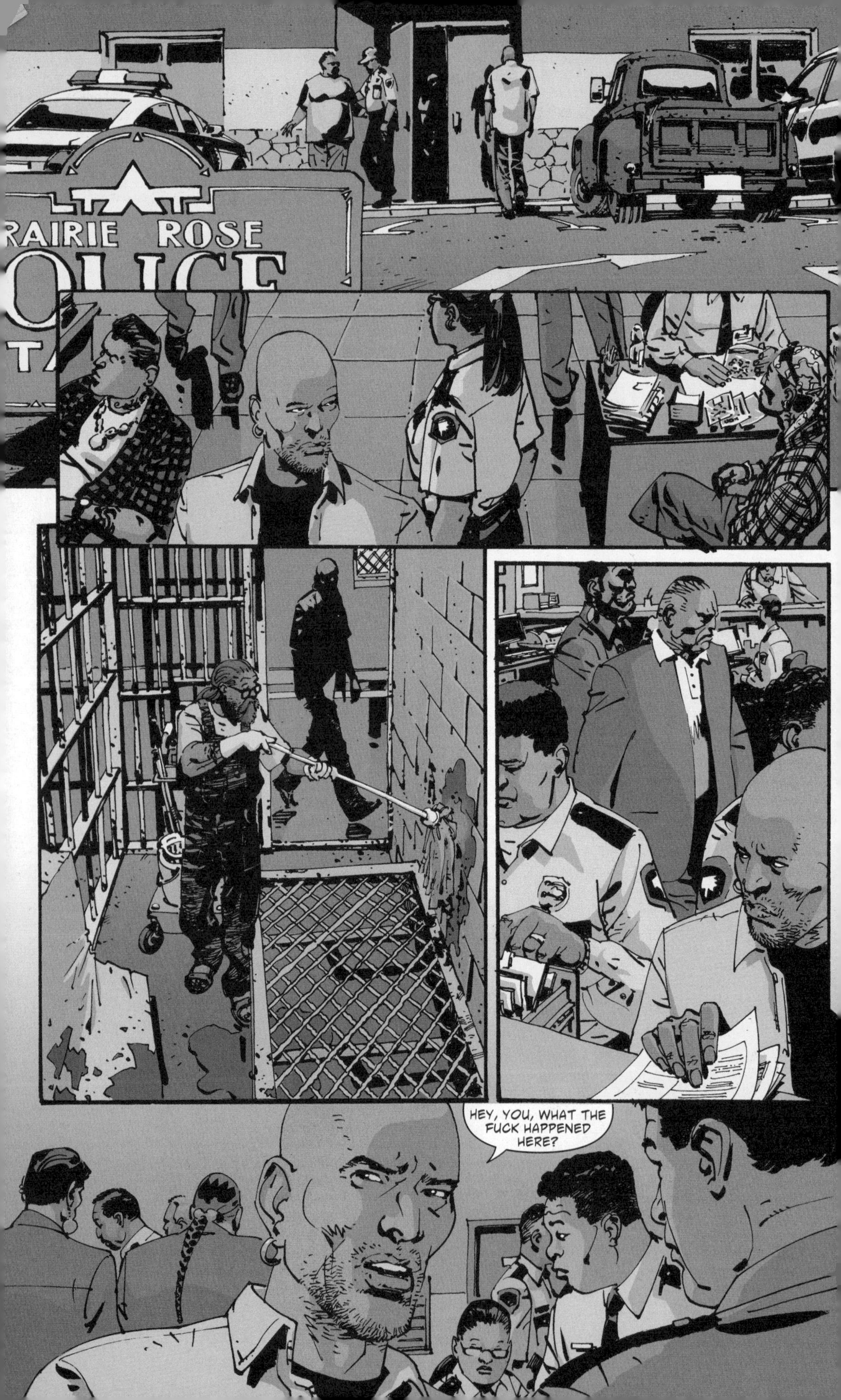

PRAIRIE ROSE
POLICE
HEY, YOU, WHAT THE FUCK HAPPENED HERE?

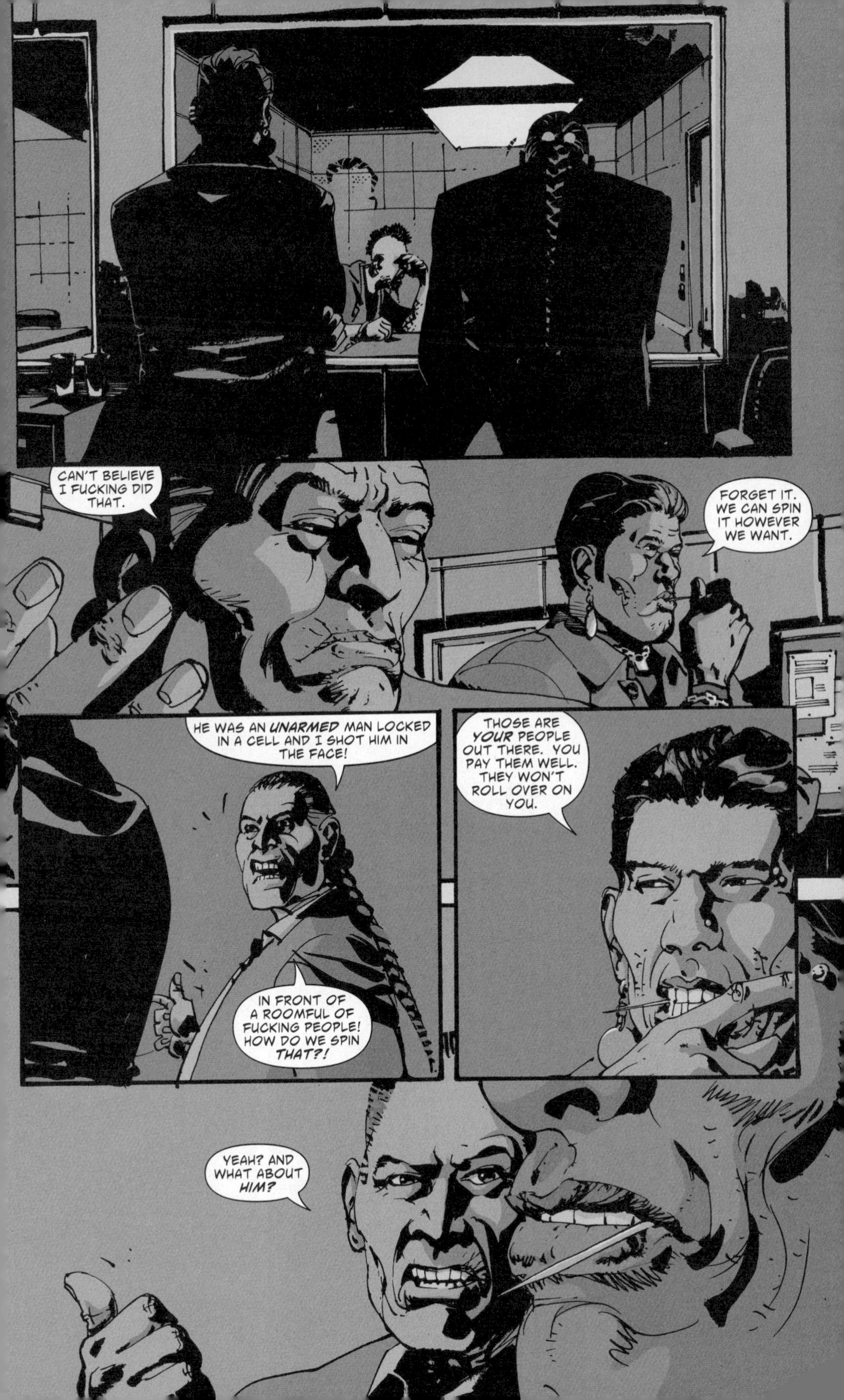

CAN'T BELIEVE I FUCKING DID THAT.
FORGET IT. WE CAN SPIN IT HOWEVER WE WANT.
HE WAS AN *UNARMED* MAN LOCKED IN A CELL AND I SHOT HIM IN THE FACE!
IN FRONT OF A ROOMFUL OF FUCKING PEOPLE! HOW DO WE SPIN *THAT?!*
THOSE ARE *YOUR* PEOPLE OUT THERE. YOU PAY THEM WELL. THEY WON'T ROLL OVER ON YOU.
YEAH? AND WHAT ABOUT *HIM?*

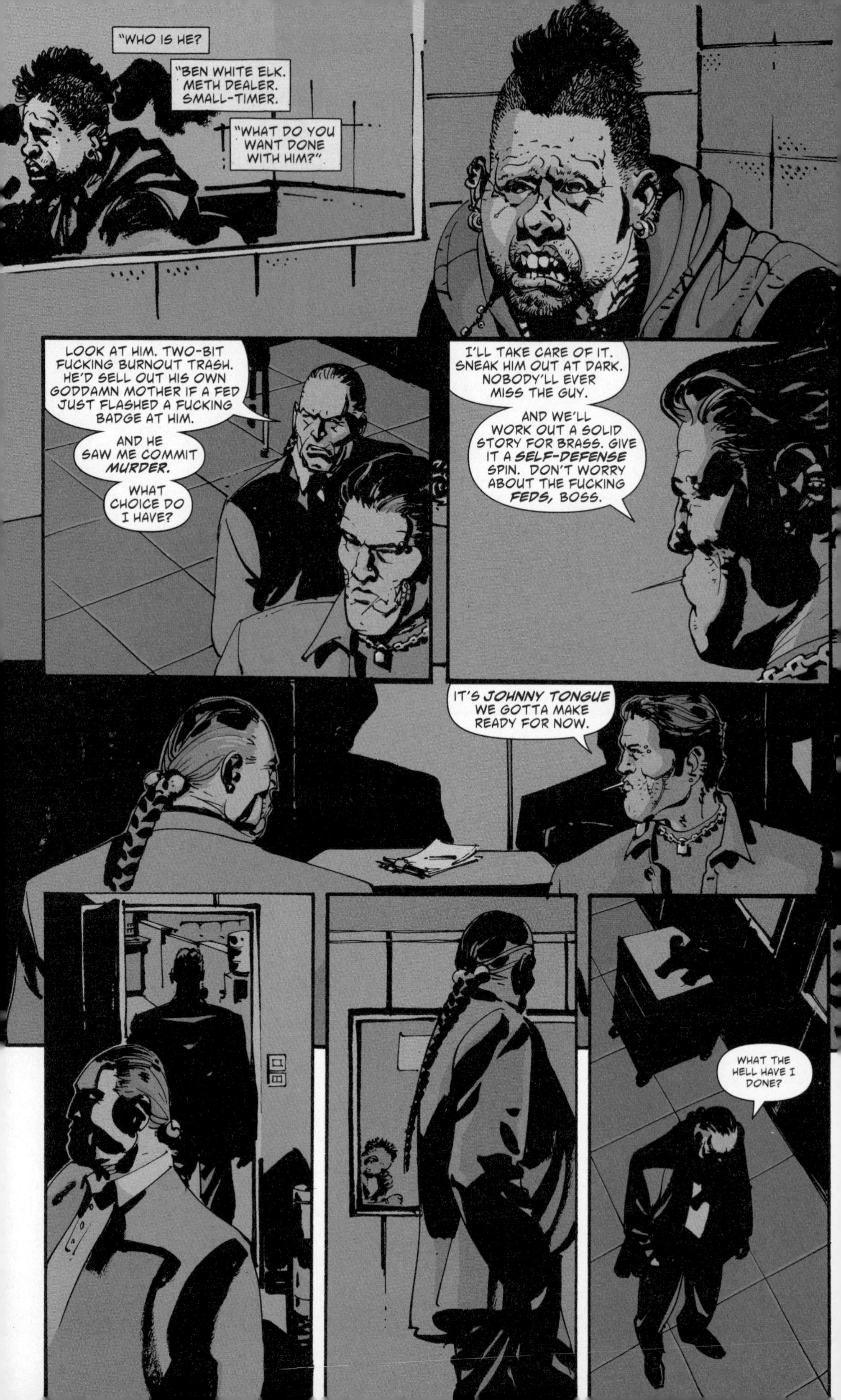
"WHO IS HE?
"BEN WHITE ELK. METH DEALER. SMALL-TIMER.
"WHAT DO YOU WANT DONE WITH HIM?"
LOOK AT HIM. TWO-BIT FUCKING BURNOUT TRASH. HE'D SELL OUT HIS OWN GODDAMN MOTHER IF A FED JUST FLASHED A FUCKING BADGE AT HIM.
AND HE SAW ME COMMIT MURDER.
WHAT CHOICE DO I HAVE?
I'LL TAKE CARE OF IT. SNEAK HIM OUT AT DARK. NOBODY'LL EVER MISS THE GUY.
AND WE'LL WORK OUT A SOLID STORY FOR BRASS. GIVE IT A SELF-DEFENSE SPIN. DON'T WORRY ABOUT THE FUCKING FEDS, BOSS.
IT'S JOHNNY TONGUE WE GOTTA MAKE READY FOR NOW.
WHAT THE HELL HAVE I DONE?

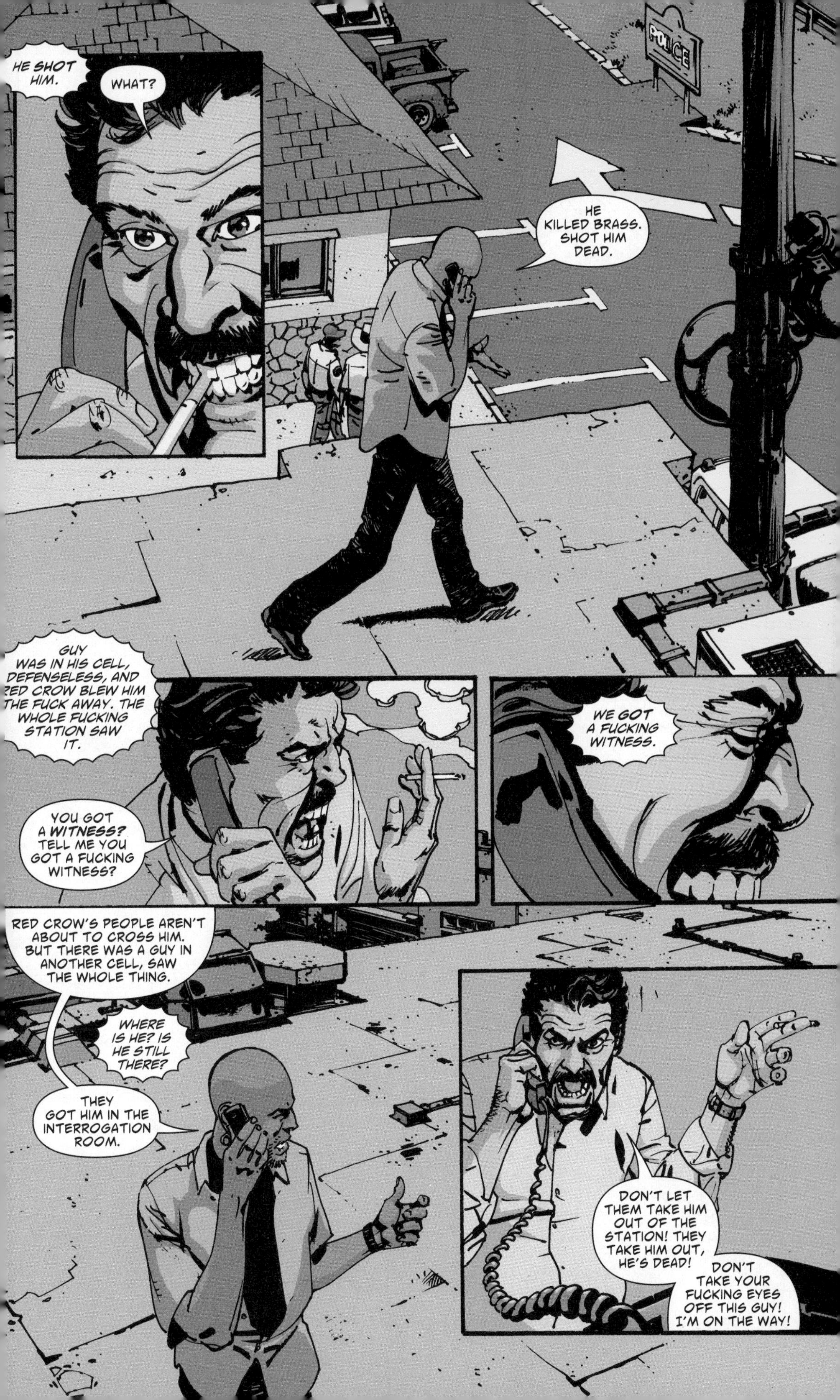
HE SHOT HIM.
WHAT?
HE KILLED BRASS. SHOT HIM DEAD.
POLICE
GUY WAS IN HIS CELL, DEFENSELESS, AND RED CROW BLEW HIM THE FUCK AWAY. THE WHOLE FUCKING STATION SAW IT.
YOU GOT A WITNESS? TELL ME YOU GOT A FUCKING WITNESS?
WE GOT A FUCKING WITNESS.
RED CROW'S PEOPLE AREN'T ABOUT TO CROSS HIM. BUT THERE WAS A GUY IN ANOTHER CELL, SAW THE WHOLE THING.
WHERE IS HE? IS HE STILL THERE?
THEY GOT HIM IN THE INTERROGATION ROOM.
DON'T LET THEM TAKE HIM OUT OF THE STATION! THEY TAKE HIM OUT, HE'S DEAD!
DON'T TAKE YOUR FUCKING EYES OFF THIS GUY! I'M ON THE WAY!

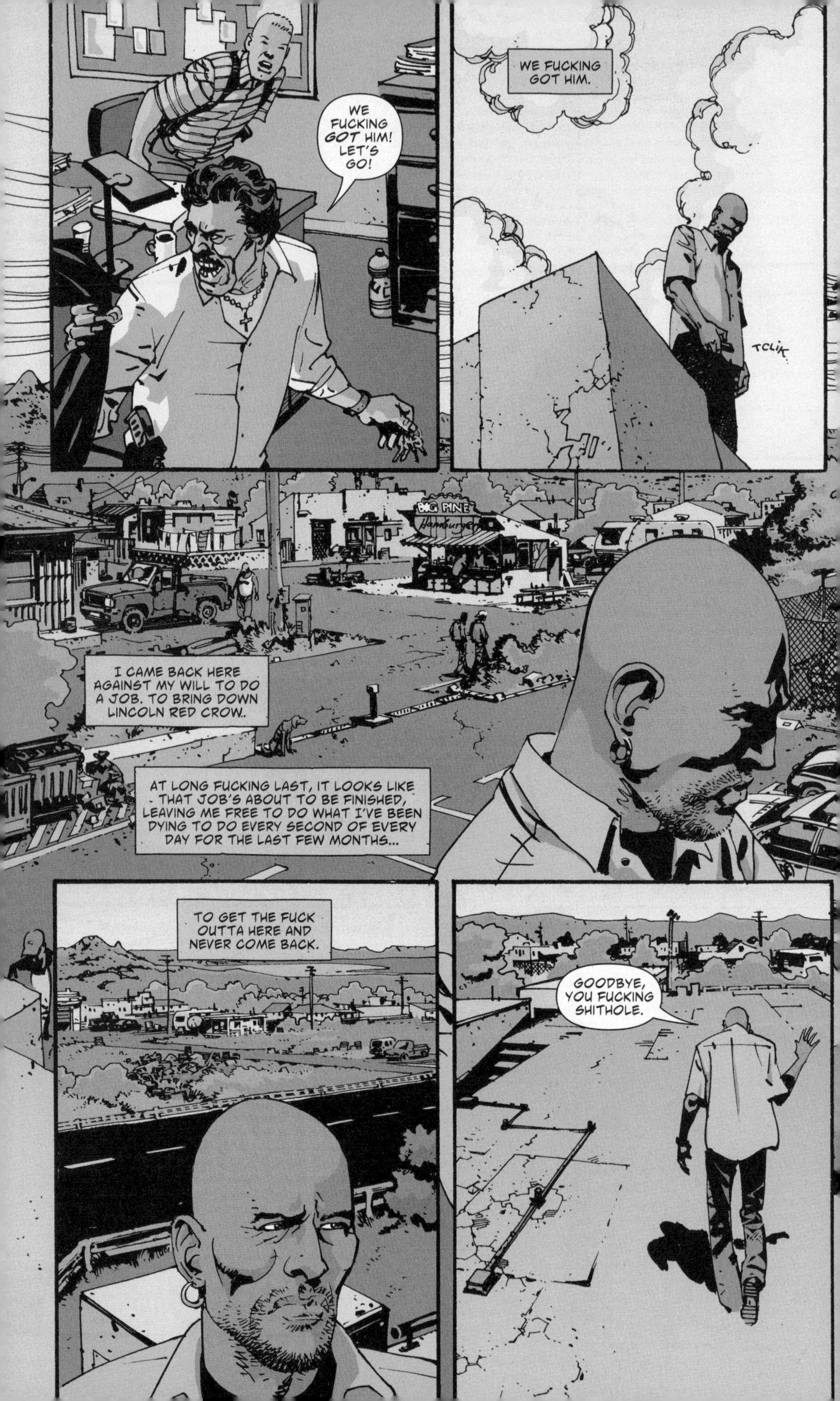
WE FUCKING GOT HIM! LET'S GO!
WE FUCKING GOT HIM.
TCLIK
BIG PINE Hamburgers
I CAME BACK HERE AGAINST MY WILL TO DO A JOB. TO BRING DOWN LINCOLN RED CROW.
AT LONG FUCKING LAST, IT LOOKS LIKE THAT JOB'S ABOUT TO BE FINISHED, LEAVING ME FREE TO DO WHAT I'VE BEEN DYING TO DO EVERY SECOND OF EVERY DAY FOR THE LAST FEW MONTHS...
TO GET THE FUCK OUTTA HERE AND NEVER COME BACK.
GOODBYE, YOU FUCKING SHITHOLE.

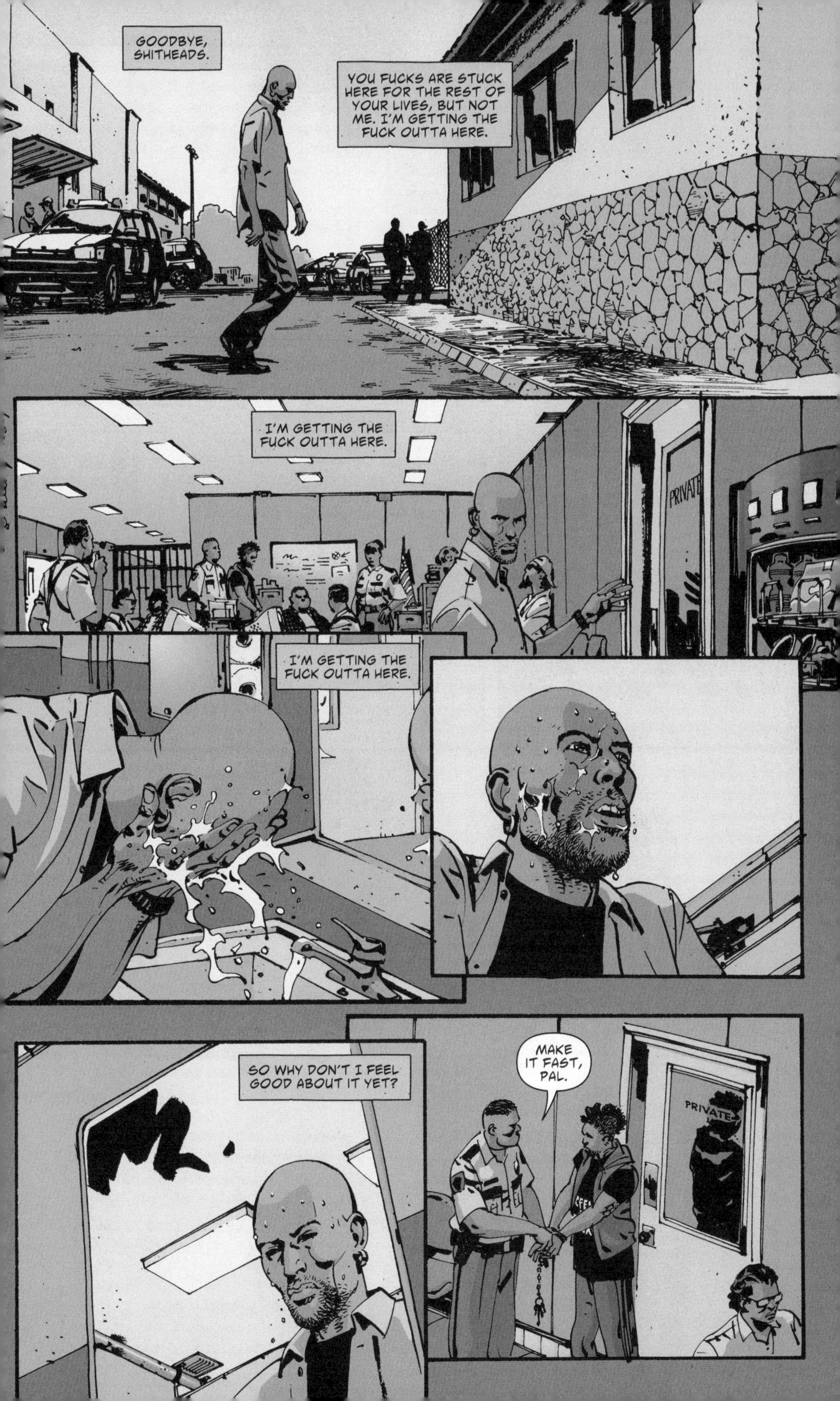
GOODBYE, SHITHEADS.
YOU FUCKS ARE STUCK HERE FOR THE REST OF YOUR LIVES, BUT NOT ME. I'M GETTING THE FUCK OUTTA HERE.
I'M GETTING THE FUCK OUTTA HERE.
PRIVATE
I'M GETTING THE FUCK OUTTA HERE.
SO WHY DON'T I FEEL GOOD ABOUT IT YET?
MAKE IT FAST, PAL.
PRIVATE

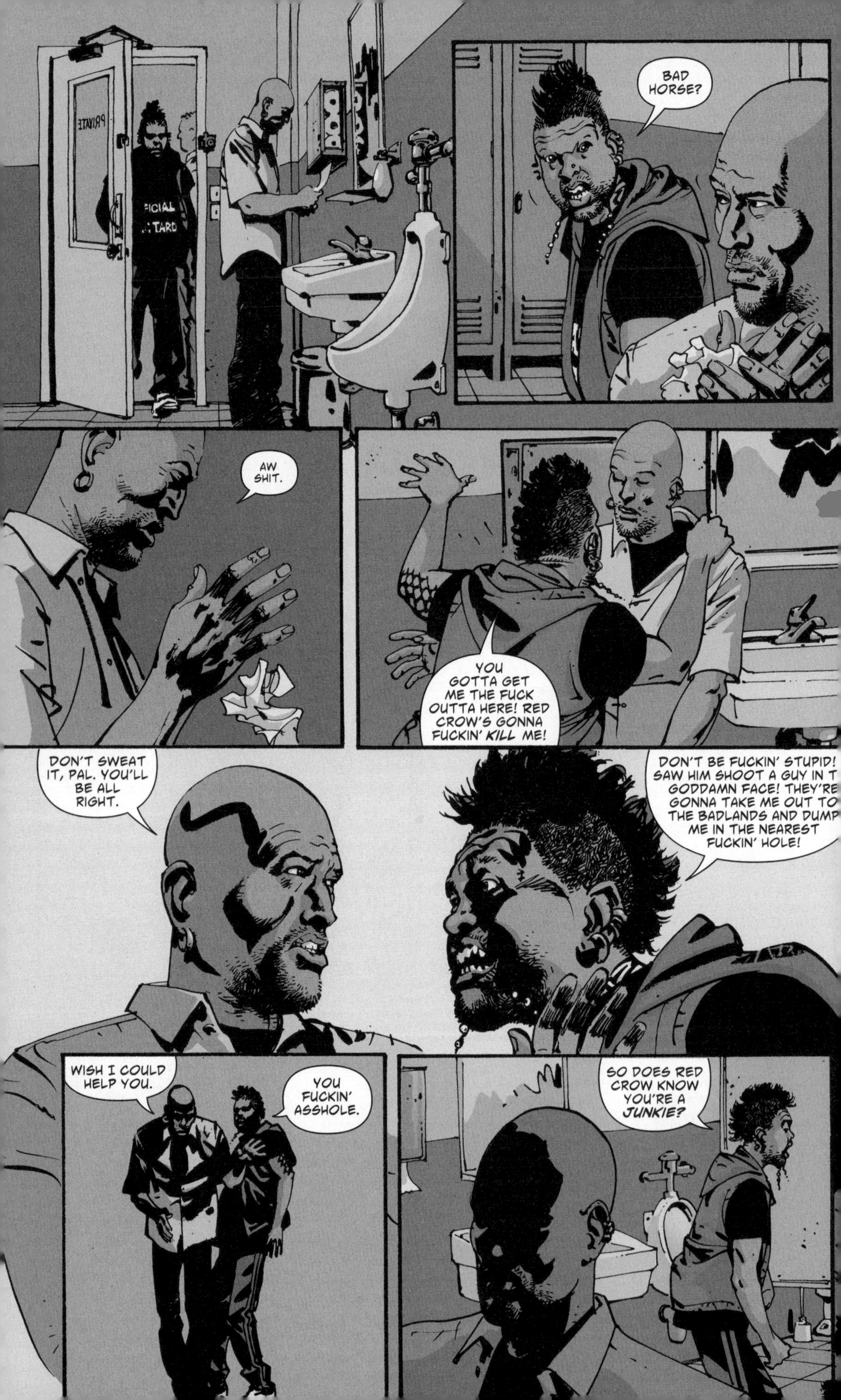
PRIVATE
FICIAL
TARD
BAD HORSE?
AW SHIT.
YOU GOTTA GET ME THE FUCK OUTTA HERE! RED CROW'S GONNA FUCKIN' KILL ME!
DON'T SWEAT IT, PAL. YOU'LL BE ALL RIGHT.
DON'T BE FUCKIN' STUPID! SAW HIM SHOOT A GUY IN T GODDAMN FACE! THEY'RE GONNA TAKE ME OUT TO THE BADLANDS AND DUMP ME IN THE NEAREST FUCKIN' HOLE!
WISH I COULD HELP YOU.
YOU FUCKIN' ASSHOLE.
SO DOES RED CROW KNOW YOU'RE A JUNKIE?

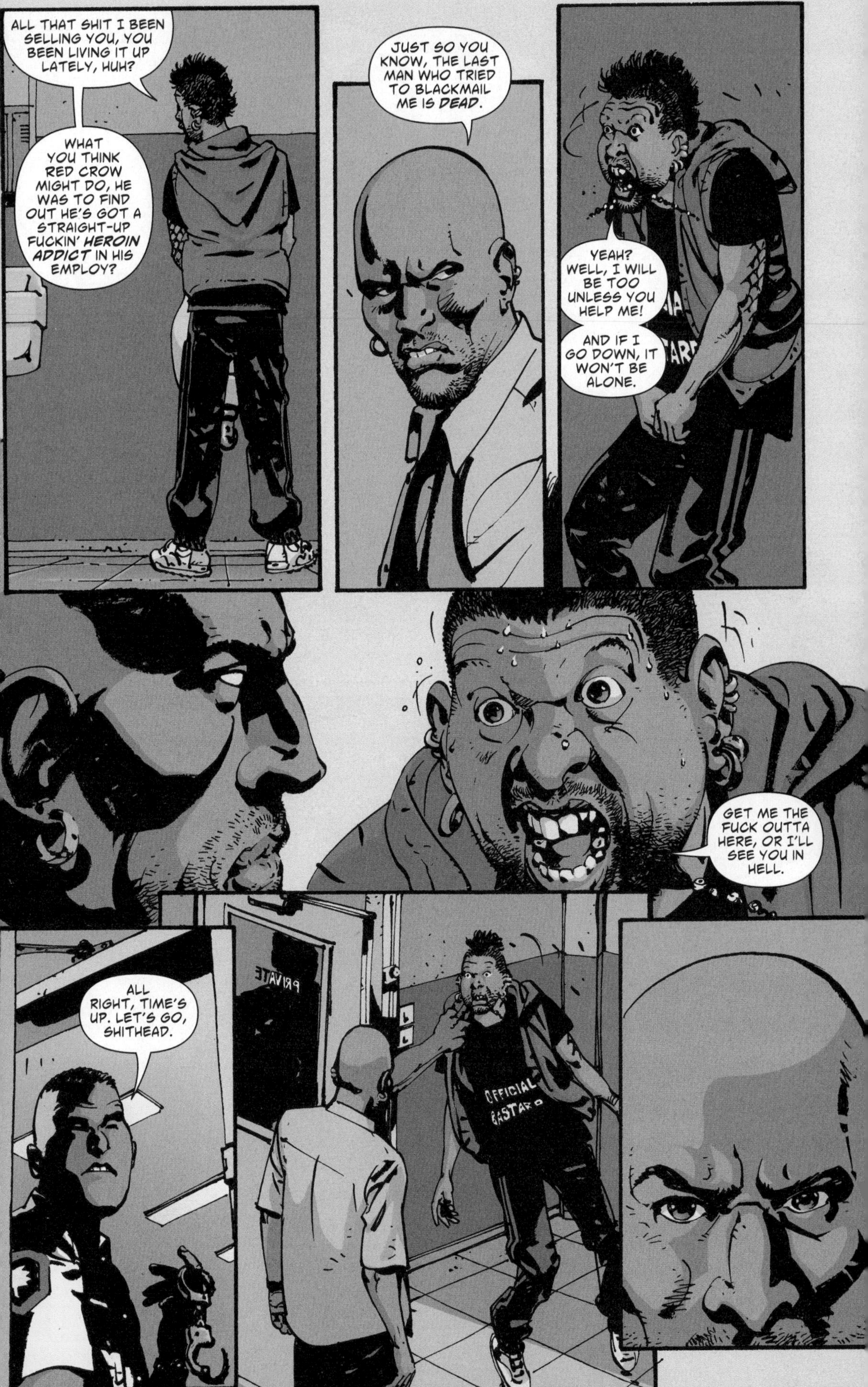
ALL THAT SHIT I BEEN SELLING YOU, YOU BEEN LIVING IT UP LATELY, HUH?
WHAT YOU THINK RED CROW MIGHT DO, HE WAS TO FIND OUT HE'S GOT A STRAIGHT-UP FUCKIN' HEROIN ADDICT IN HIS EMPLOY?
JUST SO YOU KNOW, THE LAST MAN WHO TRIED TO BLACKMAIL ME IS DEAD.
YEAH? WELL, I WILL BE TOO UNLESS YOU HELP ME!
AND IF I GO DOWN, IT WON'T BE ALONE.
GET ME THE FUCK OUTTA HERE, OR I'LL SEE YOU IN HELL.
ALL RIGHT, TIME'S UP. LET'S GO, SHITHEAD.
PRIVATE
OFFICIAL BASTARD

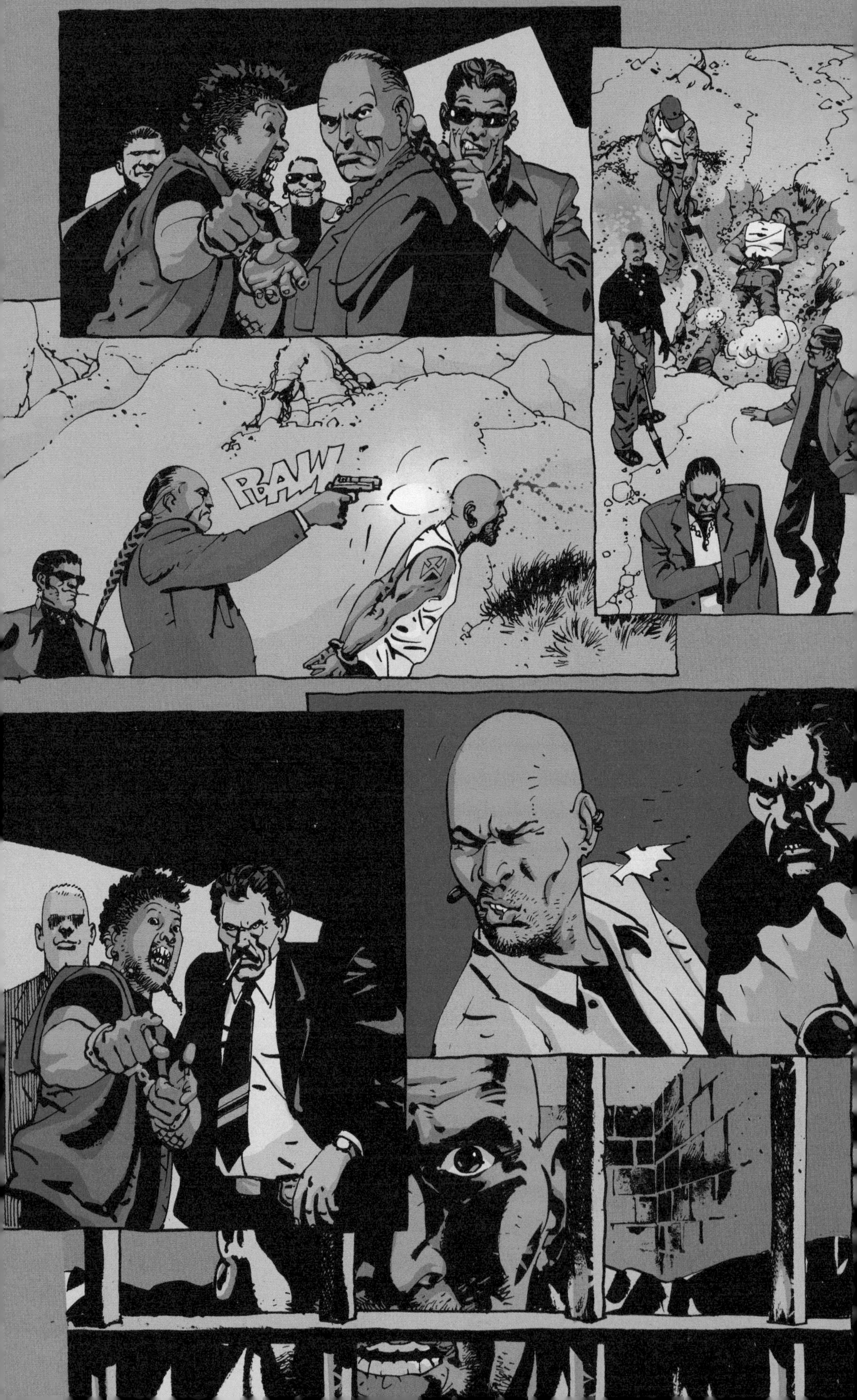
RAW

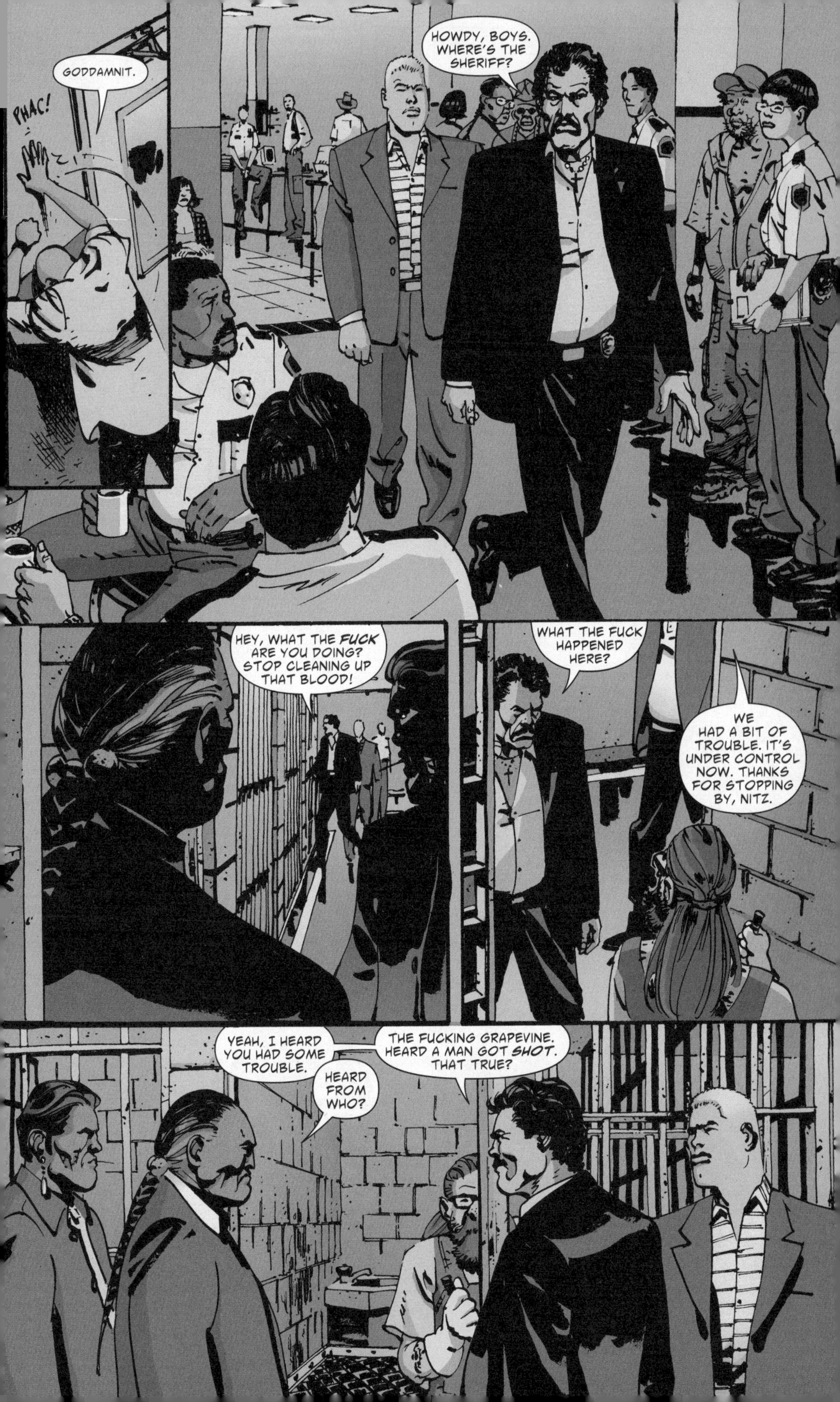
GODDAMNIT.
PHAC!
HOWDY, BOYS. WHERE'S THE SHERIFF?
HEY, WHAT THE FUCK ARE YOU DOING? STOP CLEANING UP THAT BLOOD!
WHAT THE FUCK HAPPENED HERE?
WE HAD A BIT OF TROUBLE. IT'S UNDER CONTROL NOW. THANKS FOR STOPPING BY, NITZ.
YEAH, I HEARD YOU HAD SOME TROUBLE.
HEARD FROM WHO?
THE FUCKING GRAPEVINE. HEARD A MAN GOT SHOT. THAT TRUE?

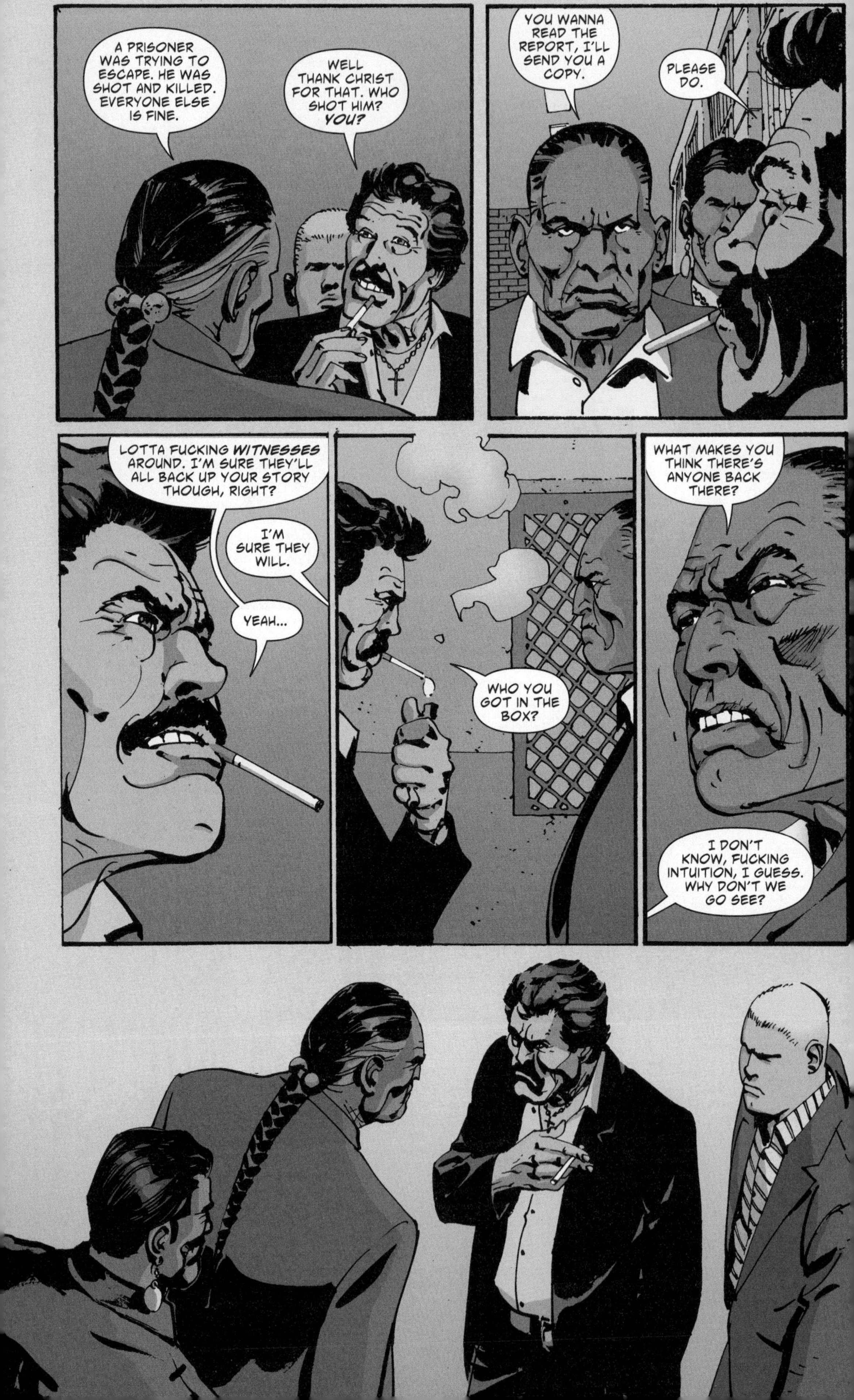
A PRISONER WAS TRYING TO ESCAPE. HE WAS SHOT AND KILLED. EVERYONE ELSE IS FINE.
WELL THANK CHRIST FOR THAT. WHO SHOT HIM? *YOU?*
YOU WANNA READ THE REPORT, I'LL SEND YOU A COPY.
PLEASE DO.
LOTTA FUCKING *WITNESSES* AROUND. I'M SURE THEY'LL ALL BACK UP YOUR STORY THOUGH, RIGHT?
I'M SURE THEY WILL.
YEAH...
WHO YOU GOT IN THE BOX?
WHAT MAKES YOU THINK THERE'S ANYONE BACK THERE?
I DON'T KNOW, FUCKING INTUITION, I GUESS. WHY DON'T WE GO SEE?

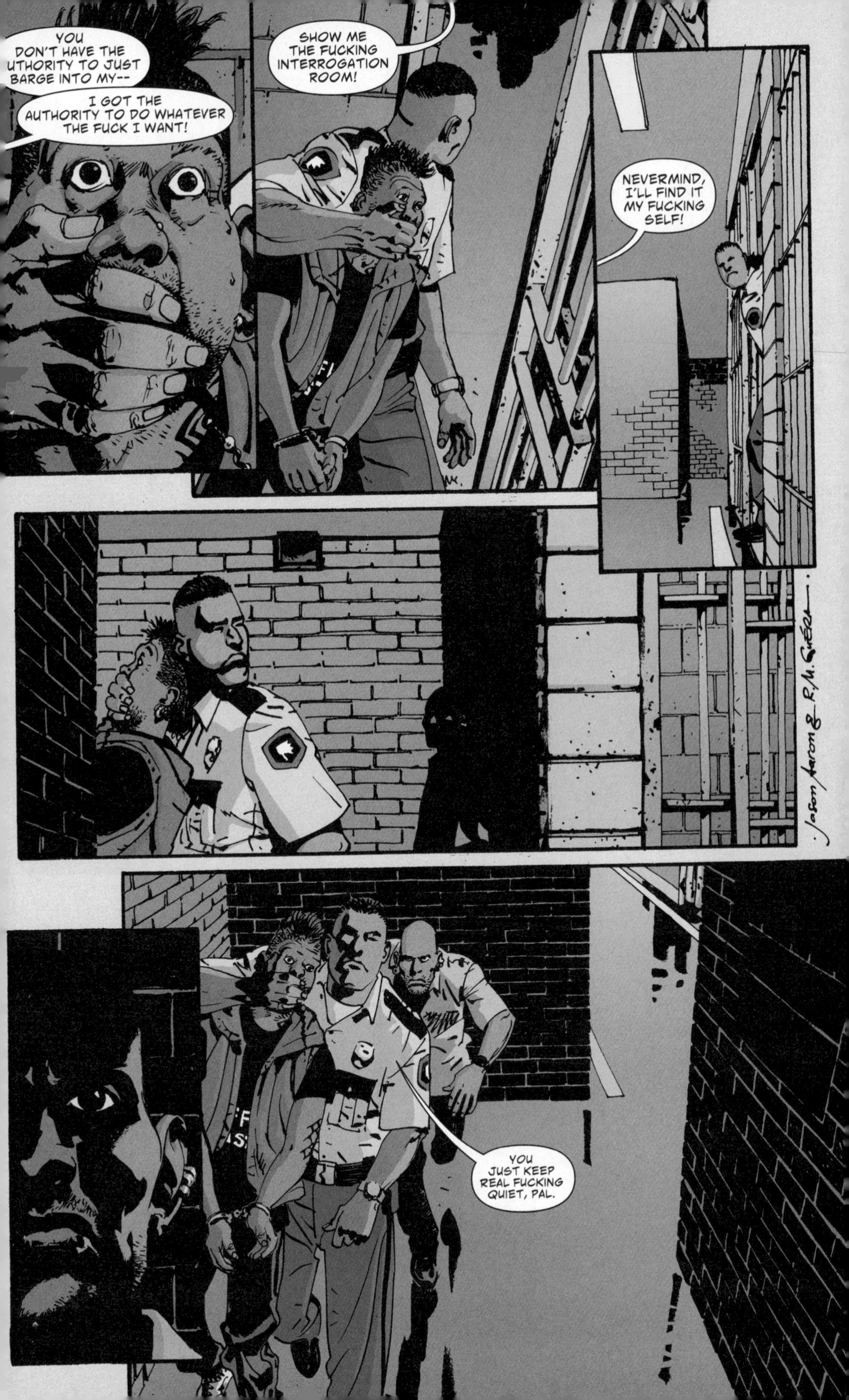
YOU DON'T HAVE THE UTHORITY TO JUST BARGE INTO MY--
I GOT THE AUTHORITY TO DO WHATEVER THE FUCK I WANT!
SHOW ME THE FUCKING INTERROGATION ROOM!
NEVERMIND, I'LL FIND IT MY FUCKING SELF!
Jason Aaron & R.M. Guéra
YOU JUST KEEP REAL FUCKING QUIET, PAL.

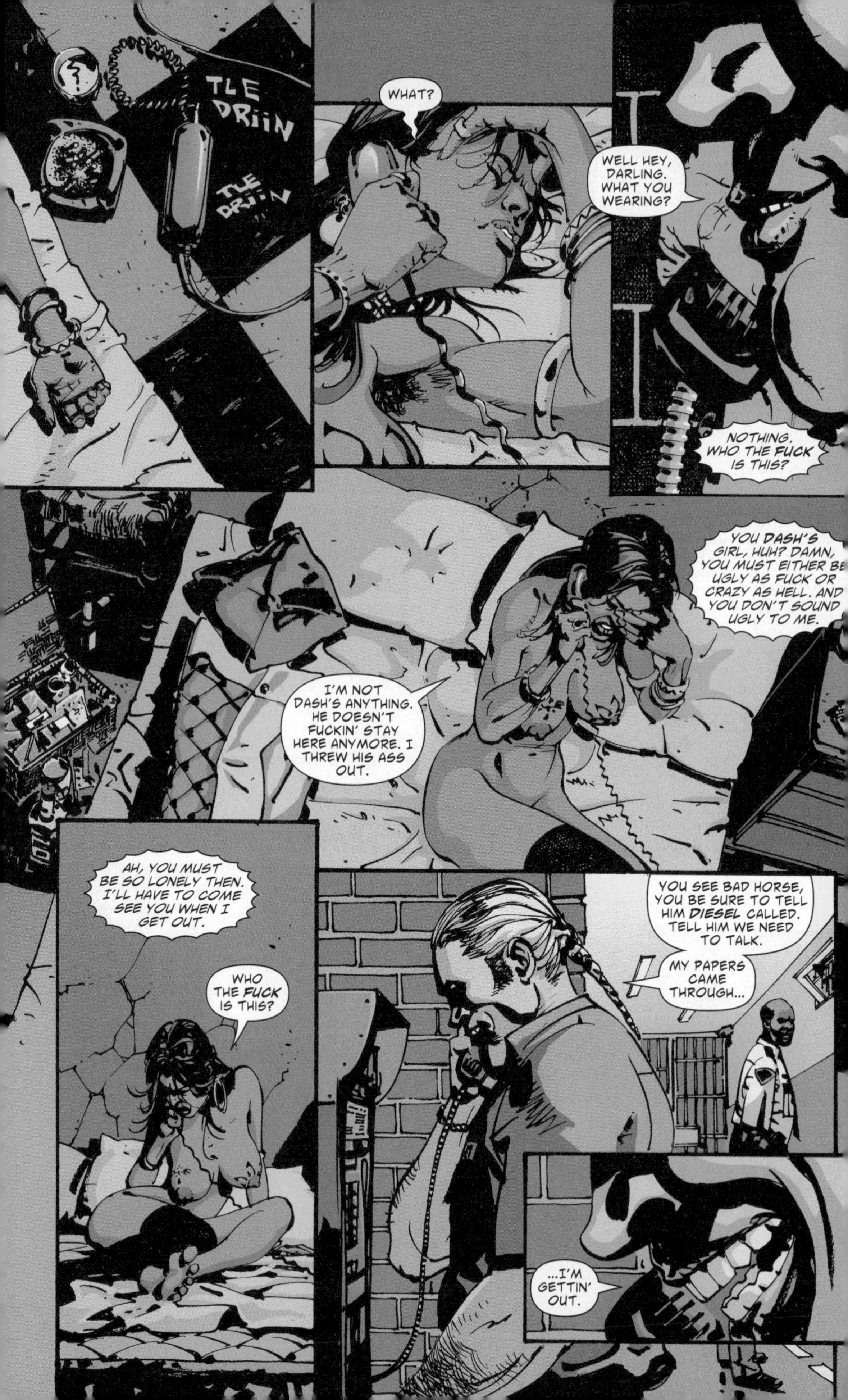
TLE DRIIN
TLE DRIIN
WHAT?
WELL HEY, DARLING. WHAT YOU WEARING?
NOTHING. WHO THE FUCK IS THIS?
YOU DASH'S GIRL, HUH? DAMN, YOU MUST EITHER BE UGLY AS FUCK OR CRAZY AS HELL. AND YOU DON'T SOUND UGLY TO ME.
I'M NOT DASH'S ANYTHING. HE DOESN'T FUCKIN' STAY HERE ANYMORE. I THREW HIS ASS OUT.
AH, YOU MUST BE SO LONELY THEN. I'LL HAVE TO COME SEE YOU WHEN I GET OUT.
WHO THE FUCK IS THIS?
YOU SEE BAD HORSE, YOU BE SURE TO TELL HIM DIESEL CALLED. TELL HIM WE NEED TO TALK.
MY PAPERS CAME THROUGH...
...I'M GETTIN' OUT.

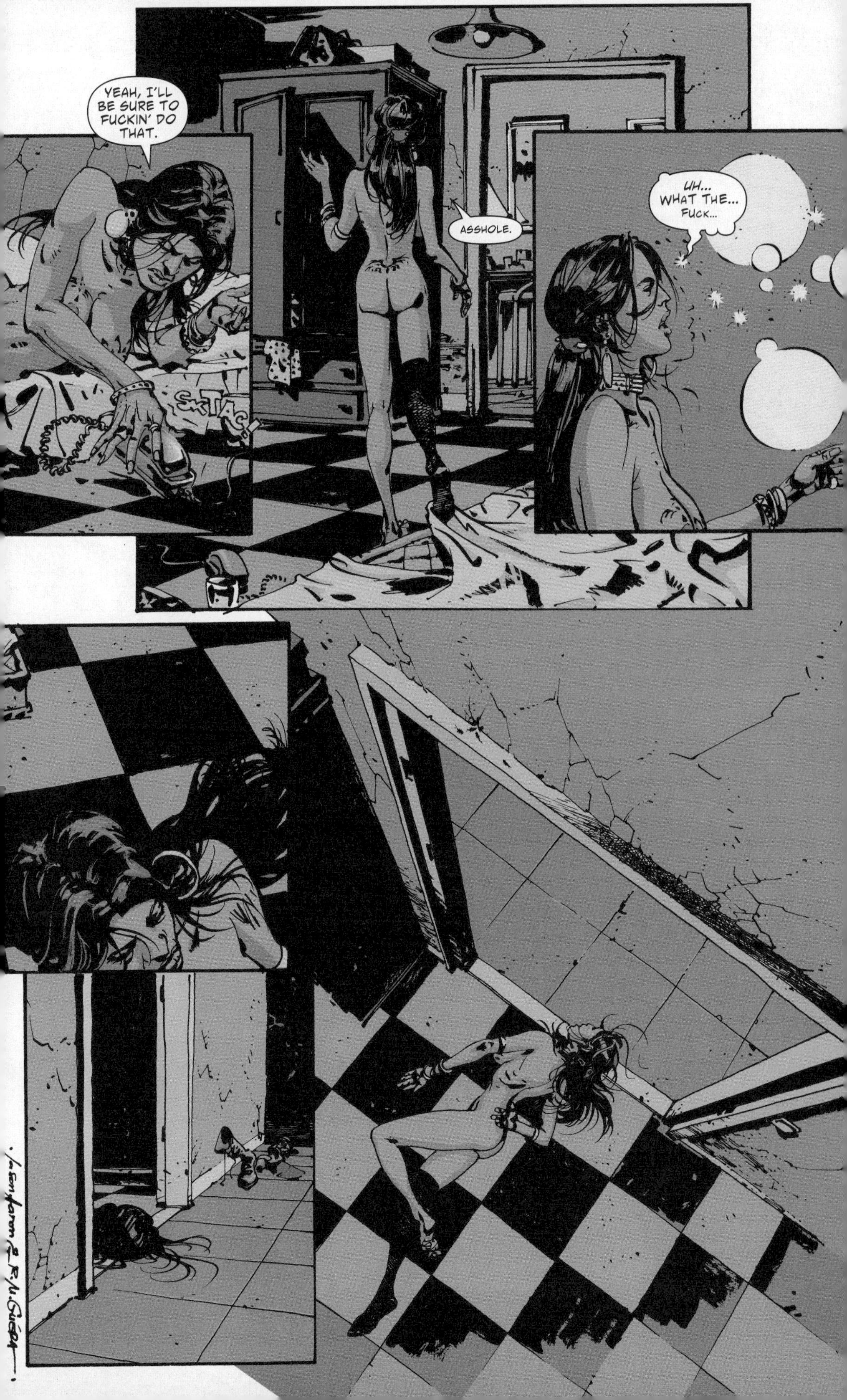
YEAH, I'LL BE SURE TO FUCKIN' DO THAT.
SKTAC!
ASSHOLE.
UH... WHAT THE... FUCK...

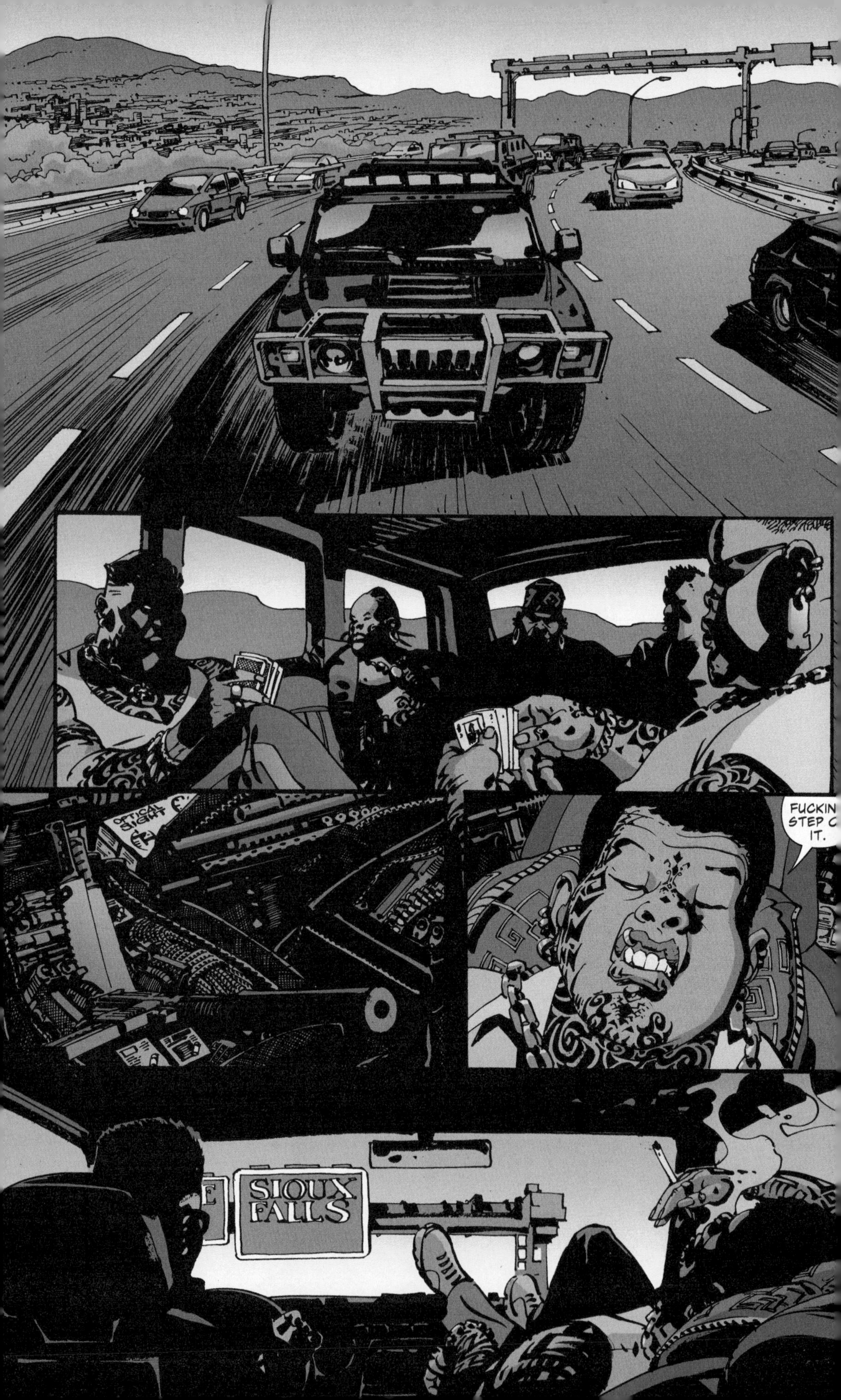

OPTICAL SIGHT
FUCKIN
STEP C
IT.
SIOUX FALLS

CHAPTER 3

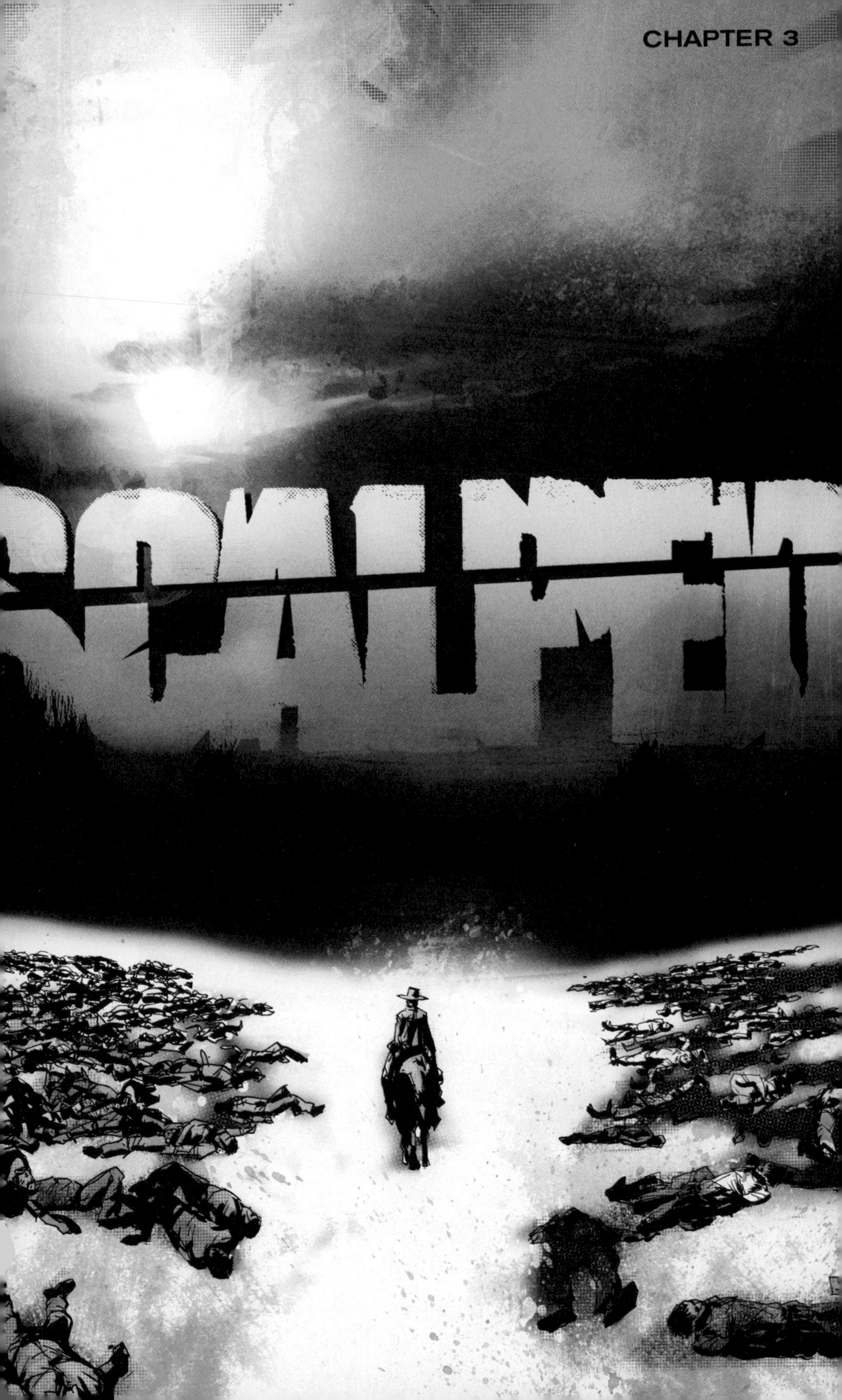

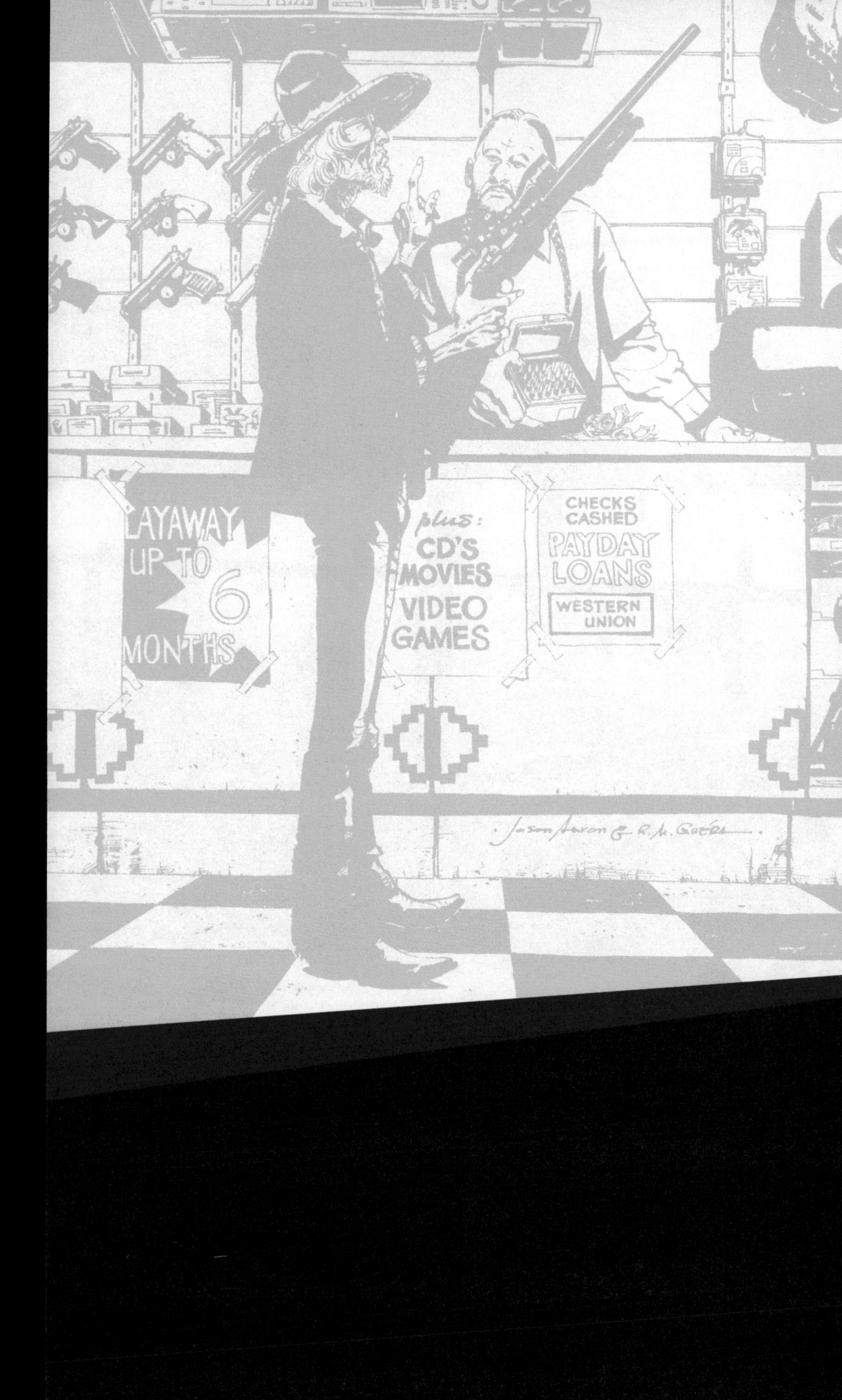
LAYAWAY
UP TO
6
MONTHS
plus:
CD'S
MOVIES
VIDEO
GAMES
CHECKS
CASHED
PAYDAY
LOANS
WESTERN
UNION

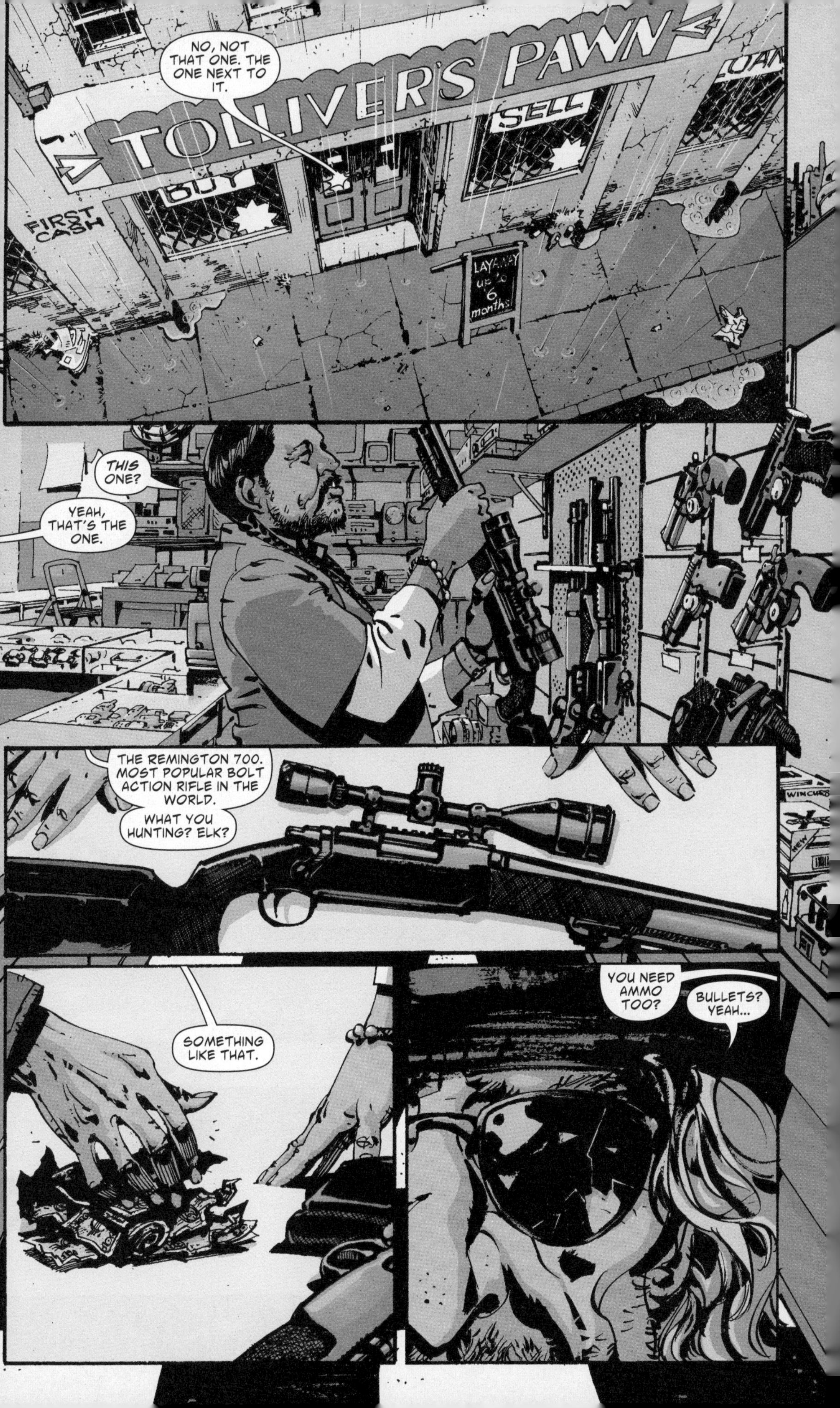
TOLLIVER'S PAWN
LOAN
SELL
BUY
FIRST CASH
NO, NOT THAT ONE. THE ONE NEXT TO IT.
LAYAWAY up to 6 months!
THIS ONE?
YEAH, THAT'S THE ONE.
THE REMINGTON 700. MOST POPULAR BOLT ACTION RIFLE IN THE WORLD.
WHAT YOU HUNTING? ELK?
SOMETHING LIKE THAT.
YOU NEED AMMO TOO?
BULLETS? YEAH...

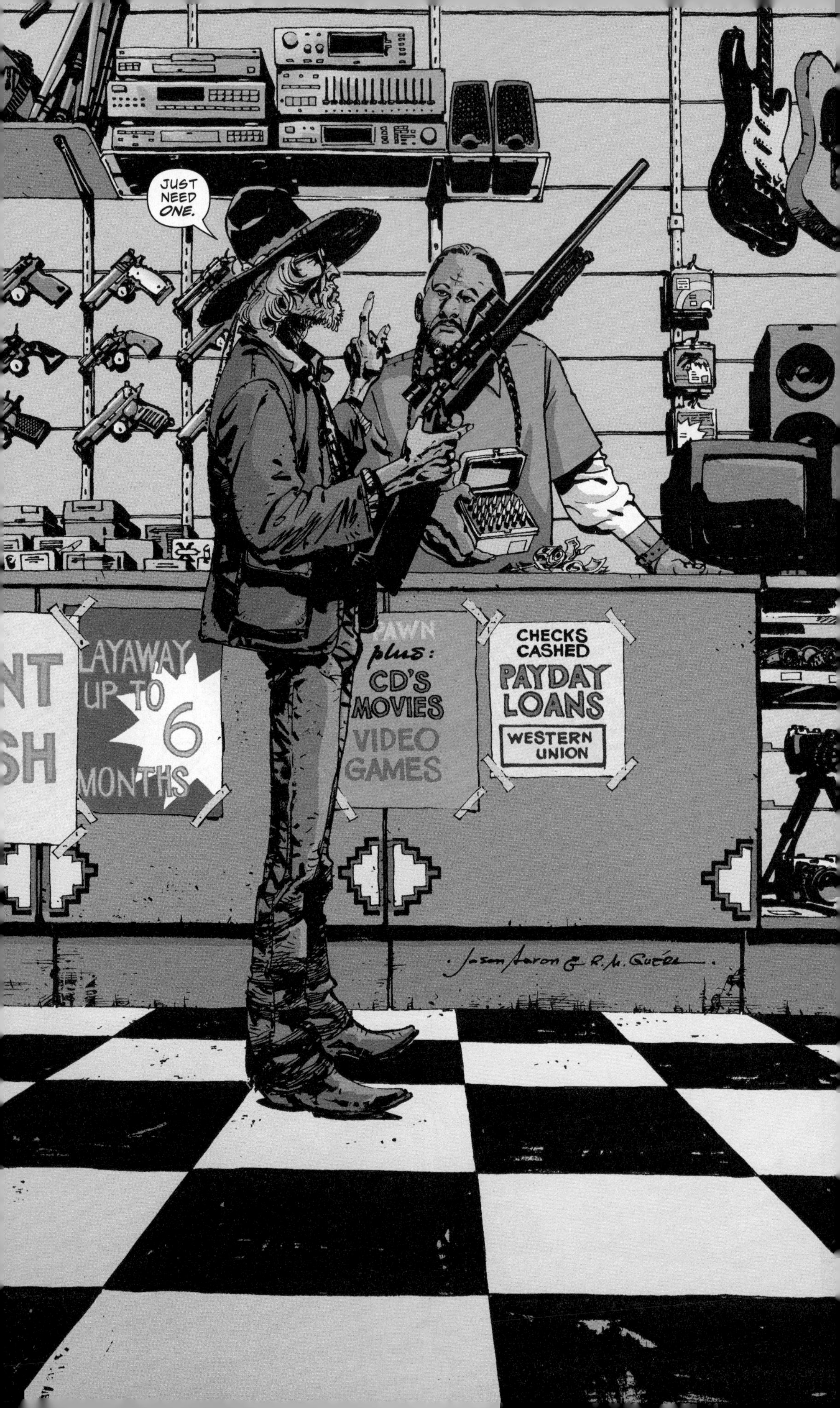

JUST NEED ONE.
LAYAWAY UP TO 6 MONTHS
PAWN plus: CD'S MOVIES VIDEO GAMES
CHECKS CASHED
PAYDAY LOANS
WESTERN UNION
Jason Aaron & R.M. Guéra

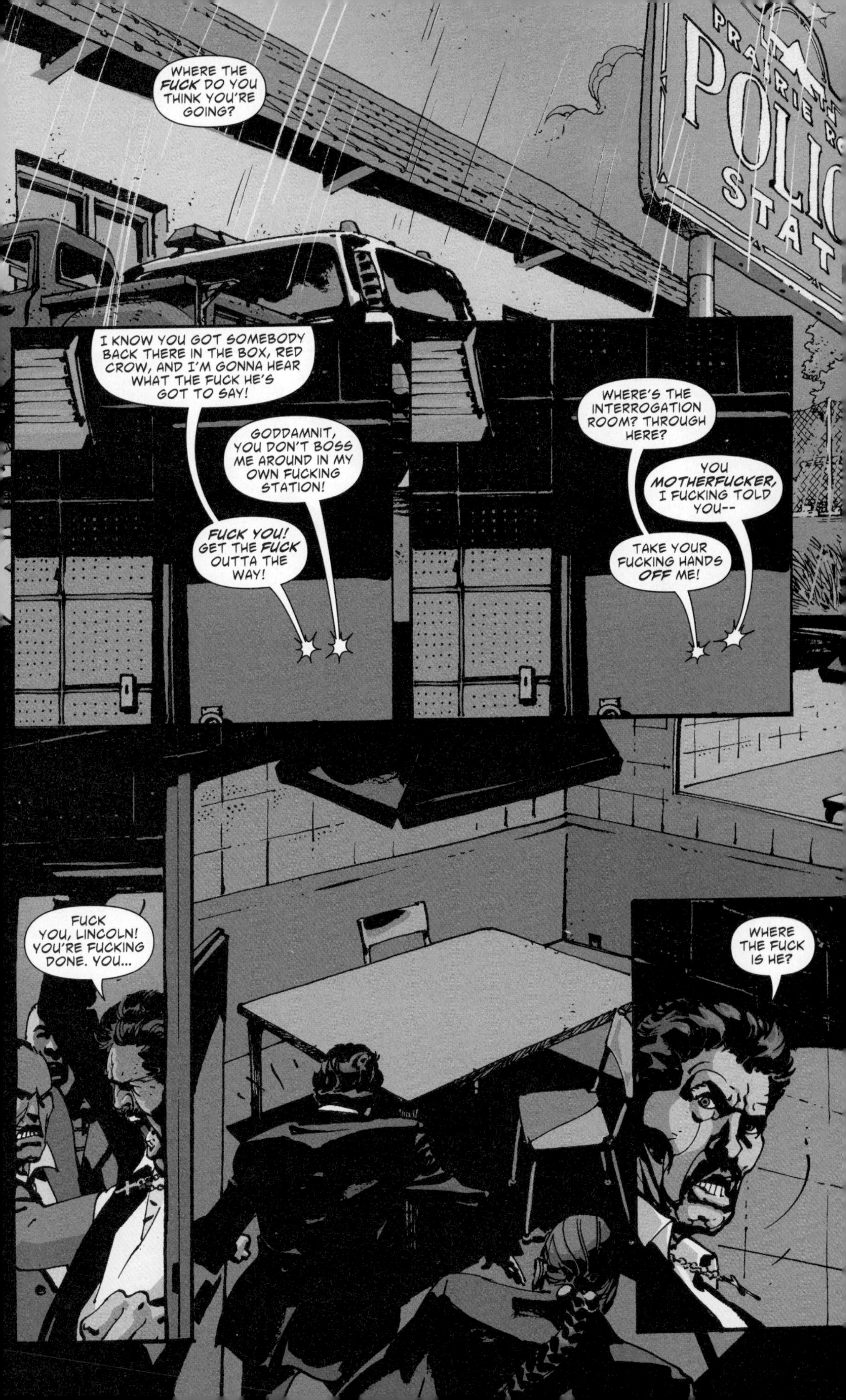
WHERE THE FUCK DO YOU THINK YOU'RE GOING?
PRAIRIE ROSE POLICE STATION
I KNOW YOU GOT SOMEBODY BACK THERE IN THE BOX, RED CROW, AND I'M GONNA HEAR WHAT THE FUCK HE'S GOT TO SAY!
GODDAMNIT, YOU DON'T BOSS ME AROUND IN MY OWN FUCKING STATION!
FUCK YOU! GET THE FUCK OUTTA THE WAY!
WHERE'S THE INTERROGATION ROOM? THROUGH HERE?
YOU MOTHERFUCKER, I FUCKING TOLD YOU--
TAKE YOUR FUCKING HANDS OFF ME!
FUCK YOU, LINCOLN! YOU'RE FUCKING DONE. YOU...
WHERE THE FUCK IS HE?

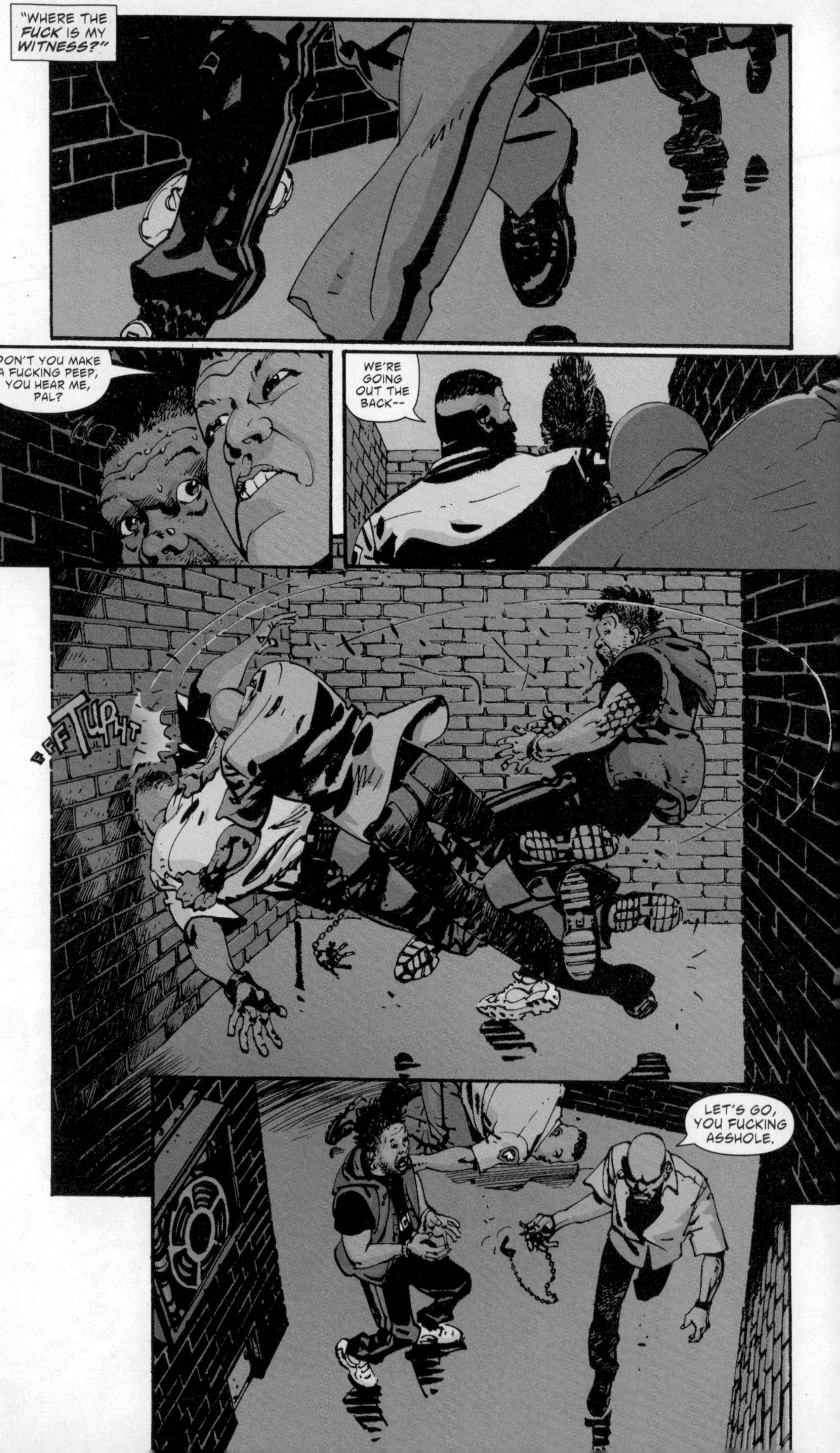
"WHERE THE FUCK IS MY WITNESS?"
DON'T YOU MAKE A FUCKING PEEP, YOU HEAR ME, PAL?
WE'RE GOING OUT THE BACK--
FFTUPHT
LET'S GO, YOU FUCKING ASSHOLE.

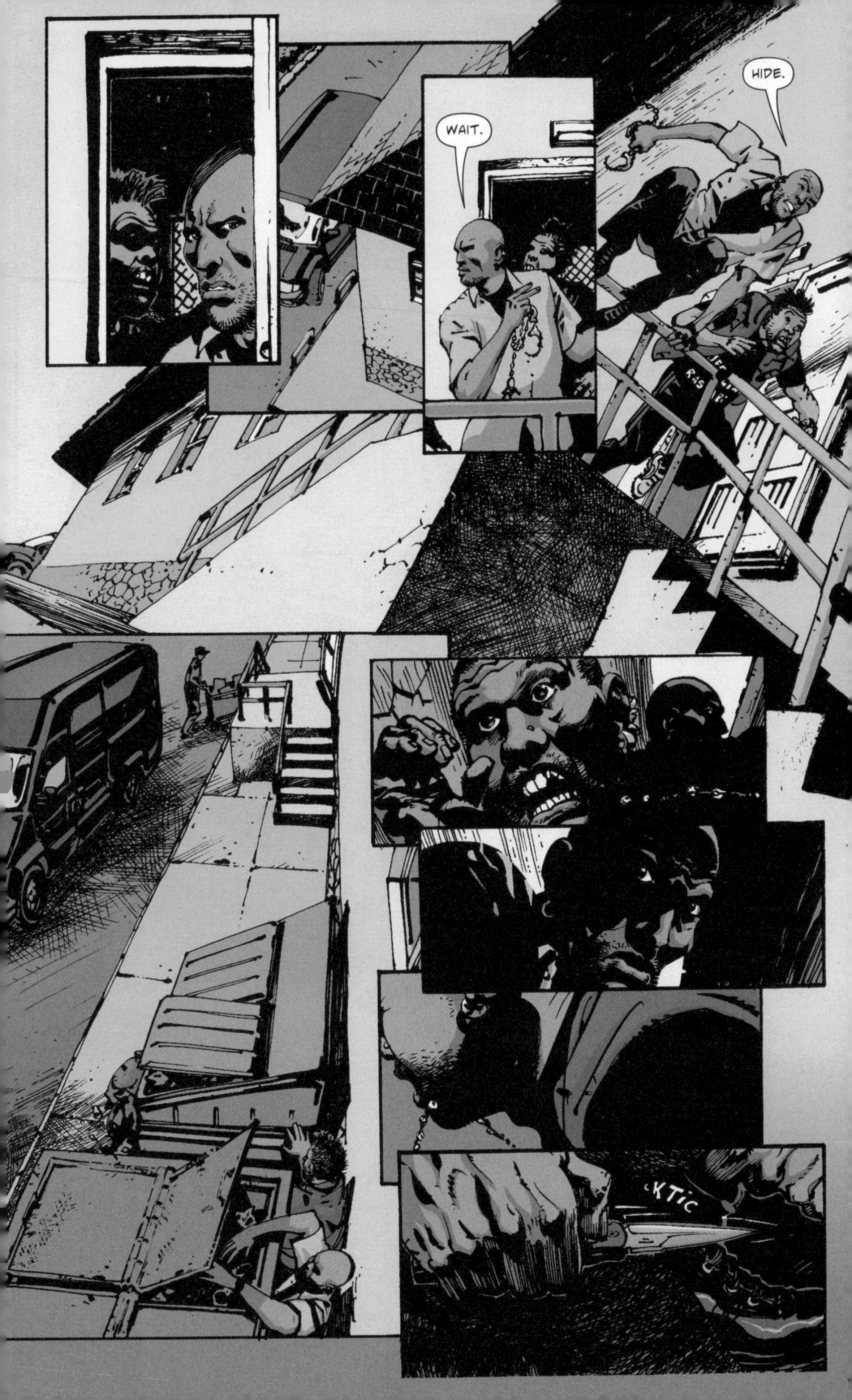
WAIT.
HIDE.
cKTic

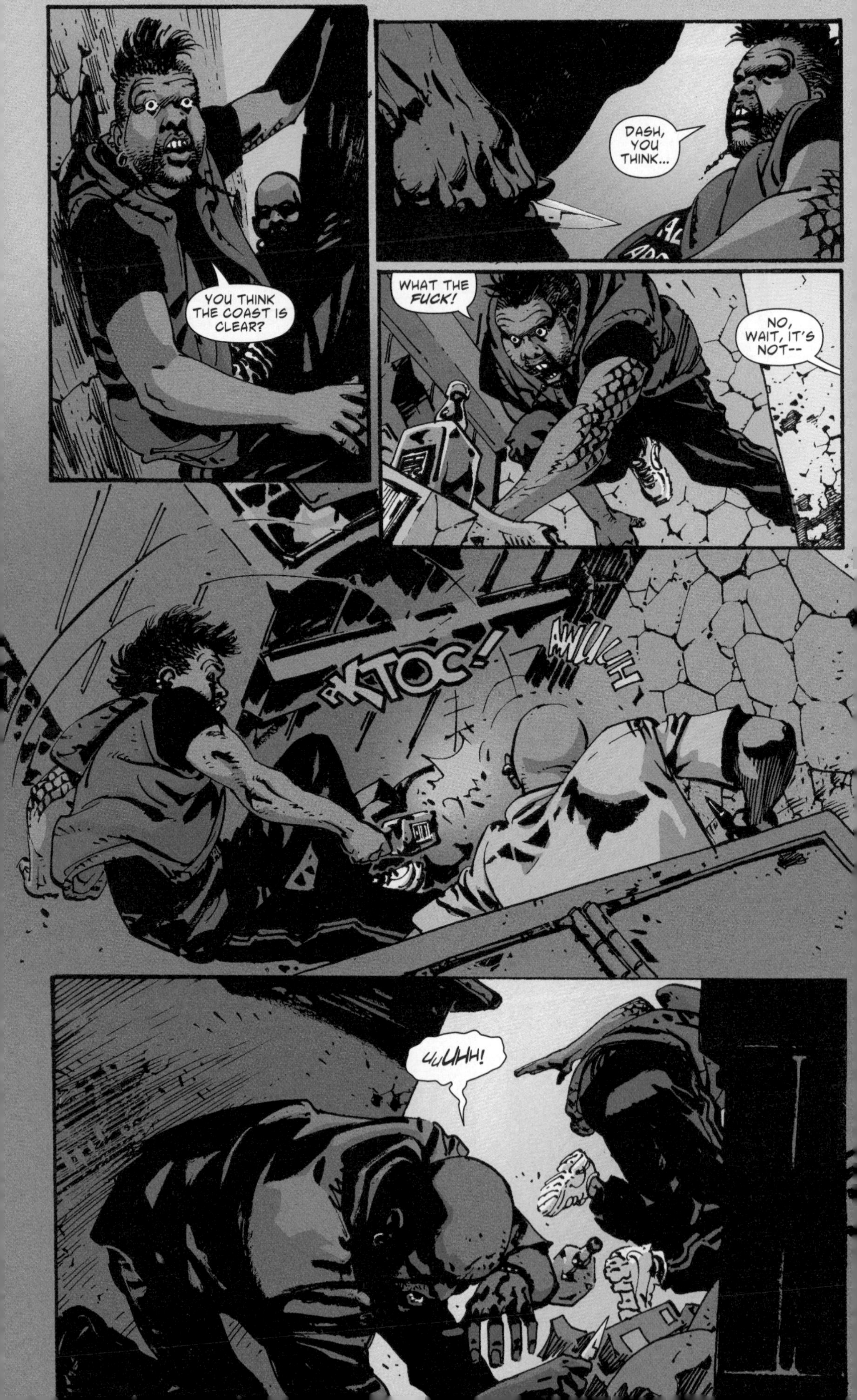
YOU THINK THE COAST IS CLEAR?
DASH, YOU THINK...
WHAT THE FUCK!
NO, WAIT, IT'S NOT--
PKTOC!
AWUUH
uuUHH!

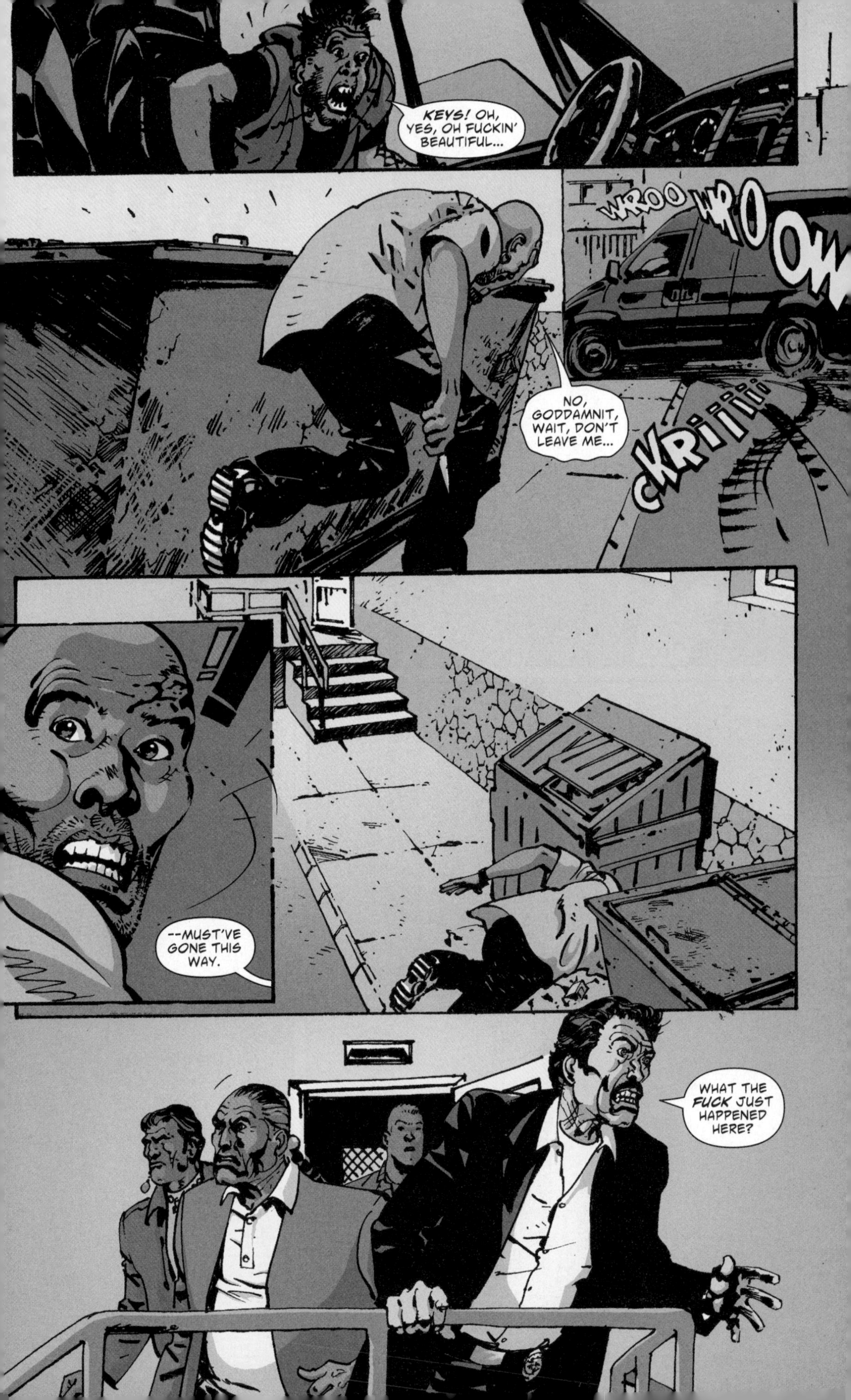
KEYS! OH, YES, OH FUCKIN' BEAUTIFUL...
WROO WROOOW
NO, GODDAMNIT, WAIT, DON'T LEAVE ME...
cKRiiiiii
--MUST'VE GONE THIS WAY.
WHAT THE FUCK JUST HAPPENED HERE?

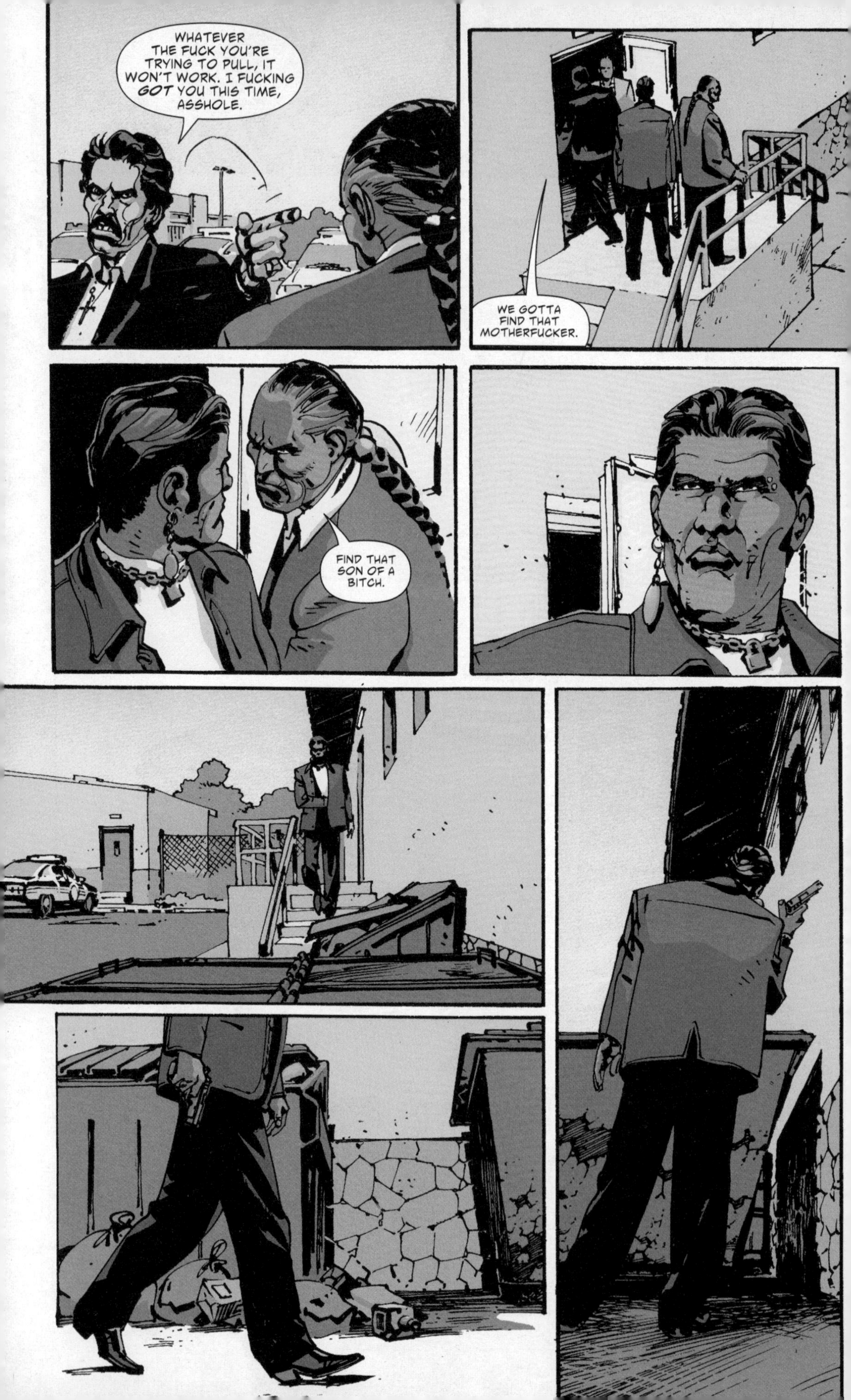
WHATEVER THE FUCK YOU'RE TRYING TO PULL, IT WON'T WORK. I FUCKING *GOT* YOU THIS TIME, ASSHOLE.
WE GOTTA FIND THAT MOTHERFUCKER.
FIND THAT SON OF A BITCH.

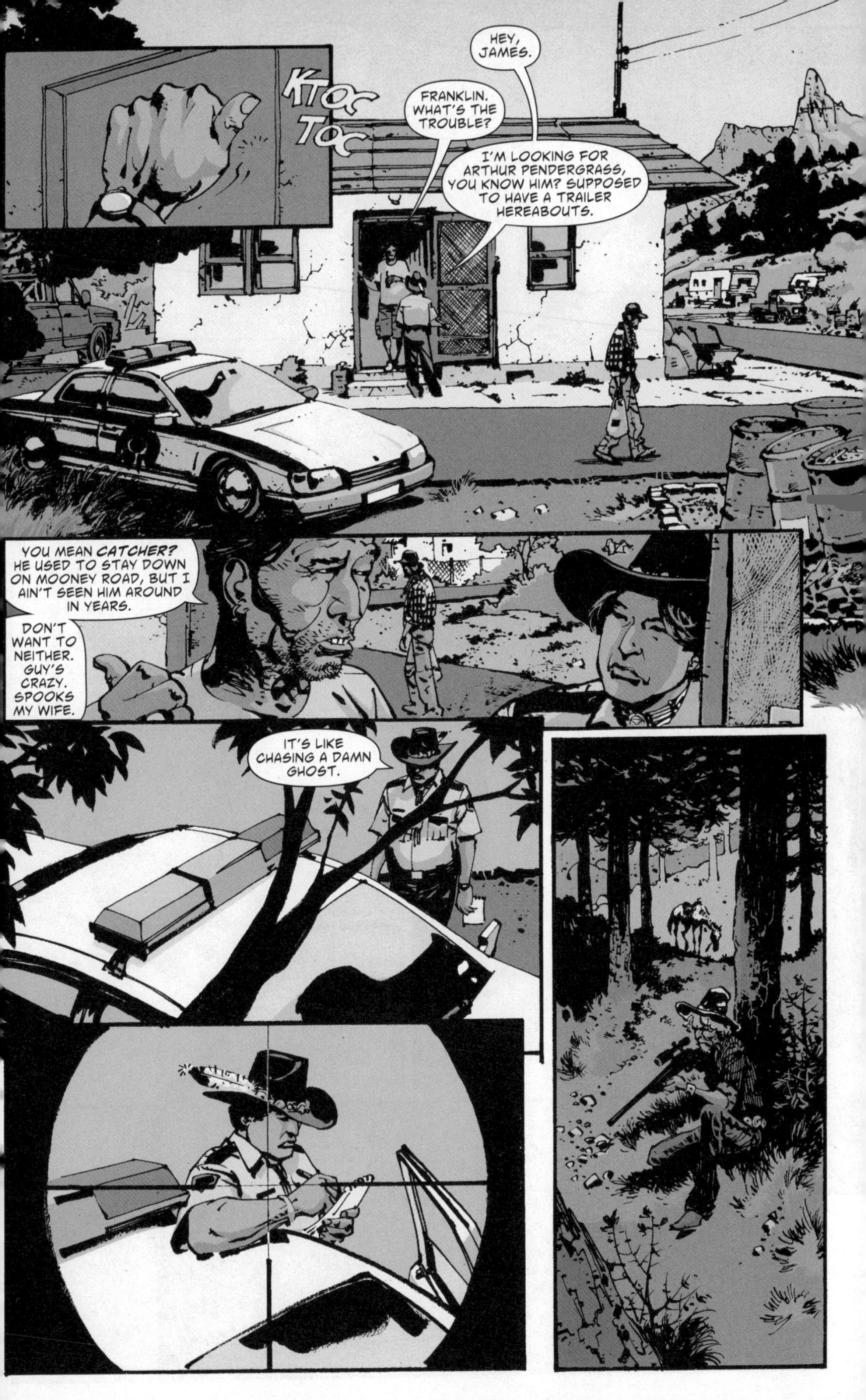
KTOC TOC
HEY, JAMES.
FRANKLIN. WHAT'S THE TROUBLE?
I'M LOOKING FOR ARTHUR PENDERGRASS, YOU KNOW HIM? SUPPOSED TO HAVE A TRAILER HEREABOUTS.
YOU MEAN *CATCHER?* HE USED TO STAY DOWN ON MOONEY ROAD, BUT I AIN'T SEEN HIM AROUND IN YEARS.
DON'T WANT TO NEITHER. GUY'S CRAZY. SPOOKS MY WIFE.
IT'S LIKE CHASING A DAMN GHOST.

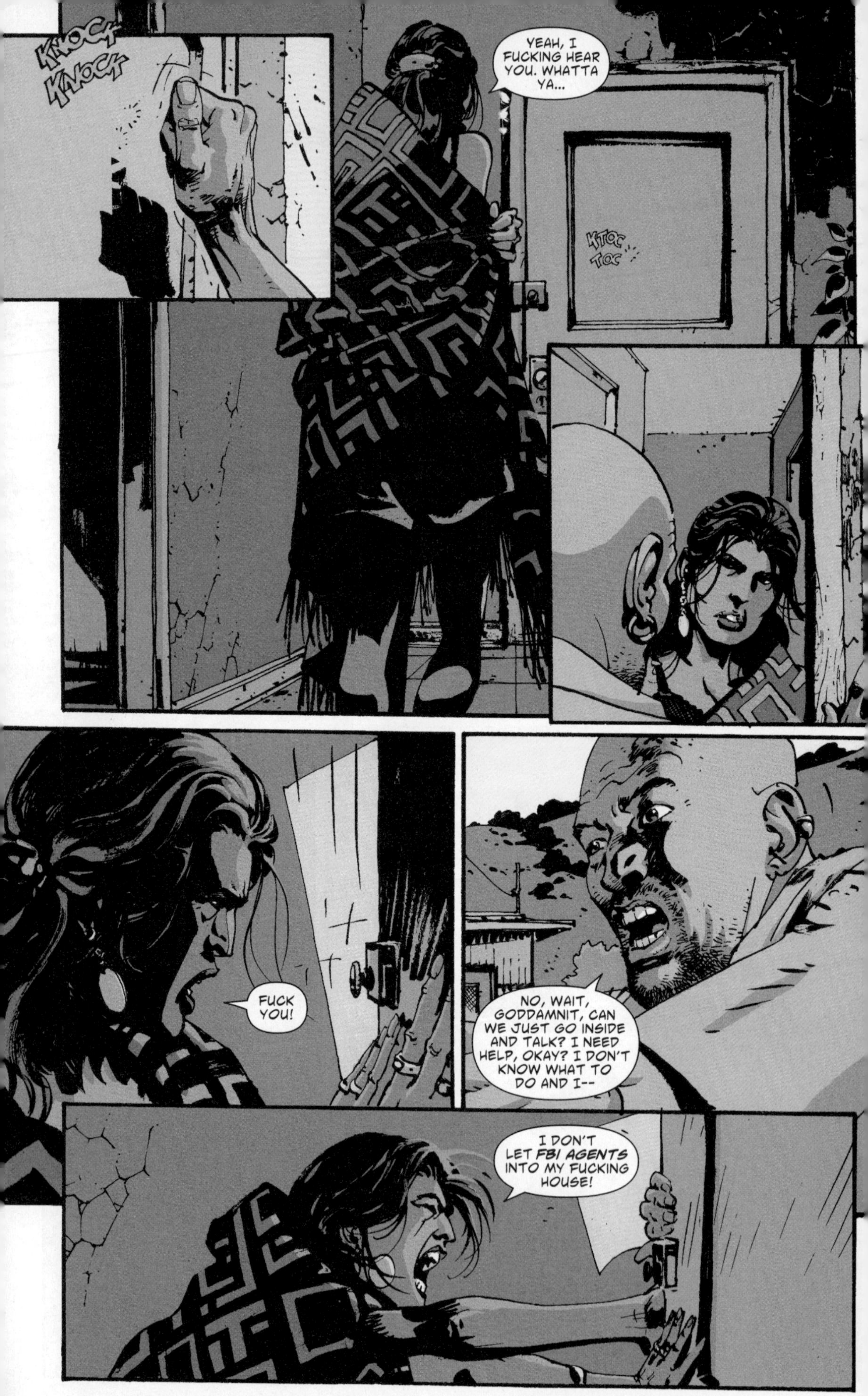
KNOCK KNOCK
YEAH, I FUCKING HEAR YOU. WHATTA YA...
KTOC TOC
FUCK YOU!
NO, WAIT, GODDAMNIT, CAN WE JUST GO INSIDE AND TALK? I NEED HELP, OKAY? I DON'T KNOW WHAT TO DO AND I--
I DON'T LET FBI AGENTS INTO MY FUCKING HOUSE!

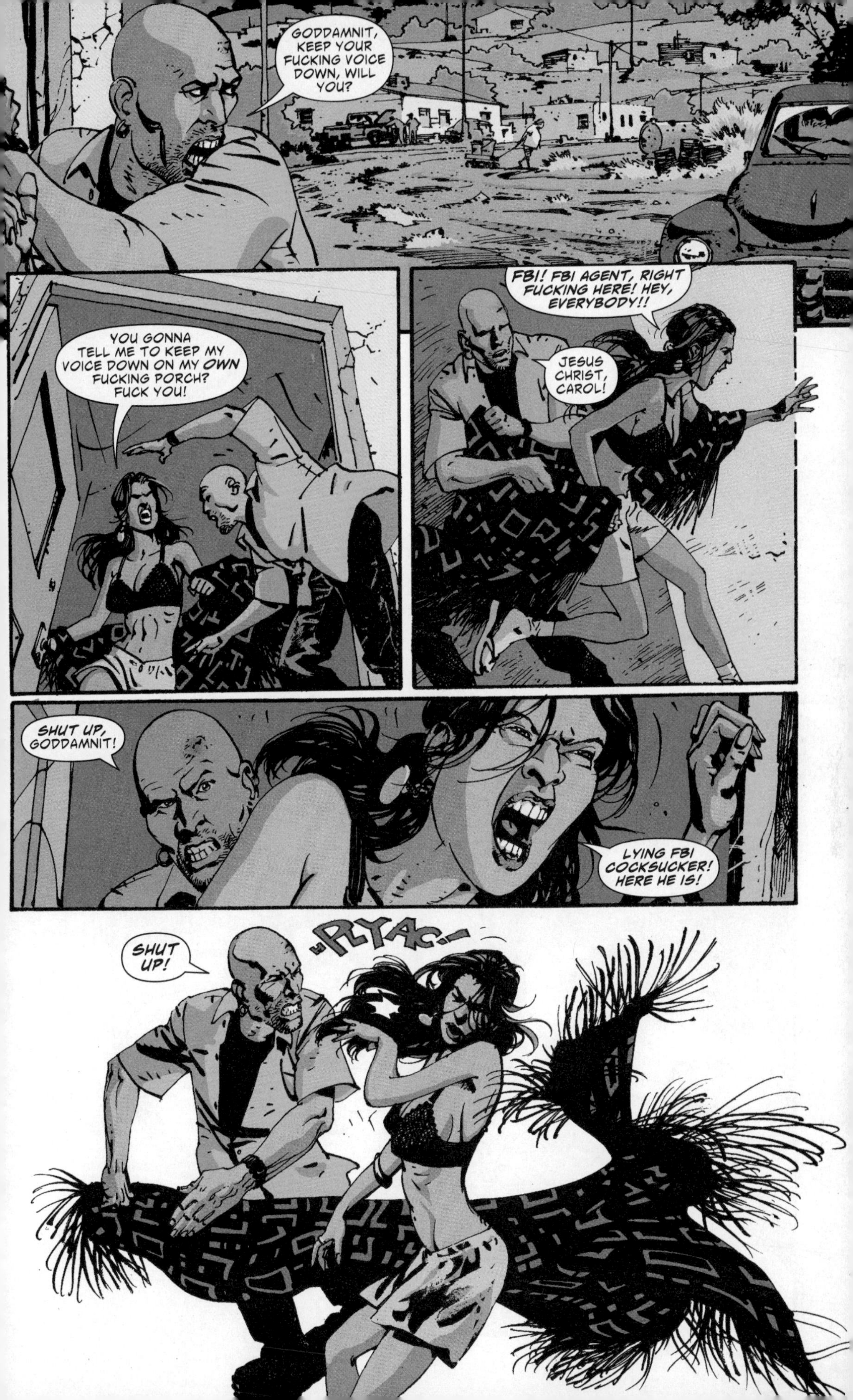
GODDAMNIT, KEEP YOUR FUCKING VOICE DOWN, WILL YOU?
YOU GONNA TELL ME TO KEEP MY VOICE DOWN ON MY OWN FUCKING PORCH? FUCK YOU!
FBI! FBI AGENT, RIGHT FUCKING HERE! HEY, EVERYBODY!!
JESUS CHRIST, CAROL!
SHUT UP, GODDAMNIT!
LYING FBI COCKSUCKER! HERE HE IS!
SHUT UP!
PLYAC

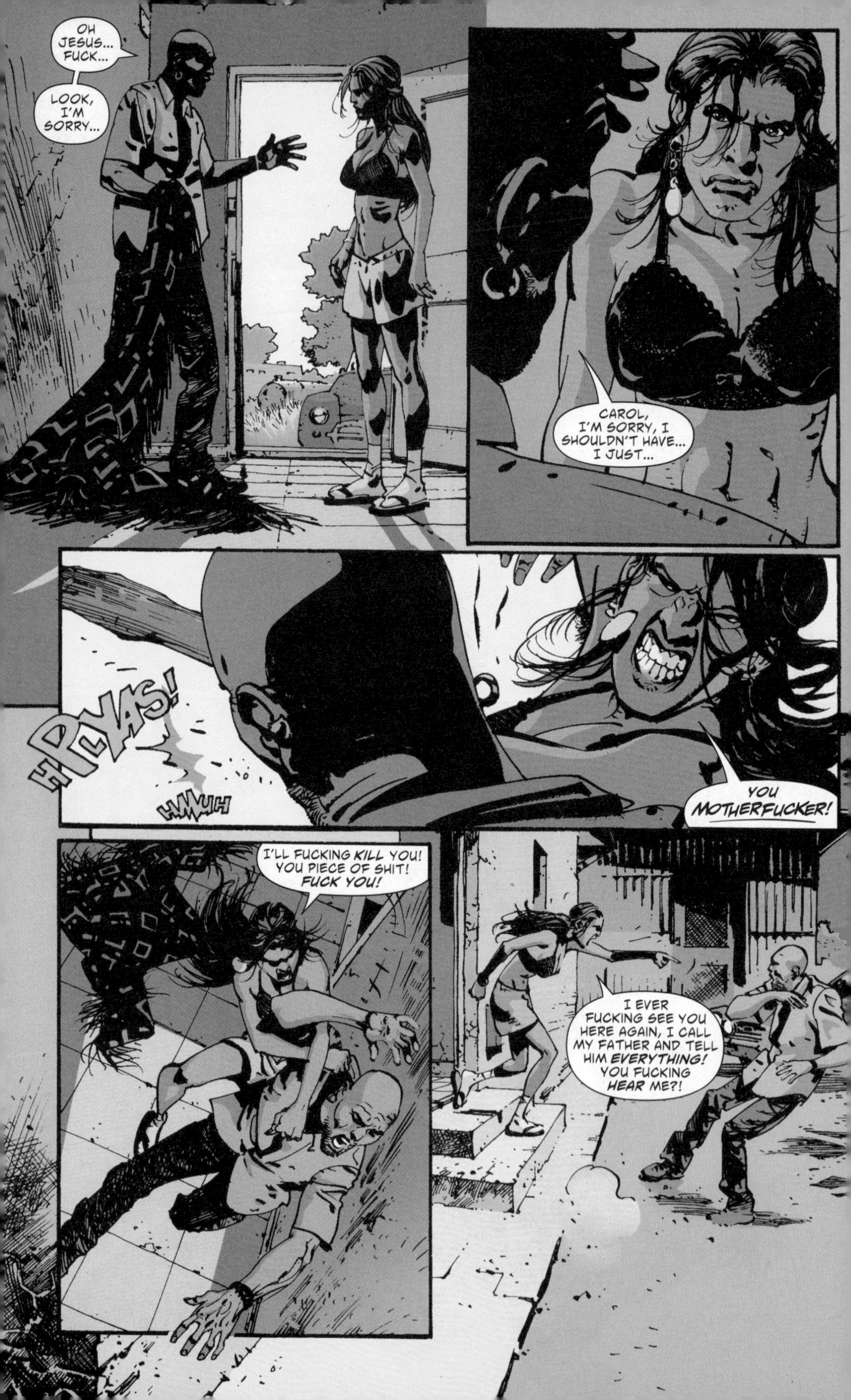
OH JESUS... FUCK...
LOOK, I'M SORRY...
CAROL, I'M SORRY, I SHOULDN'T HAVE... I JUST...
HPLYAS!
HWUH
YOU MOTHERFUCKER!
I'LL FUCKING KILL YOU! YOU PIECE OF SHIT! FUCK YOU!
I EVER FUCKING SEE YOU HERE AGAIN, I CALL MY FATHER AND TELL HIM EVERYTHING! YOU FUCKING HEAR ME?!

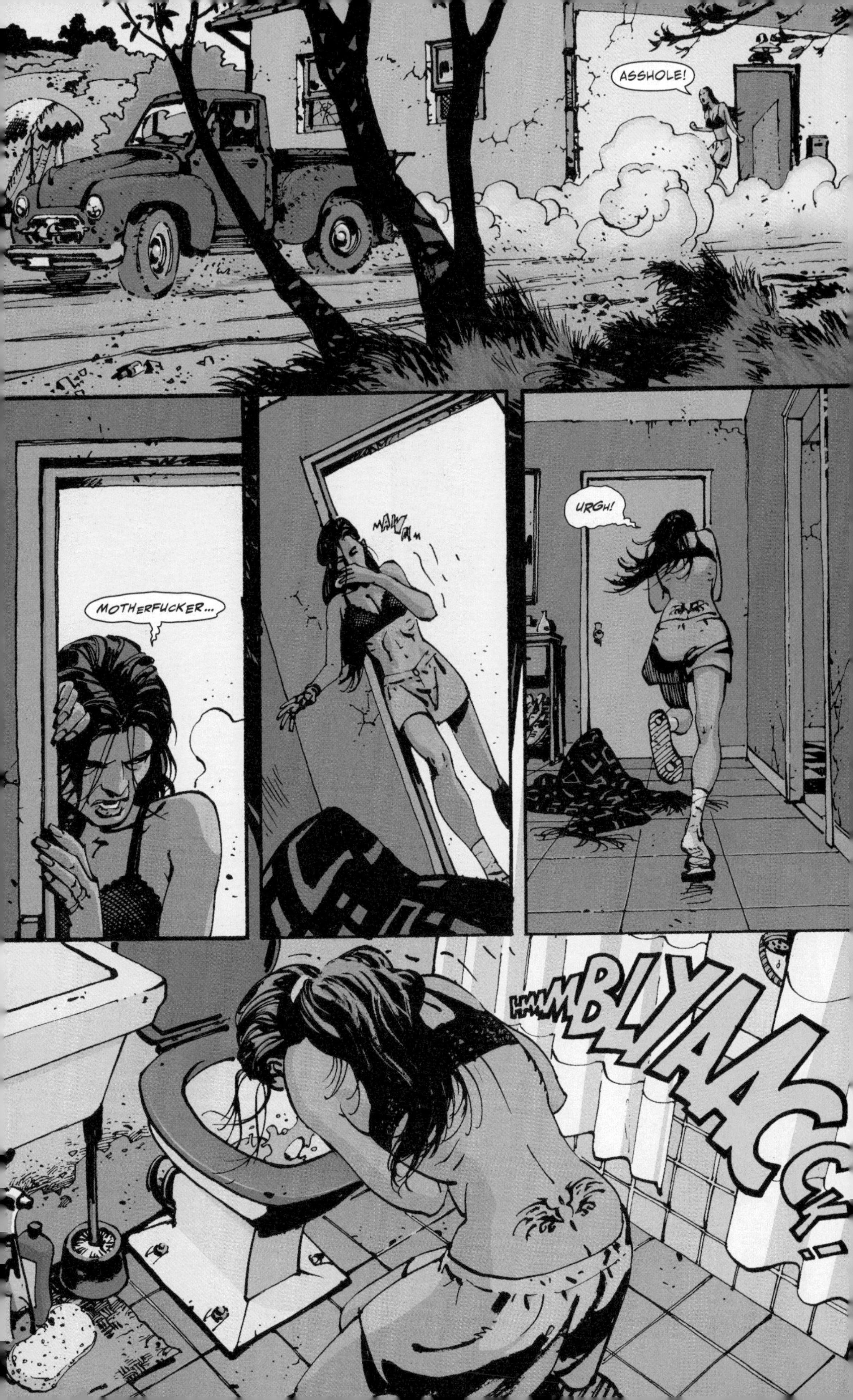
ASSHOLE!
MOTHERFUCKER...
MAW
URGH!
HWAMBLYAACGK

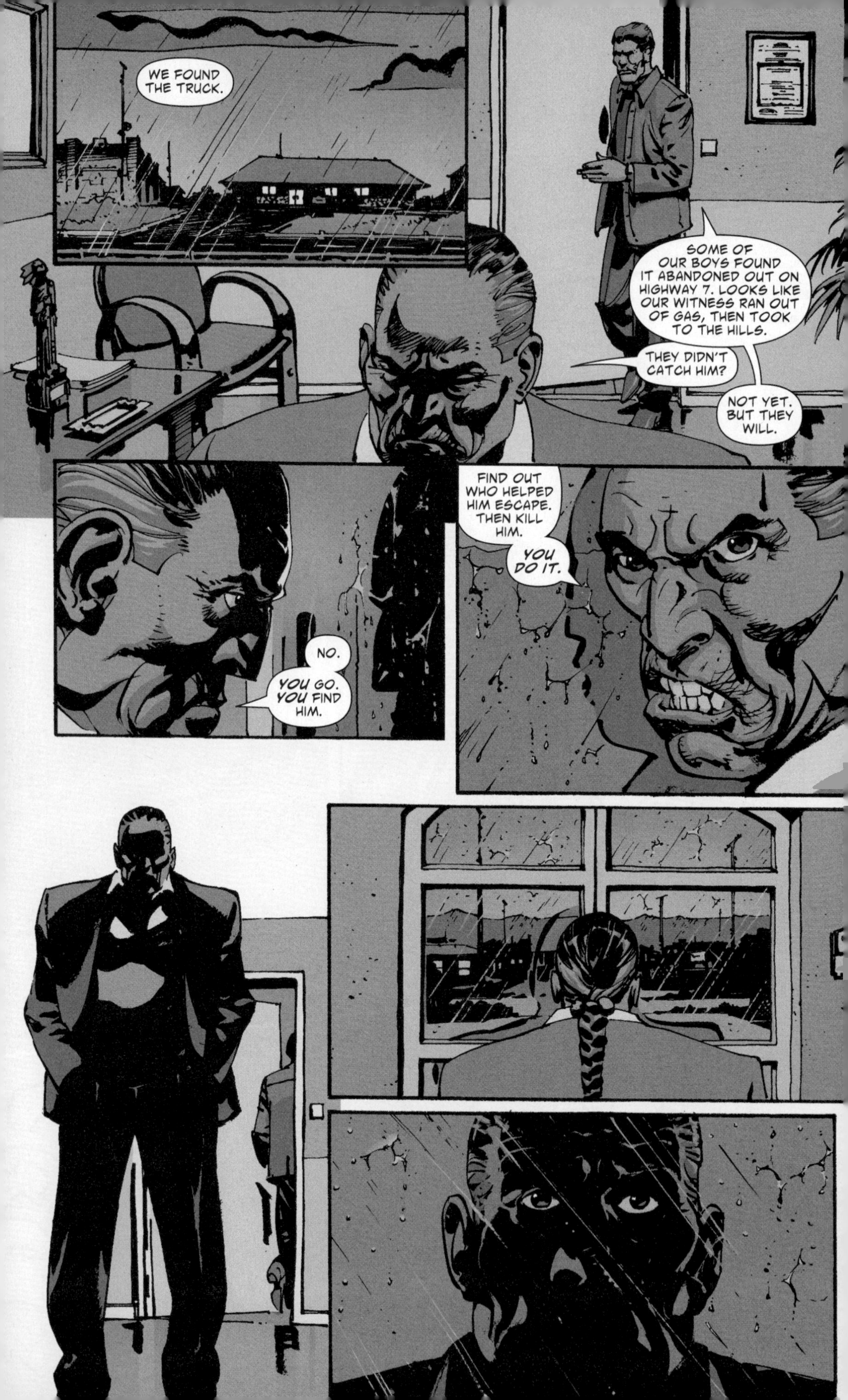
WE FOUND THE TRUCK.
SOME OF OUR BOYS FOUND IT ABANDONED OUT ON HIGHWAY 7. LOOKS LIKE OUR WITNESS RAN OUT OF GAS, THEN TOOK TO THE HILLS.
THEY DIDN'T CATCH HIM?
NOT YET. BUT THEY WILL.
FIND OUT WHO HELPED HIM ESCAPE. THEN KILL HIM.
YOU DO IT.
NO.
YOU GO. YOU FIND HIM.

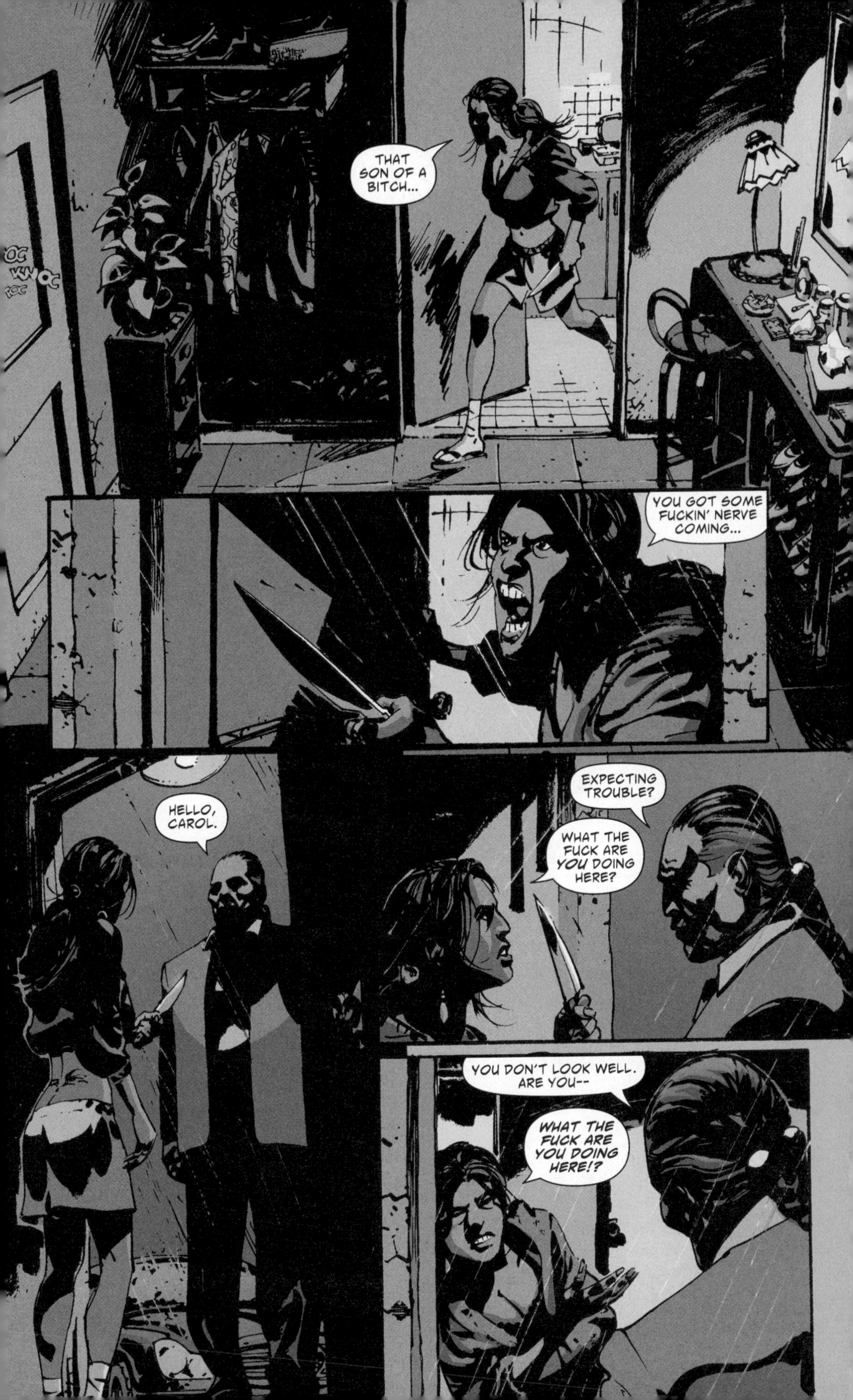
KNOC
THAT SON OF A BITCH...
YOU GOT SOME FUCKIN' NERVE COMING...
HELLO, CAROL.
EXPECTING TROUBLE?
WHAT THE FUCK ARE *YOU* DOING HERE?
YOU DON'T LOOK WELL. ARE YOU--
WHAT THE FUCK ARE YOU DOING HERE!?

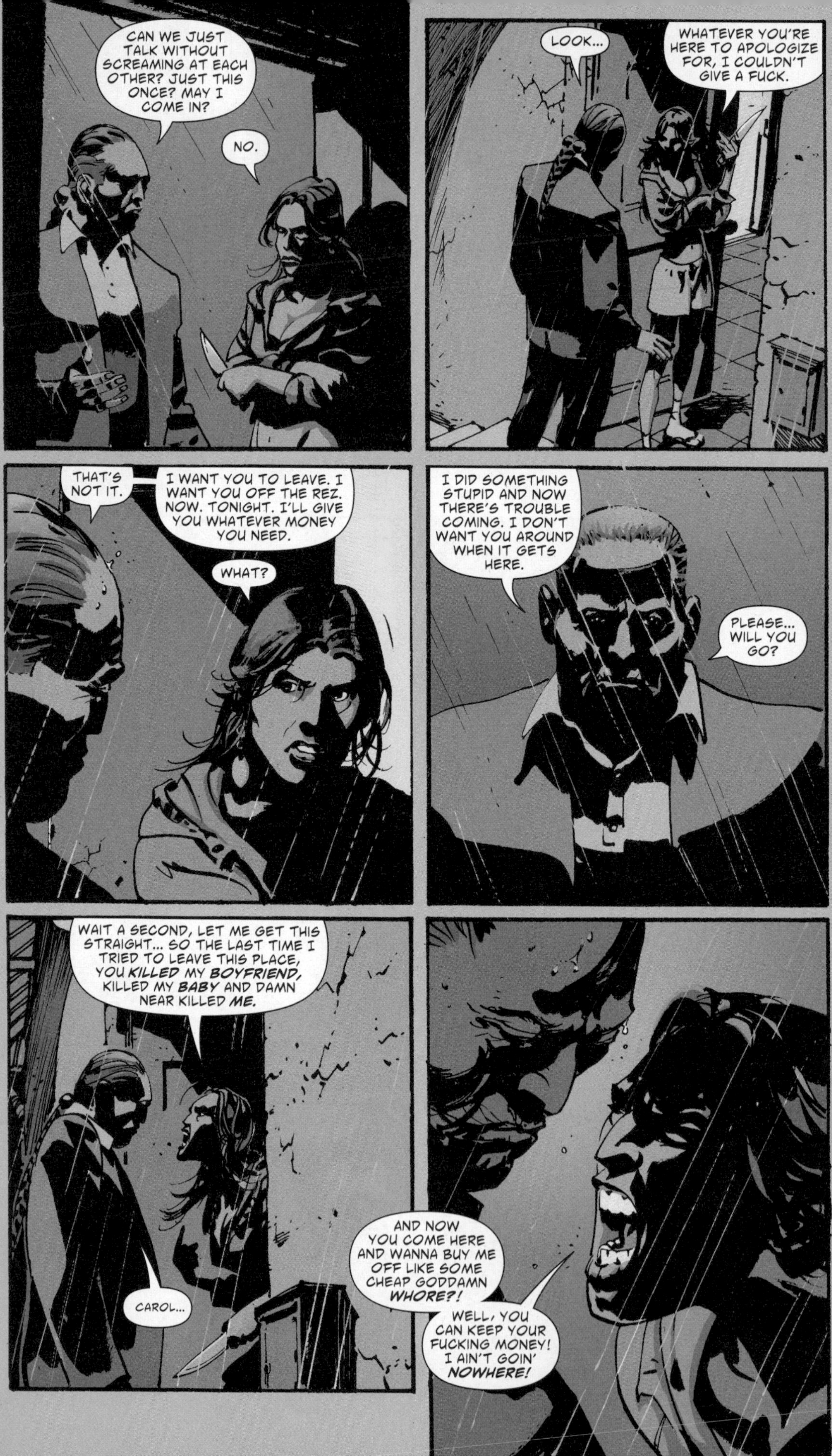
CAN WE JUST TALK WITHOUT SCREAMING AT EACH OTHER? JUST THIS ONCE? MAY I COME IN?
NO.
LOOK...
WHATEVER YOU'RE HERE TO APOLOGIZE FOR, I COULDN'T GIVE A FUCK.
THAT'S NOT IT.
I WANT YOU TO LEAVE. I WANT YOU OFF THE REZ. NOW. TONIGHT. I'LL GIVE YOU WHATEVER MONEY YOU NEED.
WHAT?
I DID SOMETHING STUPID AND NOW THERE'S TROUBLE COMING. I DON'T WANT YOU AROUND WHEN IT GETS HERE.
PLEASE... WILL YOU GO?
WAIT A SECOND, LET ME GET THIS STRAIGHT... SO THE LAST TIME I TRIED TO LEAVE THIS PLACE, YOU KILLED MY BOYFRIEND, KILLED MY BABY AND DAMN NEAR KILLED ME.
CAROL...
AND NOW YOU COME HERE AND WANNA BUY ME OFF LIKE SOME CHEAP GODDAMN WHORE?!
WELL, YOU CAN KEEP YOUR FUCKING MONEY! I AIN'T GOIN' NOWHERE!

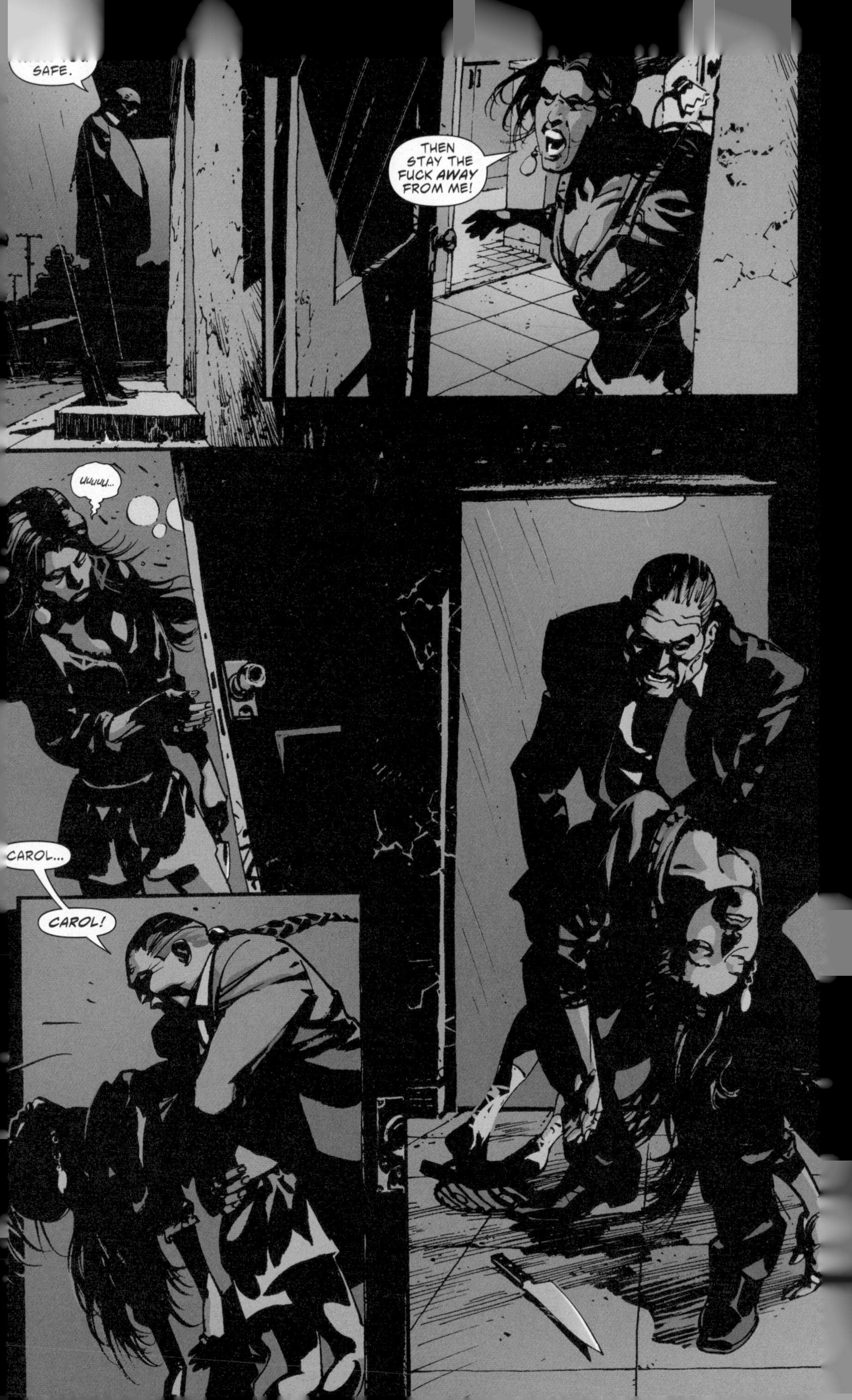
SAFE.
THEN STAY THE FUCK AWAY FROM ME!
uuuuu...
CAROL...
CAROL!

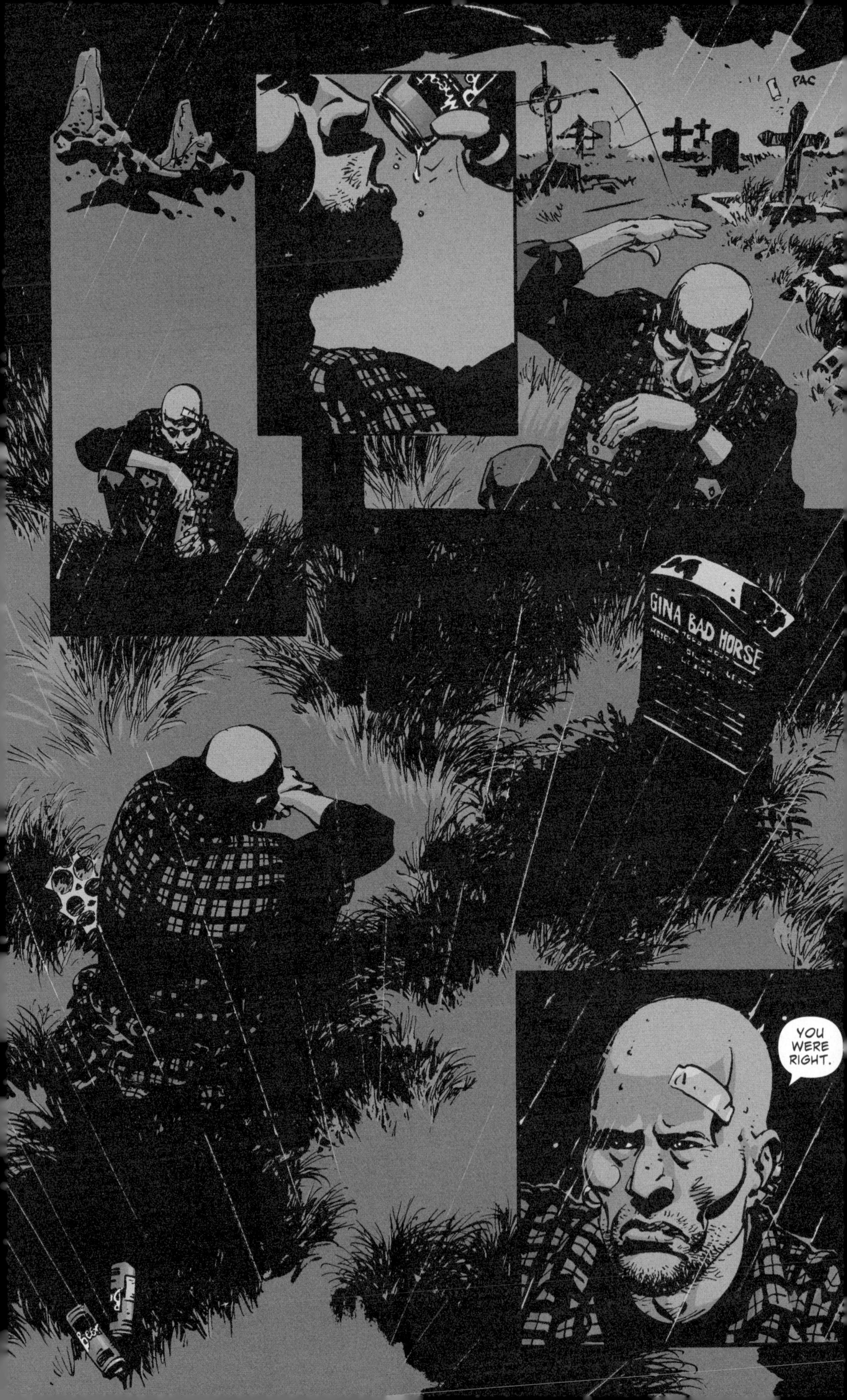
PAC
GINA BAD HORSE
YOU WERE RIGHT.

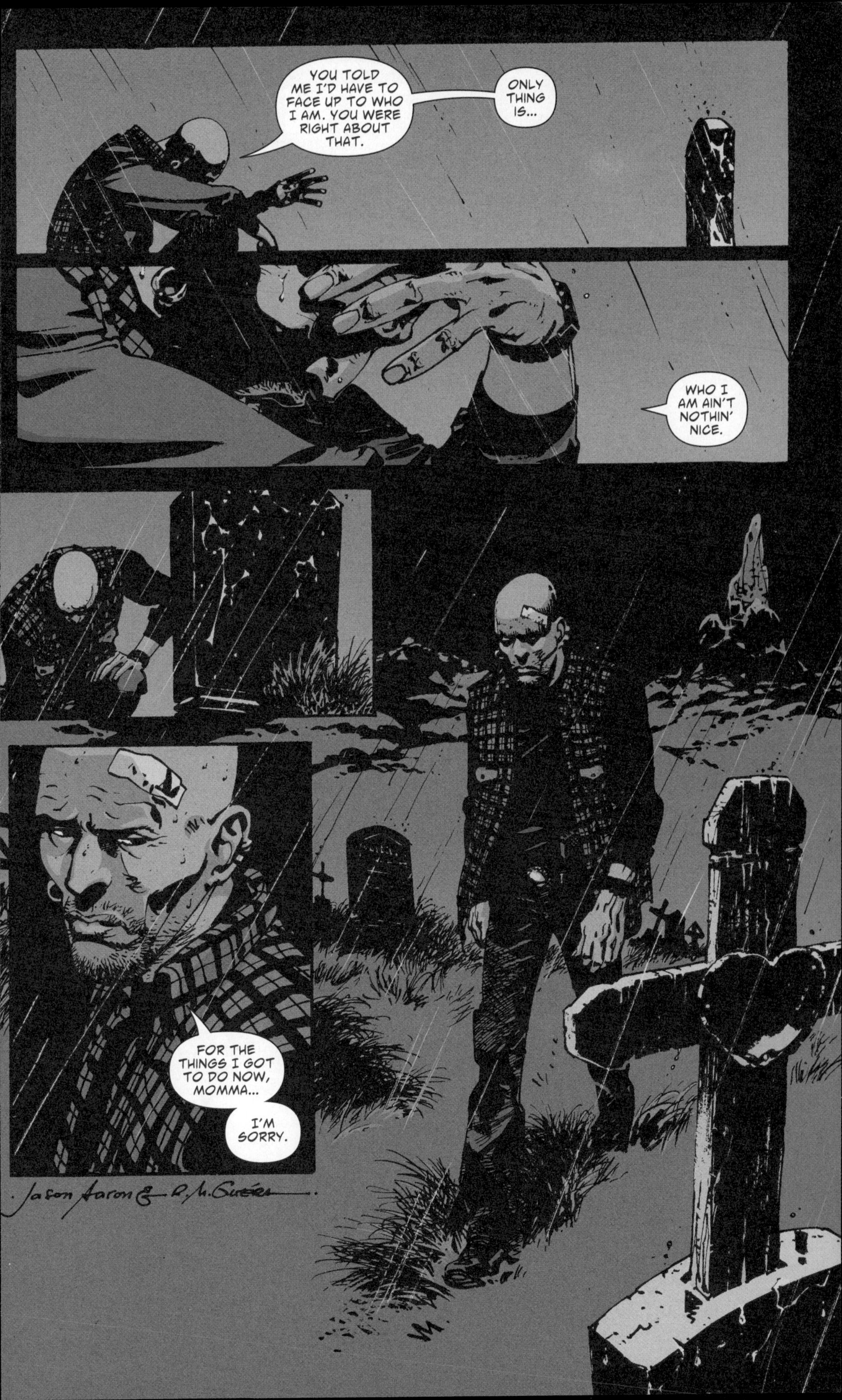

YOU TOLD ME I'D HAVE TO FACE UP TO WHO I AM. YOU WERE RIGHT ABOUT THAT.
ONLY THING IS...
WHO I AM AIN'T NOTHIN' NICE.
FOR THE THINGS I GOT TO DO NOW, MOMMA...
I'M SORRY.
Jason Aaron & R.M. Guéra

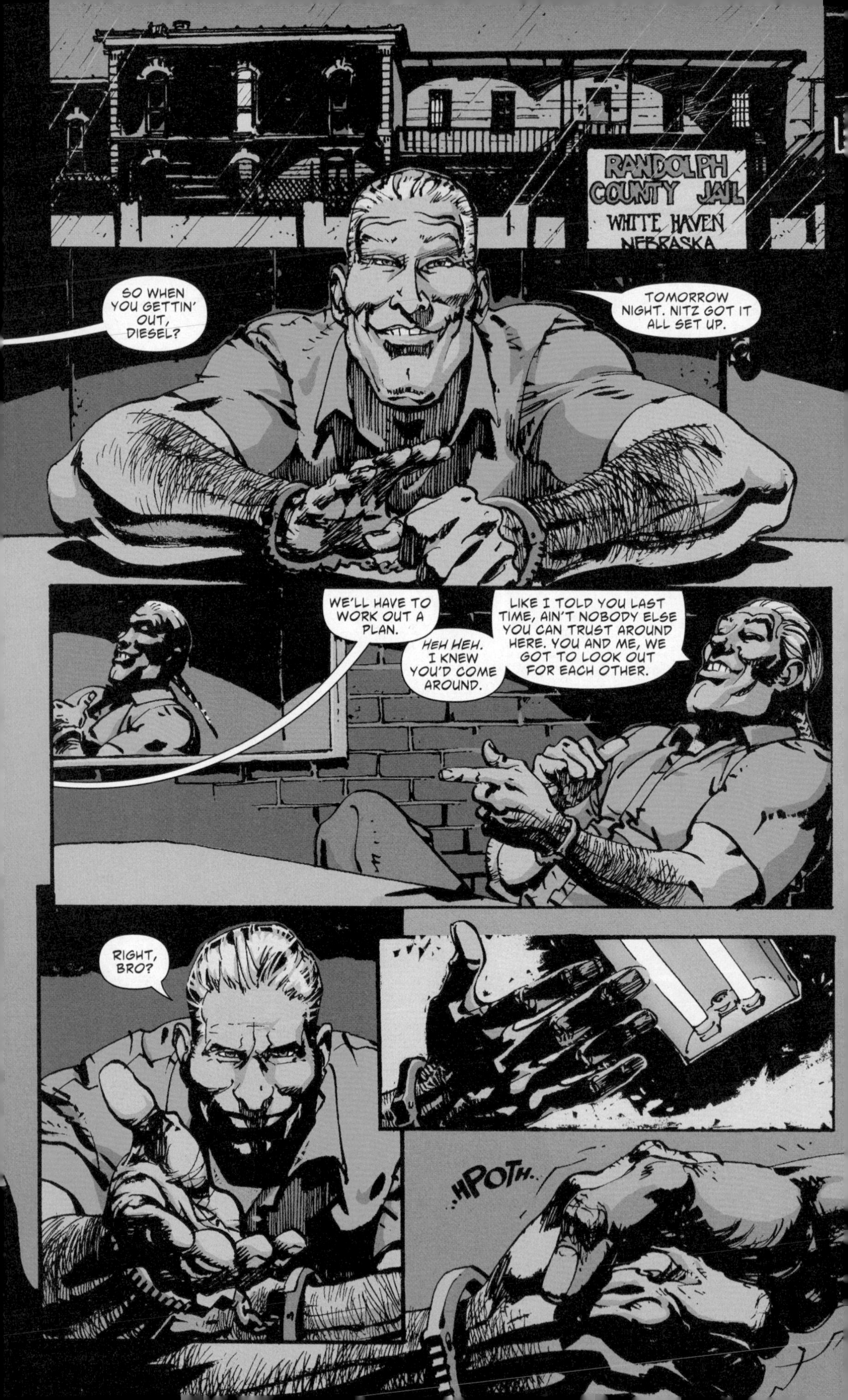
RANDOLPH COUNTY JAIL
WHITE HAVEN NEBRASKA
SO WHEN YOU GETTIN' OUT, DIESEL?
TOMORROW NIGHT. NITZ GOT IT ALL SET UP.
WE'LL HAVE TO WORK OUT A PLAN.
HEH HEH. I KNEW YOU'D COME AROUND.
LIKE I TOLD YOU LAST TIME, AIN'T NOBODY ELSE YOU CAN TRUST AROUND HERE. YOU AND ME, WE GOT TO LOOK OUT FOR EACH OTHER.
RIGHT, BRO?
HPOTH..

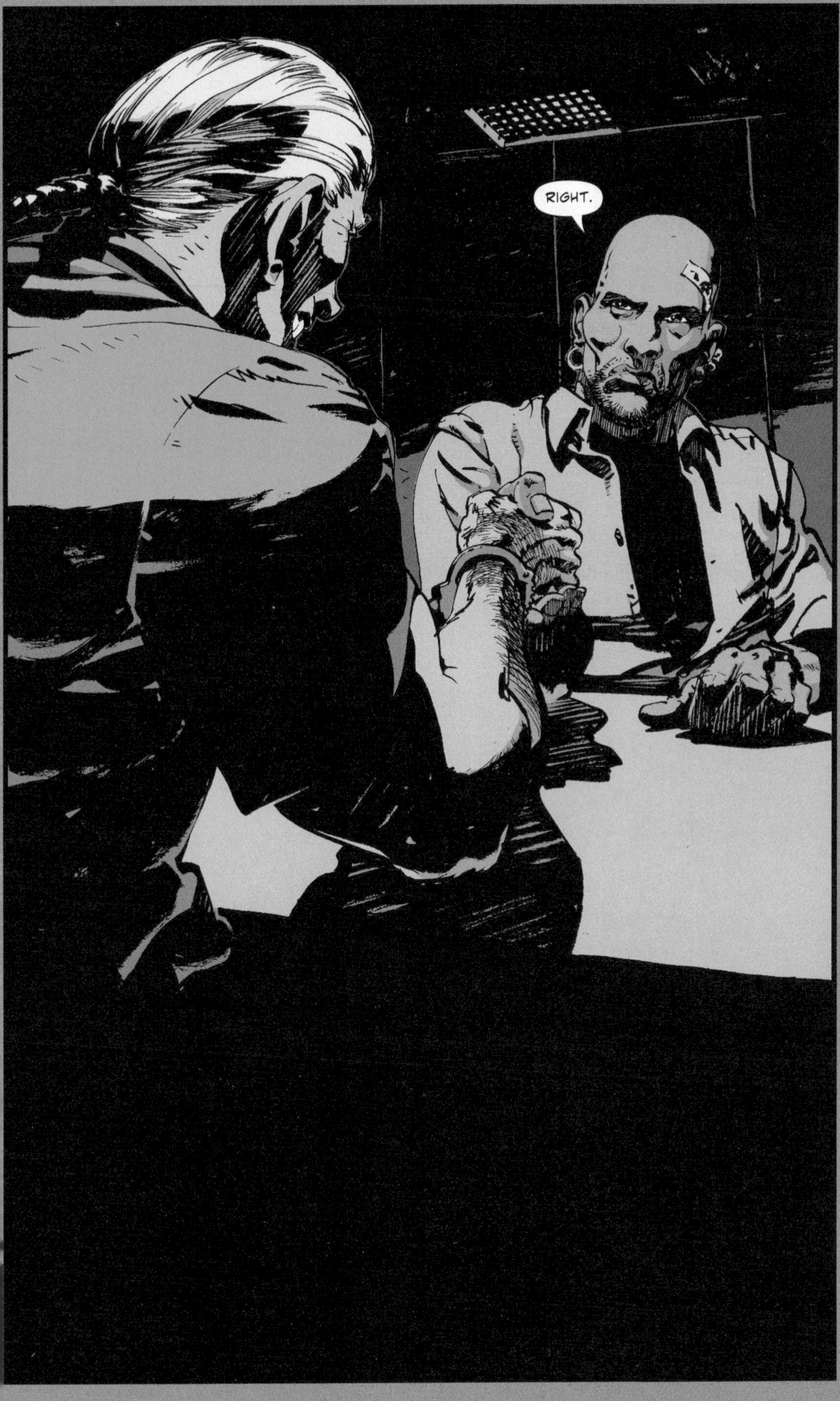
RIGHT.

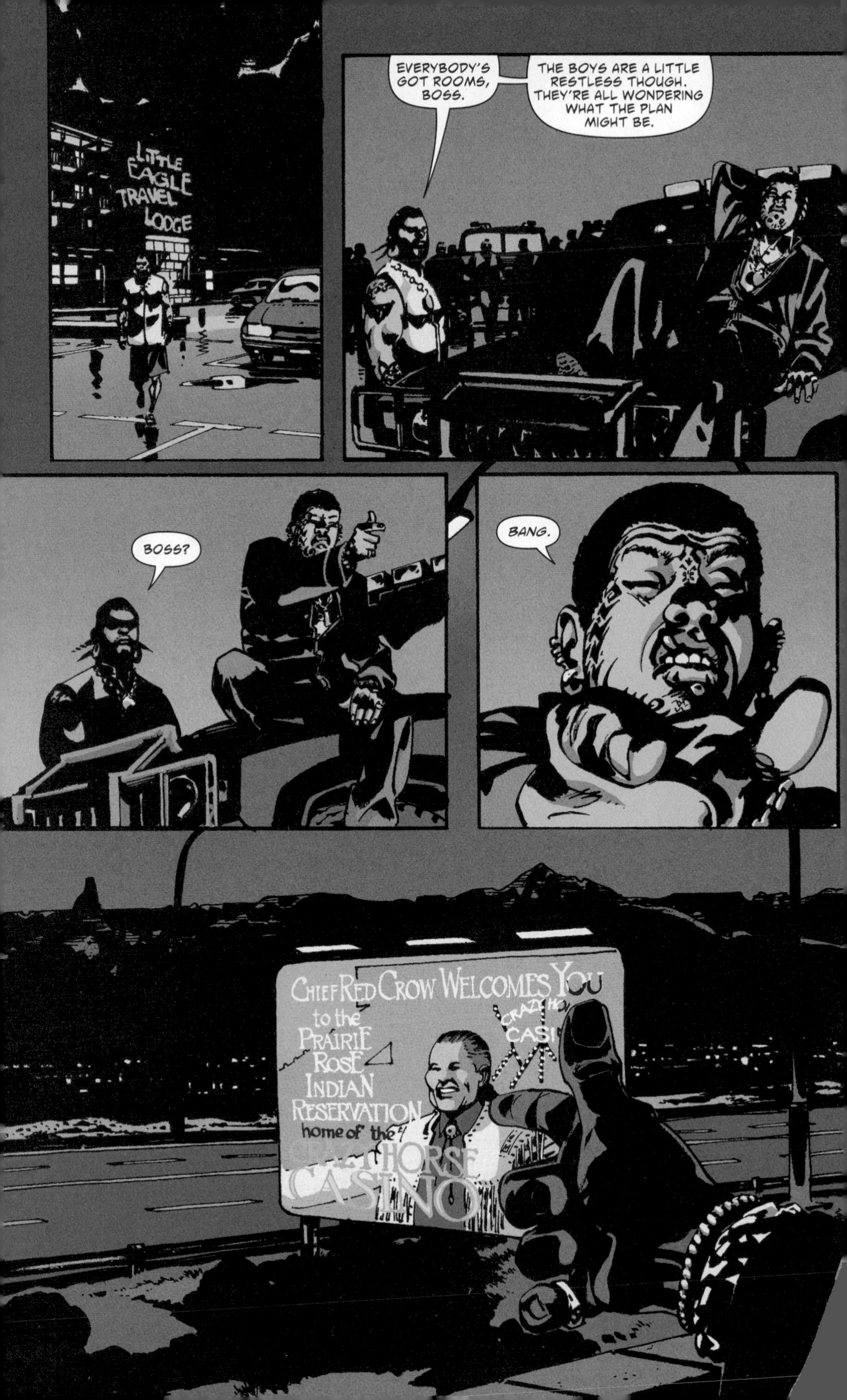
LITTLE EAGLE TRAVEL LODGE
EVERYBODY'S GOT ROOMS, BOSS.
THE BOYS ARE A LITTLE RESTLESS THOUGH. THEY'RE ALL WONDERING WHAT THE PLAN MIGHT BE.
BOSS?
BANG.
CHIEF RED CROW WELCOMES YOU to the PRAIRIE ROSE INDIAN RESERVATION home of the
CASINO

CHAPTER 4

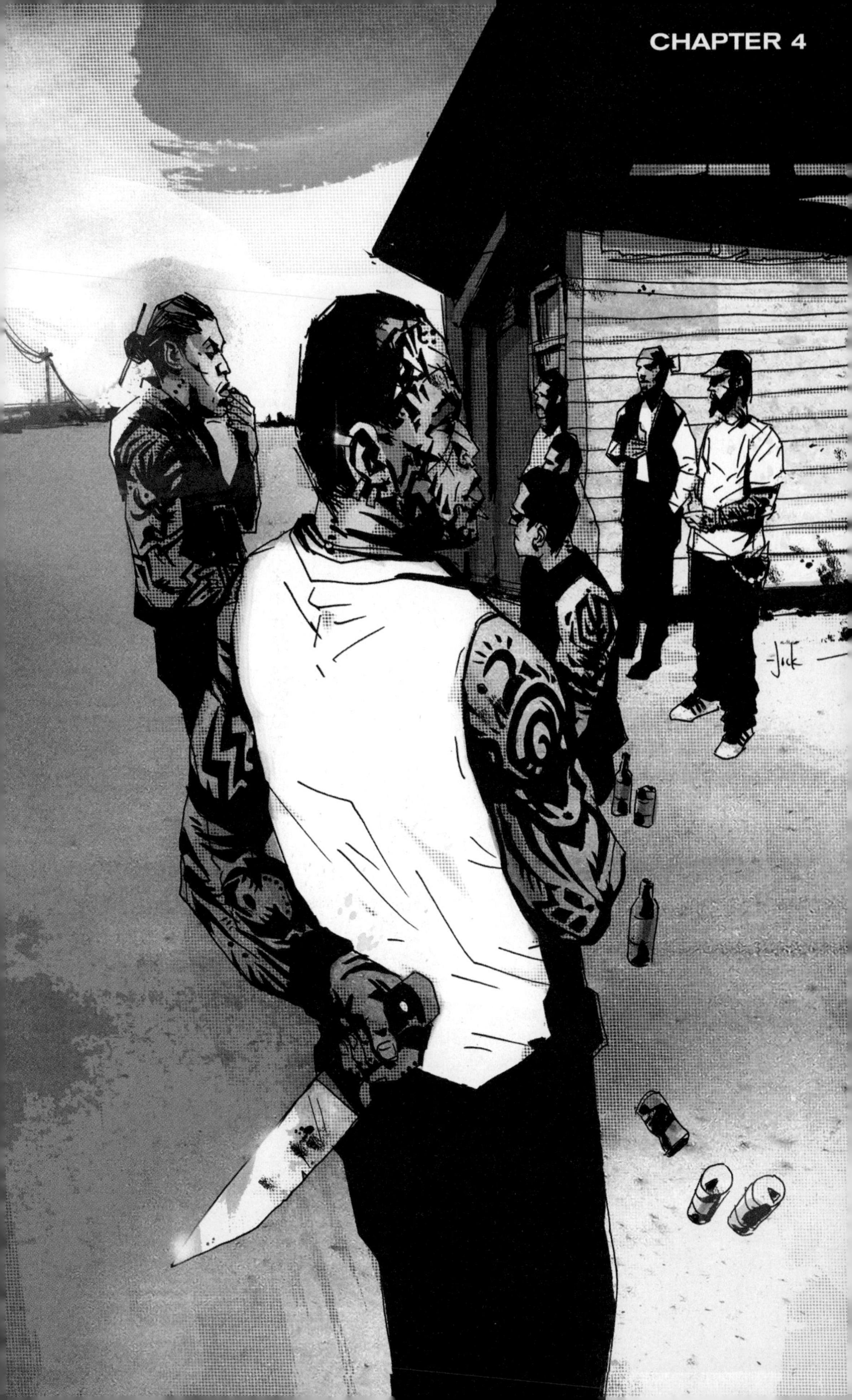

Jock

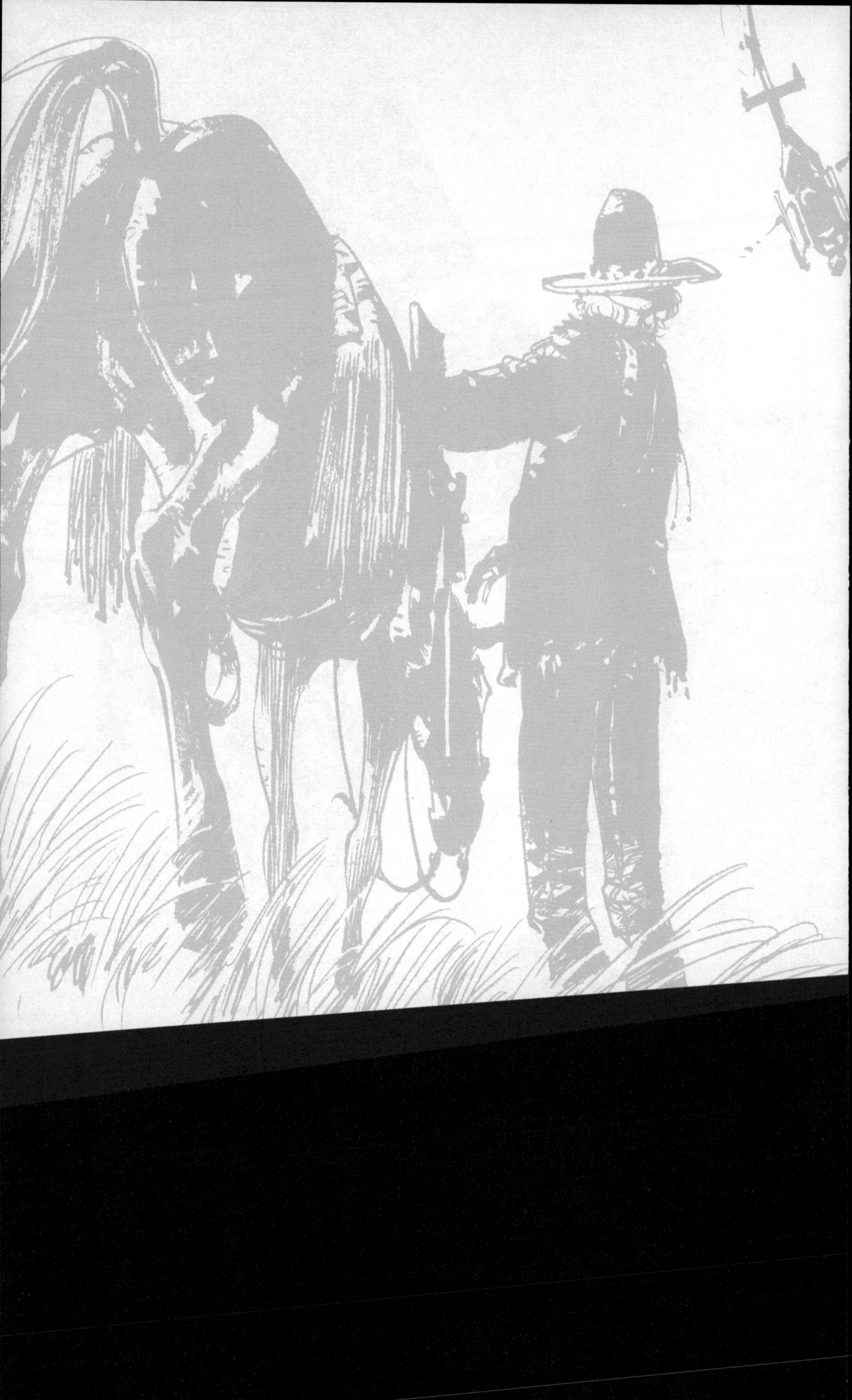

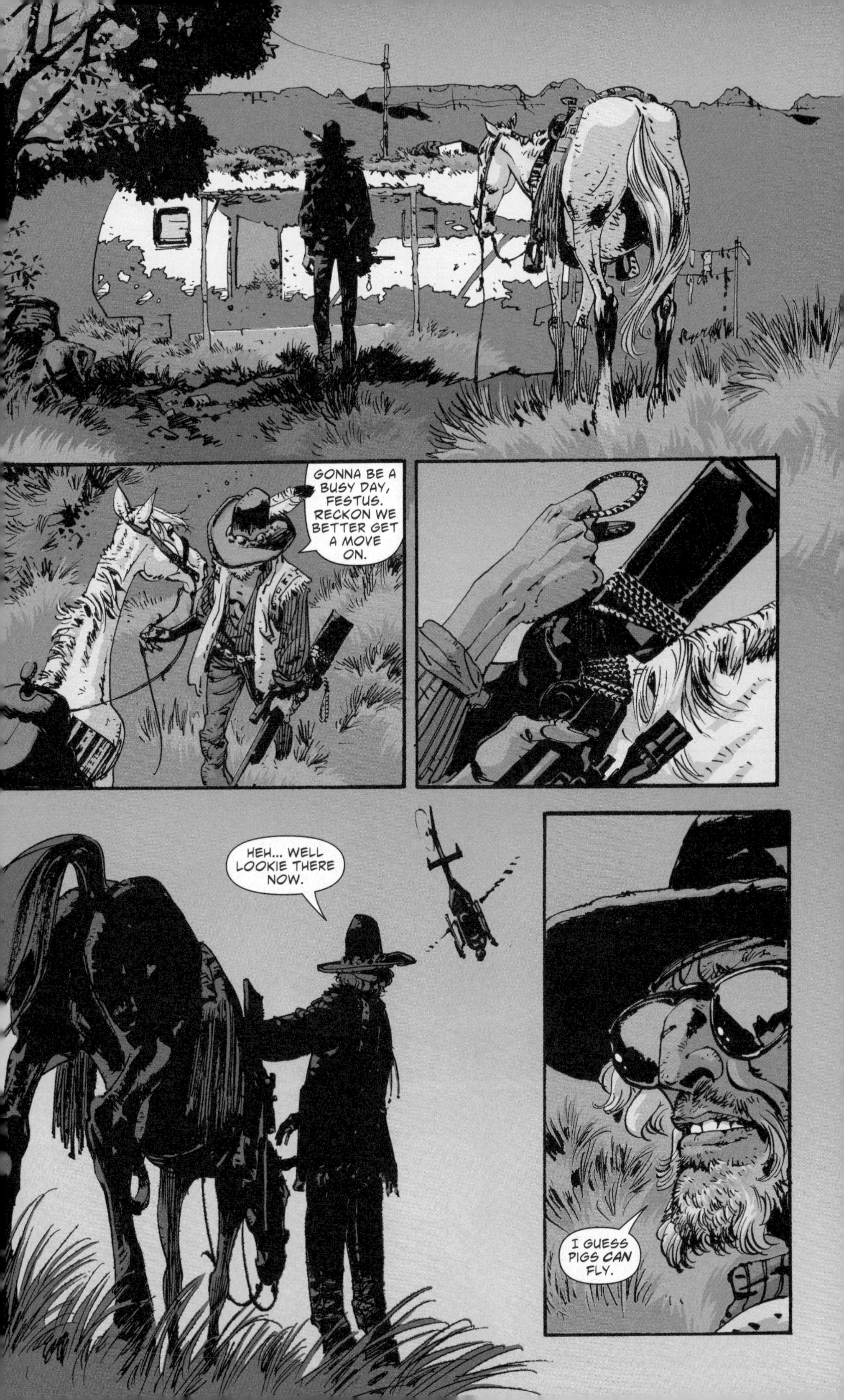
GONNA BE A BUSY DAY, FESTUS. RECKON WE BETTER GET A MOVE ON.
HEH... WELL LOOKIE THERE NOW.
I GUESS PIGS CAN FLY.

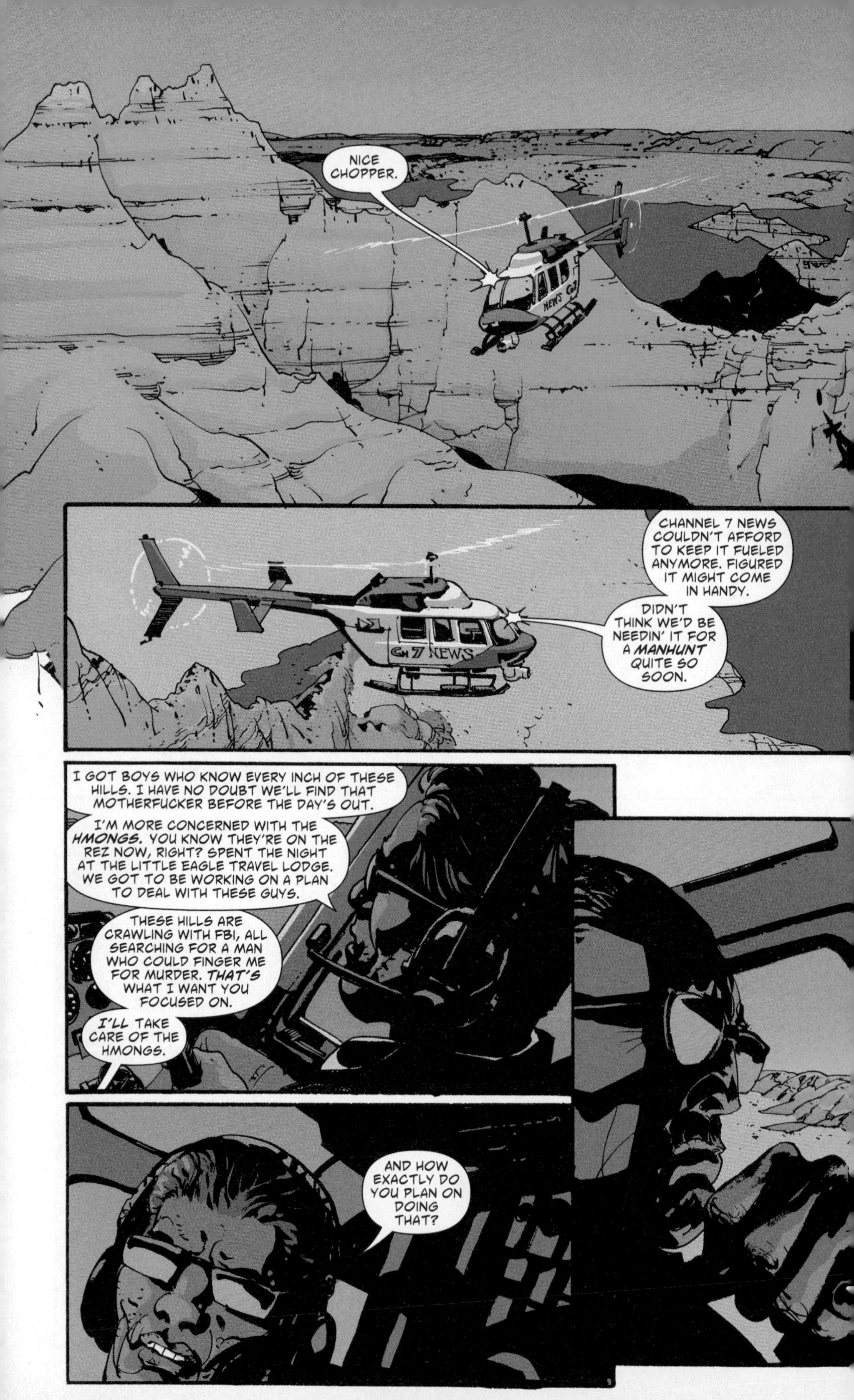
NICE CHOPPER.
CHANNEL 7 NEWS COULDN'T AFFORD TO KEEP IT FUELED ANYMORE. FIGURED IT MIGHT COME IN HANDY.
DIDN'T THINK WE'D BE NEEDIN' IT FOR A *MANHUNT* QUITE SO SOON.
NEWS
7 NEWS
I GOT BOYS WHO KNOW EVERY INCH OF THESE HILLS. I HAVE NO DOUBT WE'LL FIND THAT MOTHERFUCKER BEFORE THE DAY'S OUT.
I'M MORE CONCERNED WITH THE *HMONGS*. YOU KNOW THEY'RE ON THE REZ NOW, RIGHT? SPENT THE NIGHT AT THE LITTLE EAGLE TRAVEL LODGE. WE GOT TO BE WORKING ON A PLAN TO DEAL WITH THESE GUYS.
THESE HILLS ARE CRAWLING WITH FBI, ALL SEARCHING FOR A MAN WHO COULD FINGER ME FOR MURDER. *THAT'S* WHAT I WANT YOU FOCUSED ON.
I'LL TAKE CARE OF THE HMONGS.
AND HOW EXACTLY DO YOU PLAN ON DOING THAT?

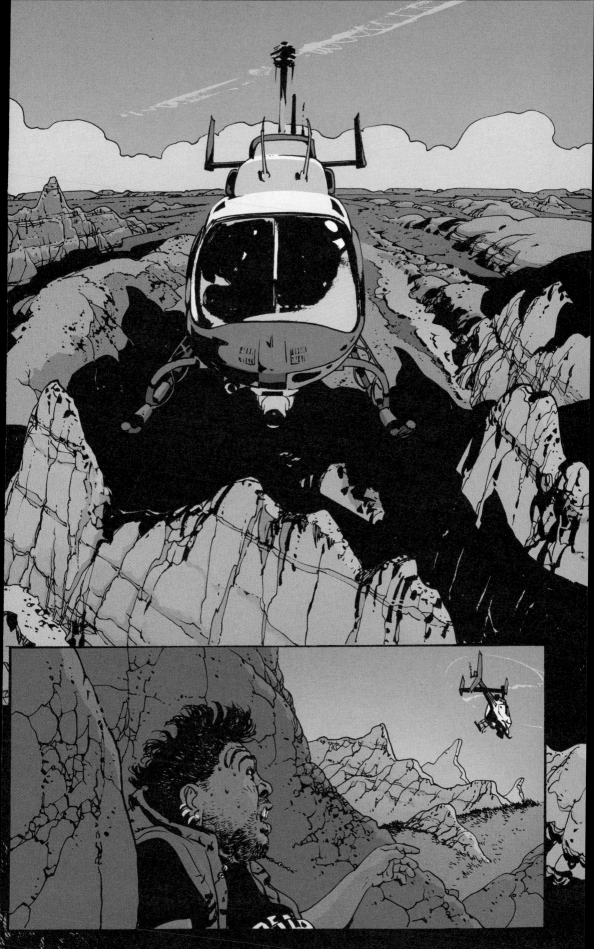

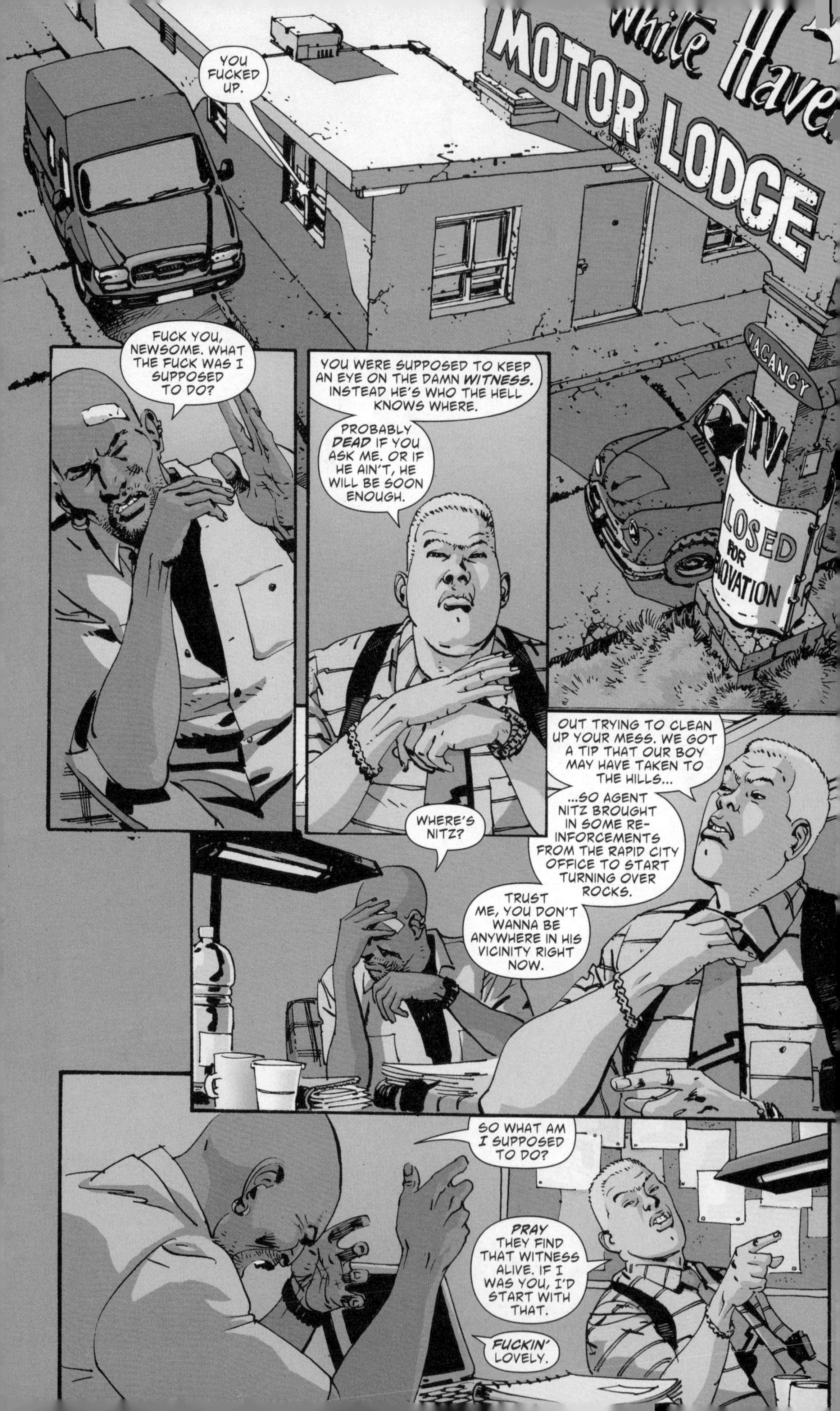
White Haven
MOTOR LODGE
YOU FUCKED UP.
VACANCY
TV
CLOSED FOR RENOVATION
FUCK YOU, NEWSOME. WHAT THE FUCK WAS I SUPPOSED TO DO?
YOU WERE SUPPOSED TO KEEP AN EYE ON THE DAMN *WITNESS.* INSTEAD HE'S WHO THE HELL KNOWS WHERE.
PROBABLY *DEAD* IF YOU ASK ME. OR IF HE AIN'T, HE WILL BE SOON ENOUGH.
WHERE'S NITZ?
OUT TRYING TO CLEAN UP YOUR MESS. WE GOT A TIP THAT OUR BOY MAY HAVE TAKEN TO THE HILLS...
...SO AGENT NITZ BROUGHT IN SOME RE-INFORCEMENTS FROM THE RAPID CITY OFFICE TO START TURNING OVER ROCKS.
TRUST ME, YOU DON'T WANNA BE ANYWHERE IN HIS VICINITY RIGHT NOW.
SO WHAT AM *I* SUPPOSED TO DO?
PRAY THEY FIND THAT WITNESS ALIVE. IF I WAS YOU, I'D START WITH THAT.
FUCKIN' LOVELY.

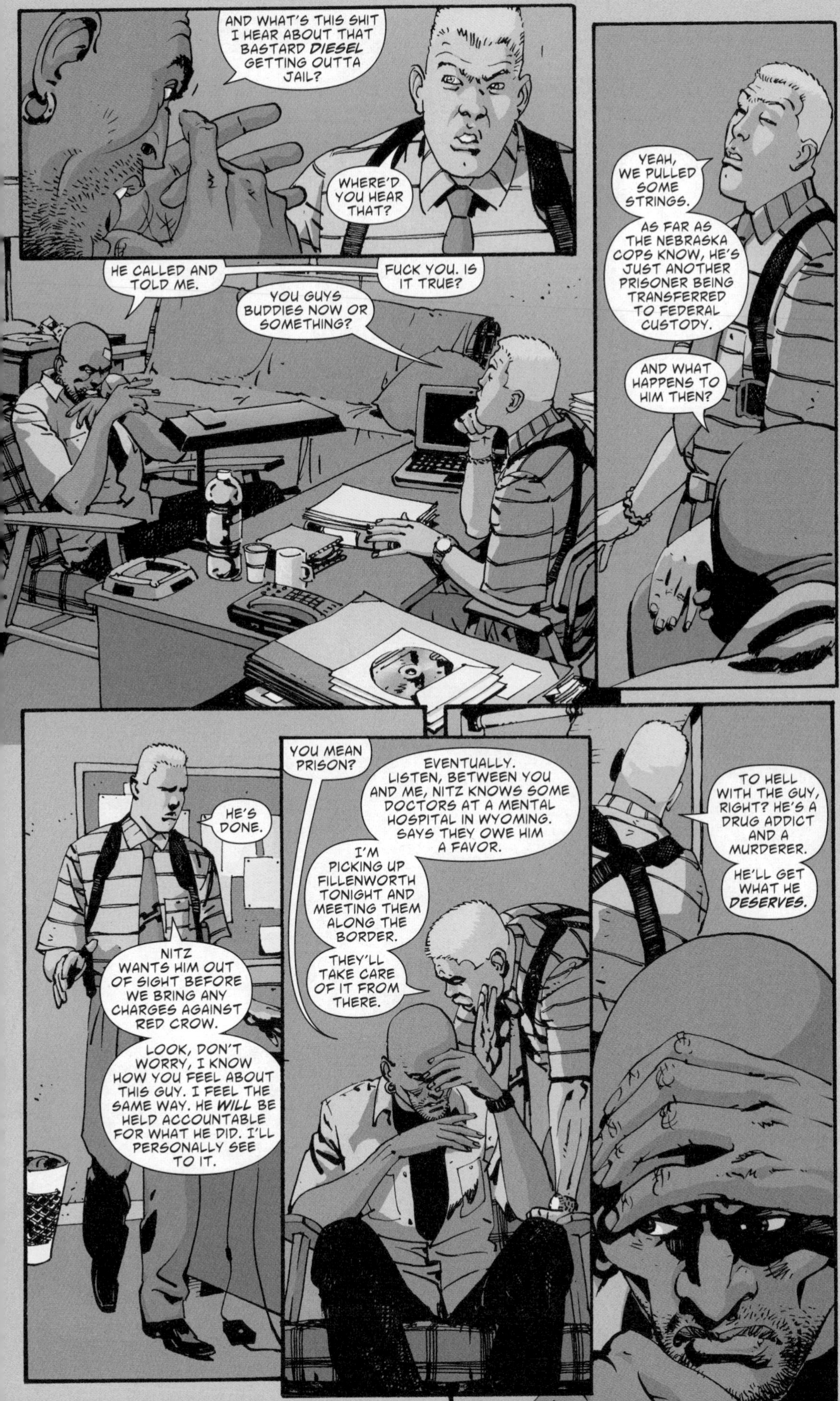
AND WHAT'S THIS SHIT I HEAR ABOUT THAT BASTARD *DIESEL* GETTING OUTTA JAIL?
WHERE'D YOU HEAR THAT?
HE CALLED AND TOLD ME.
YOU GUYS BUDDIES NOW OR SOMETHING?
FUCK YOU. IS IT TRUE?
YEAH, WE PULLED SOME STRINGS.
AS FAR AS THE NEBRASKA COPS KNOW, HE'S JUST ANOTHER PRISONER BEING TRANSFERRED TO FEDERAL CUSTODY.
AND WHAT HAPPENS TO HIM THEN?
HE'S DONE.
NITZ WANTS HIM OUT OF SIGHT BEFORE WE BRING ANY CHARGES AGAINST RED CROW.
LOOK, DON'T WORRY, I KNOW HOW YOU FEEL ABOUT THIS GUY. I FEEL THE SAME WAY. HE *WILL* BE HELD ACCOUNTABLE FOR WHAT HE DID. I'LL PERSONALLY SEE TO IT.
YOU MEAN PRISON?
EVENTUALLY. LISTEN, BETWEEN YOU AND ME, NITZ KNOWS SOME DOCTORS AT A MENTAL HOSPITAL IN WYOMING. SAYS THEY OWE HIM A FAVOR.
I'M PICKING UP FILLENWORTH TONIGHT AND MEETING THEM ALONG THE BORDER.
THEY'LL TAKE CARE OF IT FROM THERE.
TO HELL WITH THE GUY, RIGHT? HE'S A DRUG ADDICT AND A MURDERER.
HE'LL GET WHAT HE *DESERVES*.

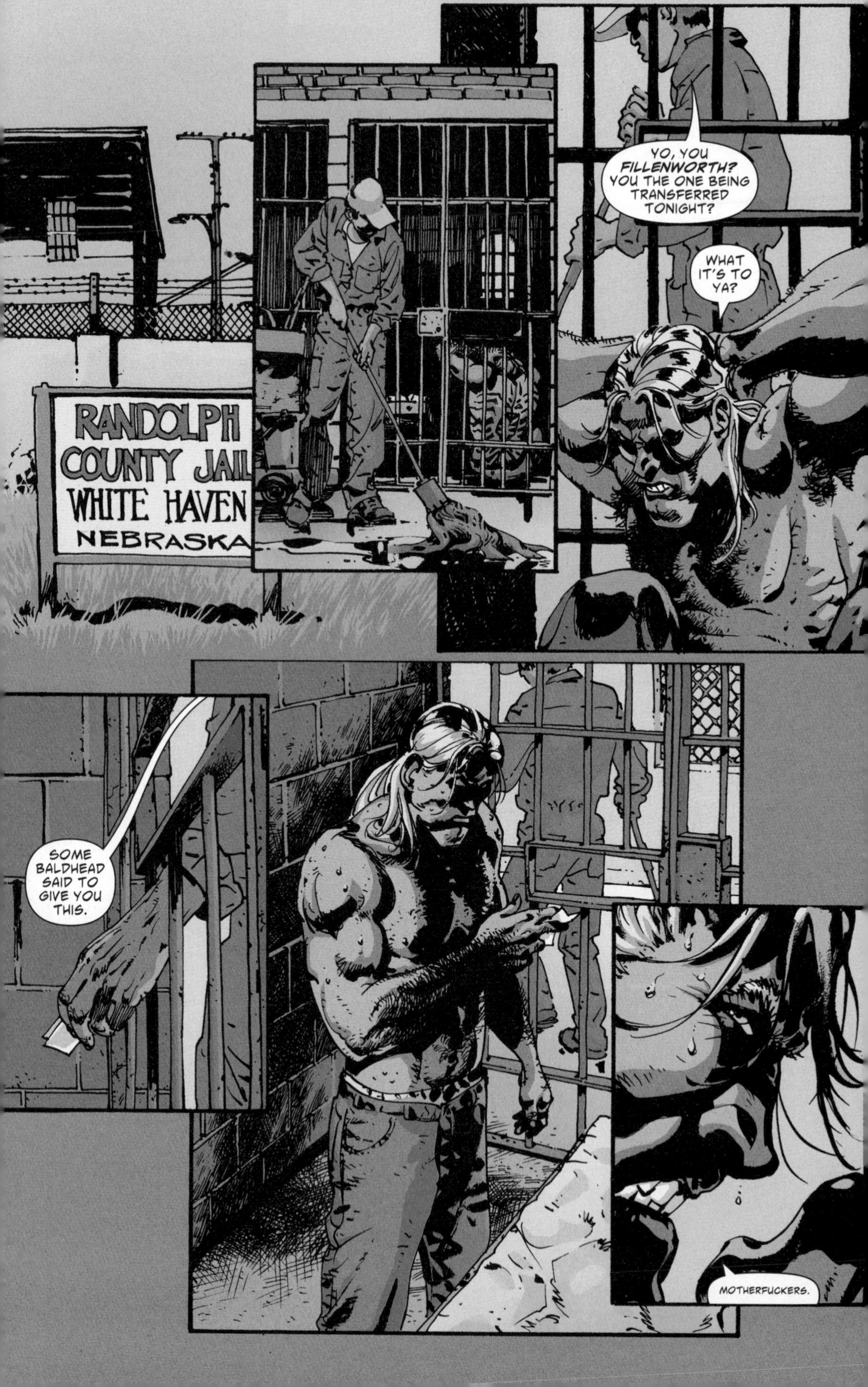

RANDOLPH
COUNTY JAIL
WHITE HAVEN
NEBRASKA
YO, YOU FILLENWORTH? YOU THE ONE BEING TRANSFERRED TONIGHT?
WHAT IT'S TO YA?
SOME BALDHEAD SAID TO GIVE YOU THIS.
MOTHERFUCKERS.

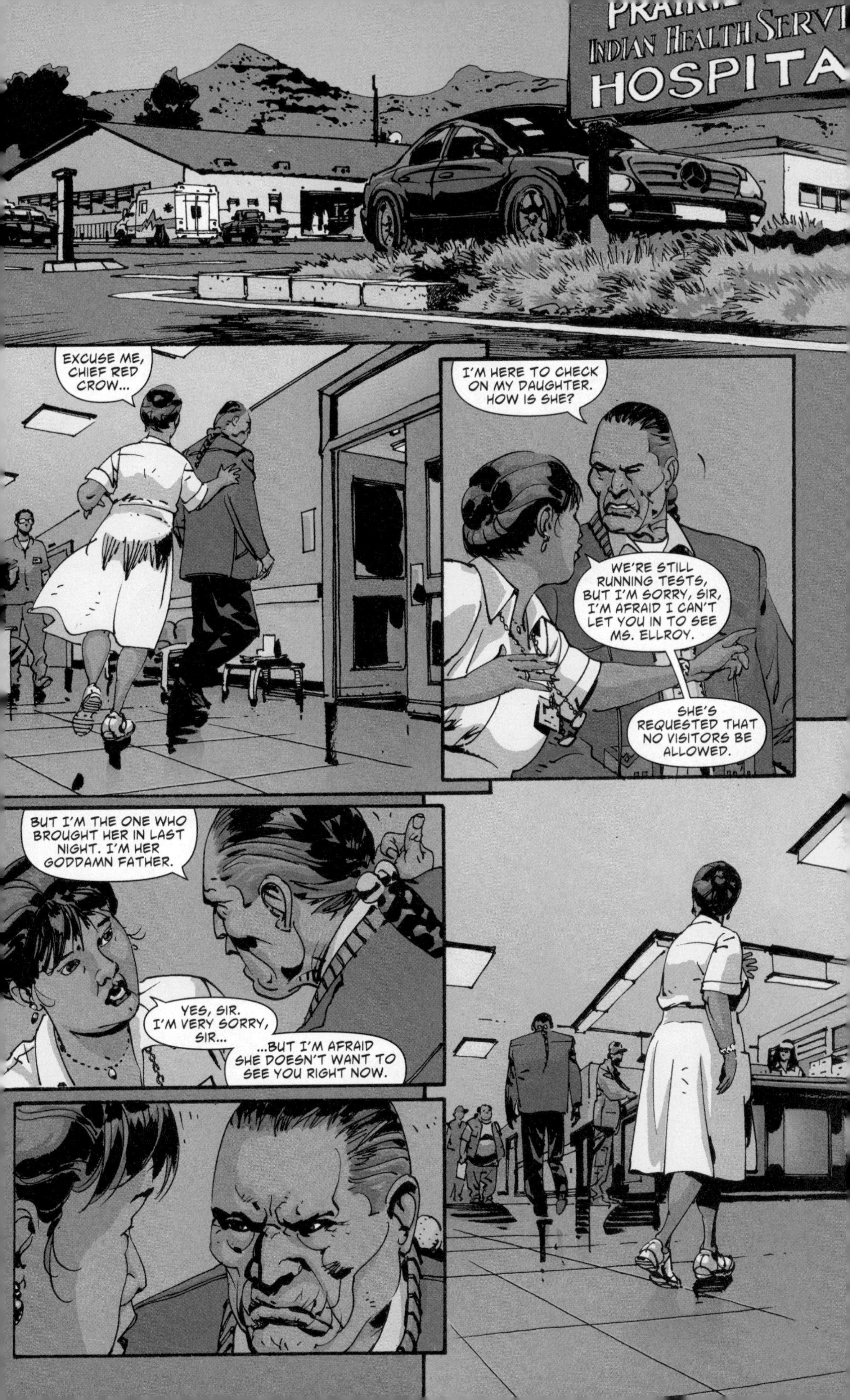
PRAIRIE
INDIAN HEALTH SERVI
HOSPITA
EXCUSE ME, CHIEF RED CROW...
I'M HERE TO CHECK ON MY DAUGHTER. HOW IS SHE?
WE'RE STILL RUNNING TESTS, BUT I'M SORRY, SIR, I'M AFRAID I CAN'T LET YOU IN TO SEE MS. ELLROY.
SHE'S REQUESTED THAT NO VISITORS BE ALLOWED.
BUT I'M THE ONE WHO BROUGHT HER IN LAST NIGHT. I'M HER GODDAMN FATHER.
YES, SIR. I'M VERY SORRY, SIR...
...BUT I'M AFRAID SHE DOESN'T WANT TO SEE YOU RIGHT NOW.

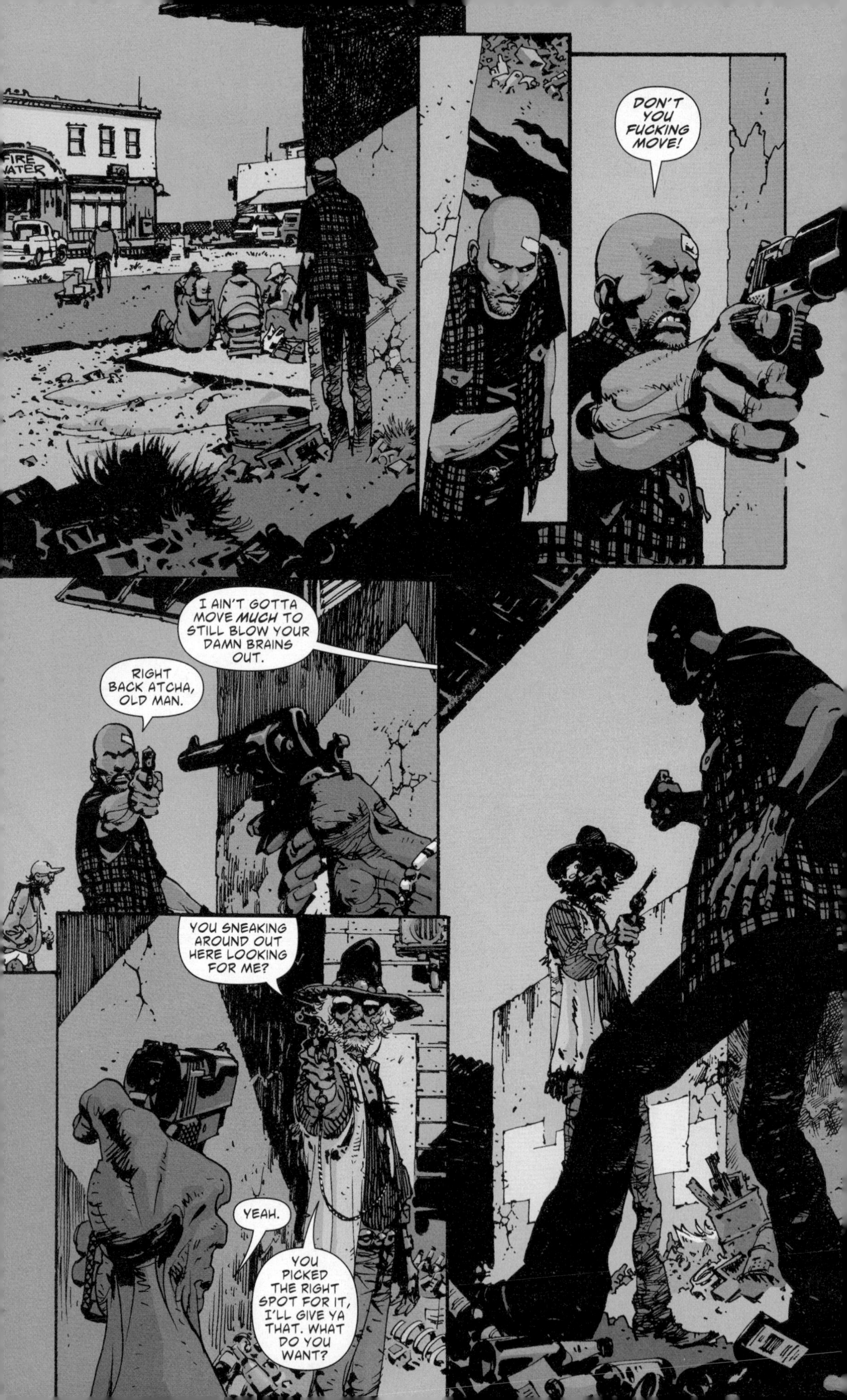
FIRE WATER
DON'T YOU FUCKING MOVE!
I AIN'T GOTTA MOVE MUCH TO STILL BLOW YOUR DAMN BRAINS OUT.
RIGHT BACK ATCHA, OLD MAN.
YOU SNEAKING AROUND OUT HERE LOOKING FOR ME?
YEAH.
YOU PICKED THE RIGHT SPOT FOR IT, I'LL GIVE YA THAT. WHAT DO YOU WANT?

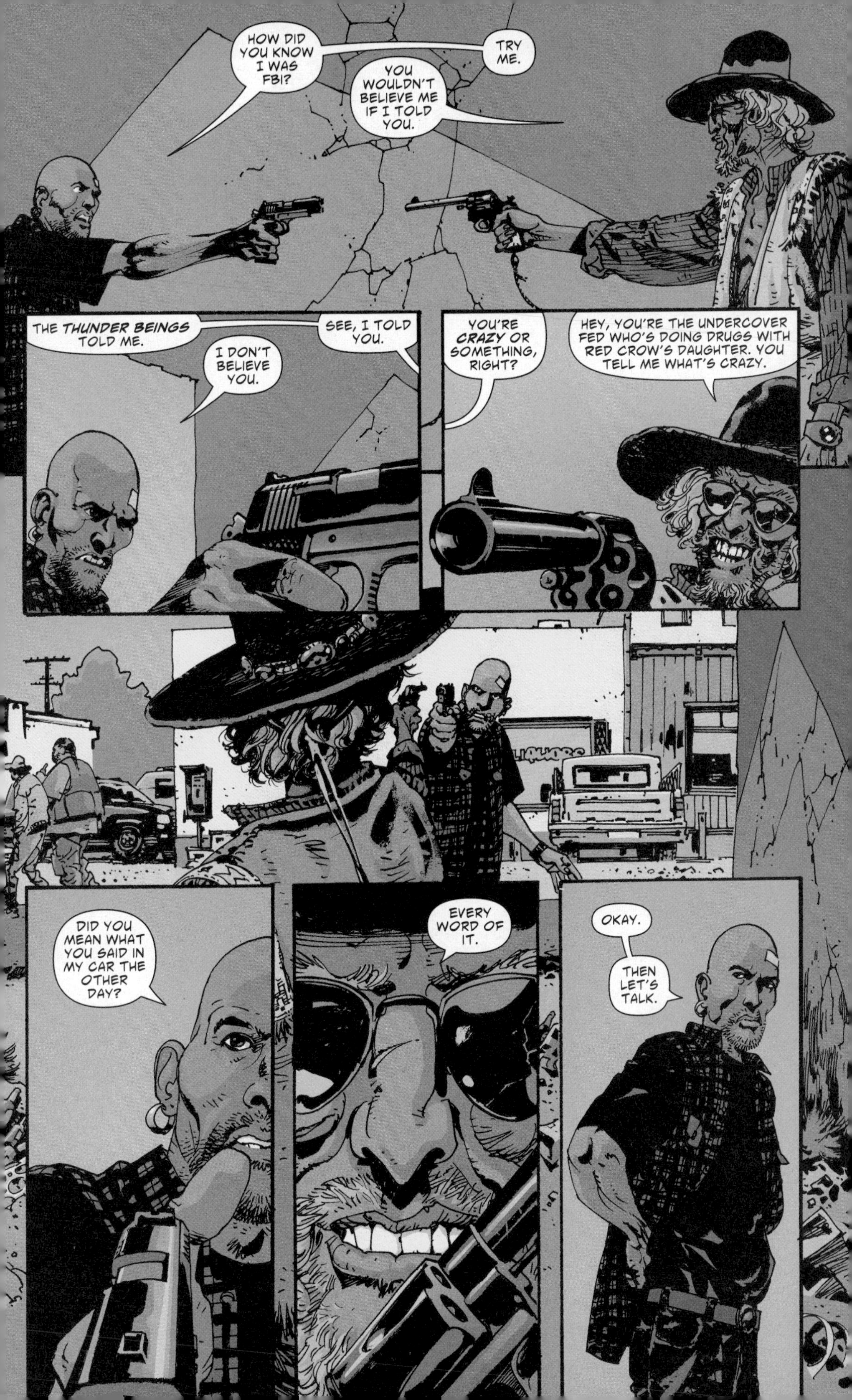
HOW DID YOU KNOW I WAS FBI?
TRY ME.
YOU WOULDN'T BELIEVE ME IF I TOLD YOU.
THE *THUNDER BEINGS* TOLD ME.
SEE, I TOLD YOU.
I DON'T BELIEVE YOU.
YOU'RE *CRAZY* OR SOMETHING, RIGHT?
HEY, YOU'RE THE UNDERCOVER FED WHO'S DOING DRUGS WITH RED CROW'S DAUGHTER. YOU TELL ME WHAT'S CRAZY.
DID YOU MEAN WHAT YOU SAID IN MY CAR THE OTHER DAY?
EVERY WORD OF IT.
OKAY.
THEN LET'S TALK.

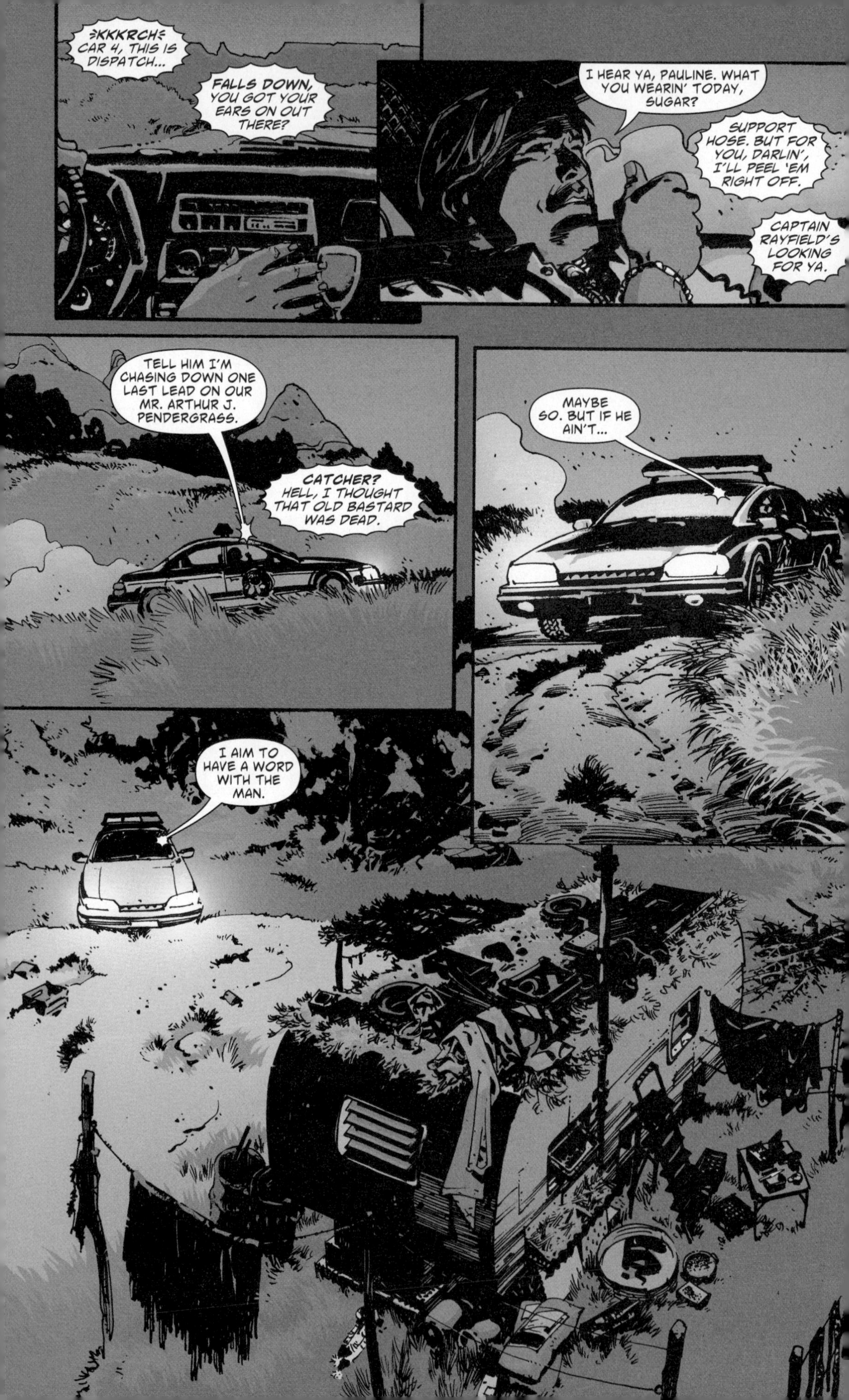

=KKKRCH= CAR 4, THIS IS DISPATCH...
FALLS DOWN, YOU GOT YOUR EARS ON OUT THERE?
I HEAR YA, PAULINE. WHAT YOU WEARIN' TODAY, SUGAR?
SUPPORT HOSE. BUT FOR YOU, DARLIN', I'LL PEEL 'EM RIGHT OFF.
CAPTAIN RAYFIELD'S LOOKING FOR YA.
TELL HIM I'M CHASING DOWN ONE LAST LEAD ON OUR MR. ARTHUR J. PENDERGRASS.
CATCHER? HELL, I THOUGHT THAT OLD BASTARD WAS DEAD.
MAYBE SO. BUT IF HE AIN'T...
I AIM TO HAVE A WORD WITH THE MAN.

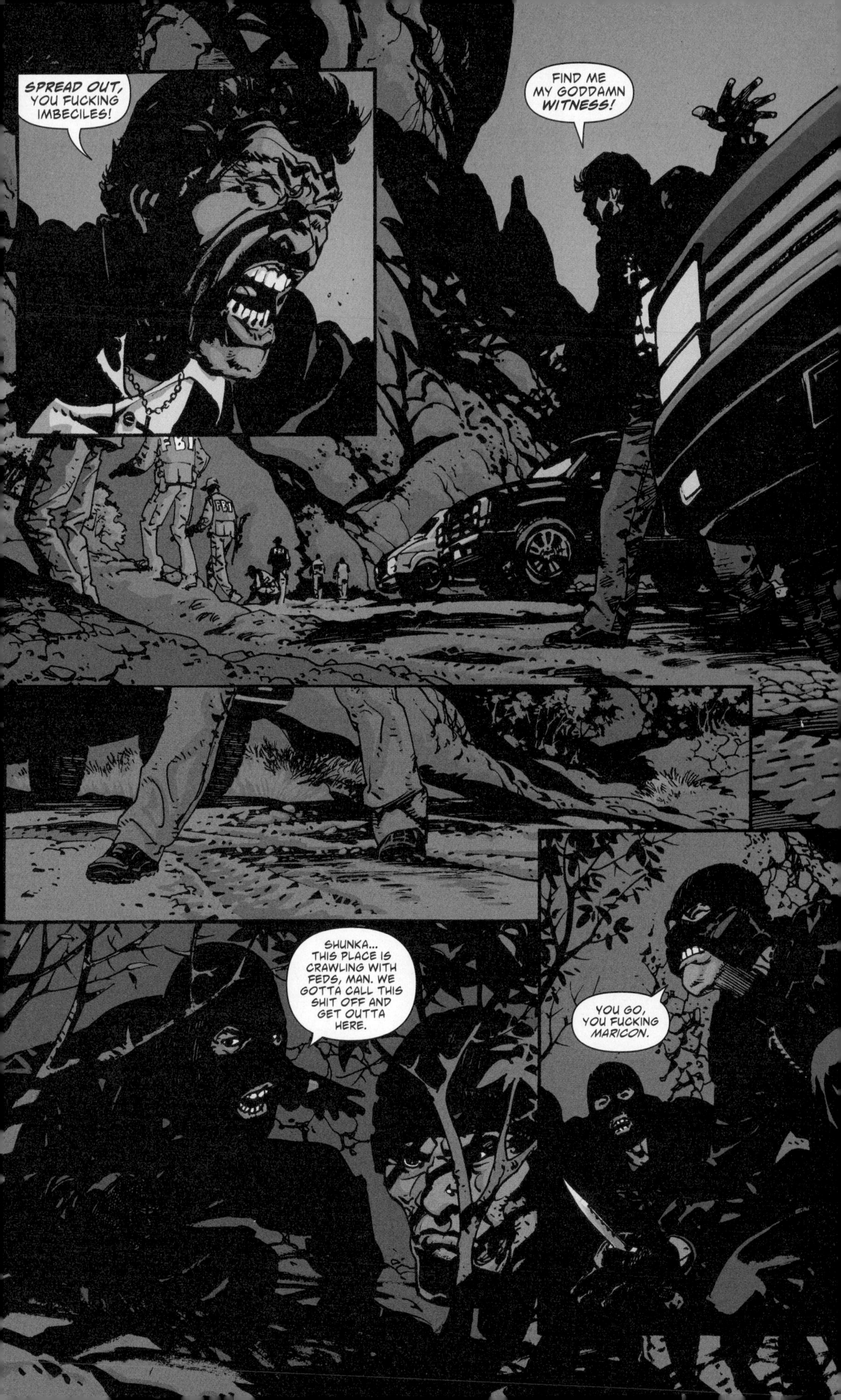
SPREAD OUT, YOU FUCKING IMBECILES!
FIND ME MY GODDAMN WITNESS!
SHUNKA... THIS PLACE IS CRAWLING WITH FEDS, MAN. WE GOTTA CALL THIS SHIT OFF AND GET OUTTA HERE.
YOU GO, YOU FUCKING MARICON.
FBI

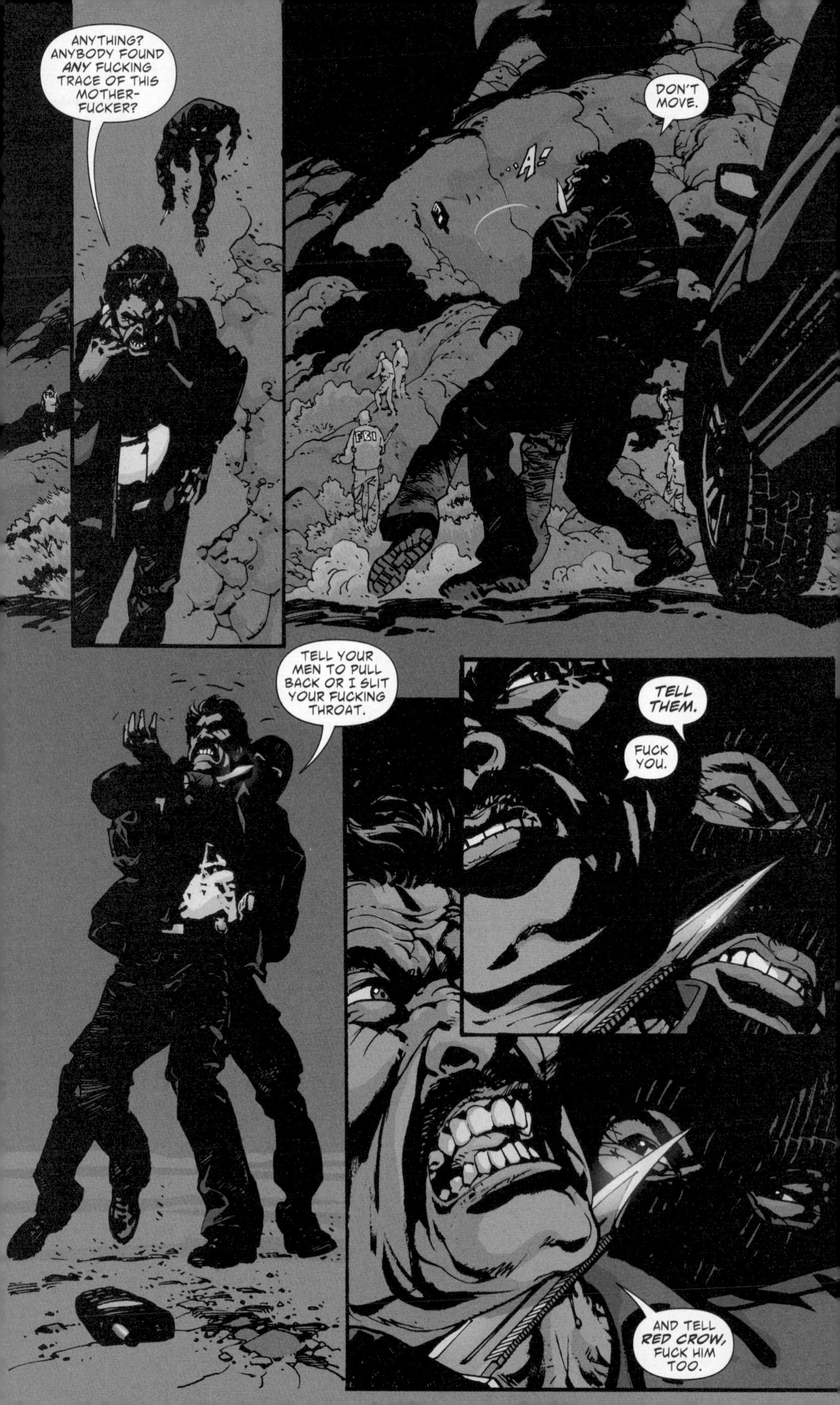
ANYTHING? ANYBODY FOUND ANY FUCKING TRACE OF THIS MOTHER-FUCKER?
DON'T MOVE.
A!
TELL YOUR MEN TO PULL BACK OR I SLIT YOUR FUCKING THROAT.
TELL THEM.
FUCK YOU.
AND TELL RED CROW, FUCK HIM TOO.

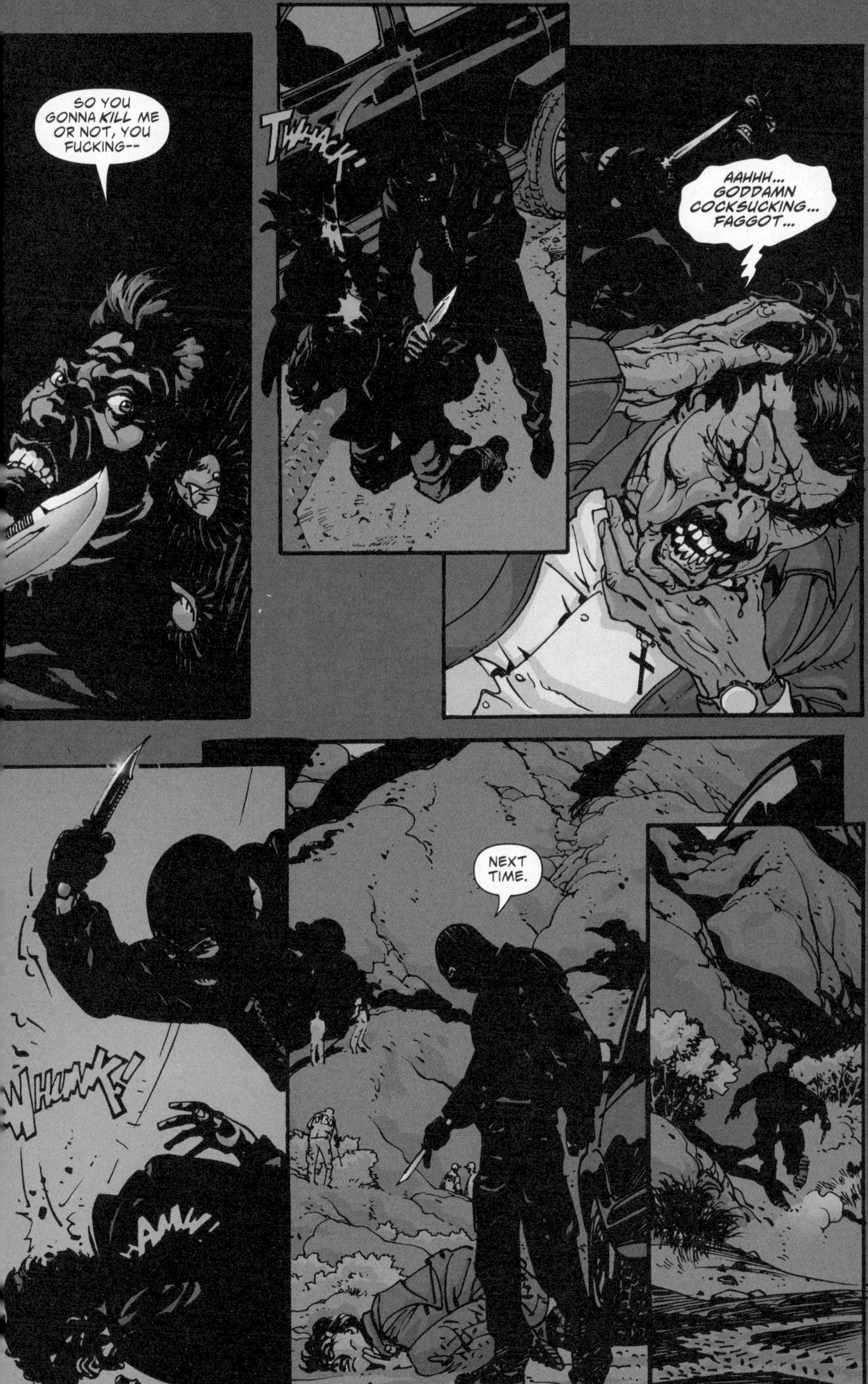
SO YOU GONNA KILL ME OR NOT, YOU FUCKING--
THWACK
AAHHH... GODDAMN COCKSUCKING... FAGGOT...
WHUNK!
NEXT TIME.

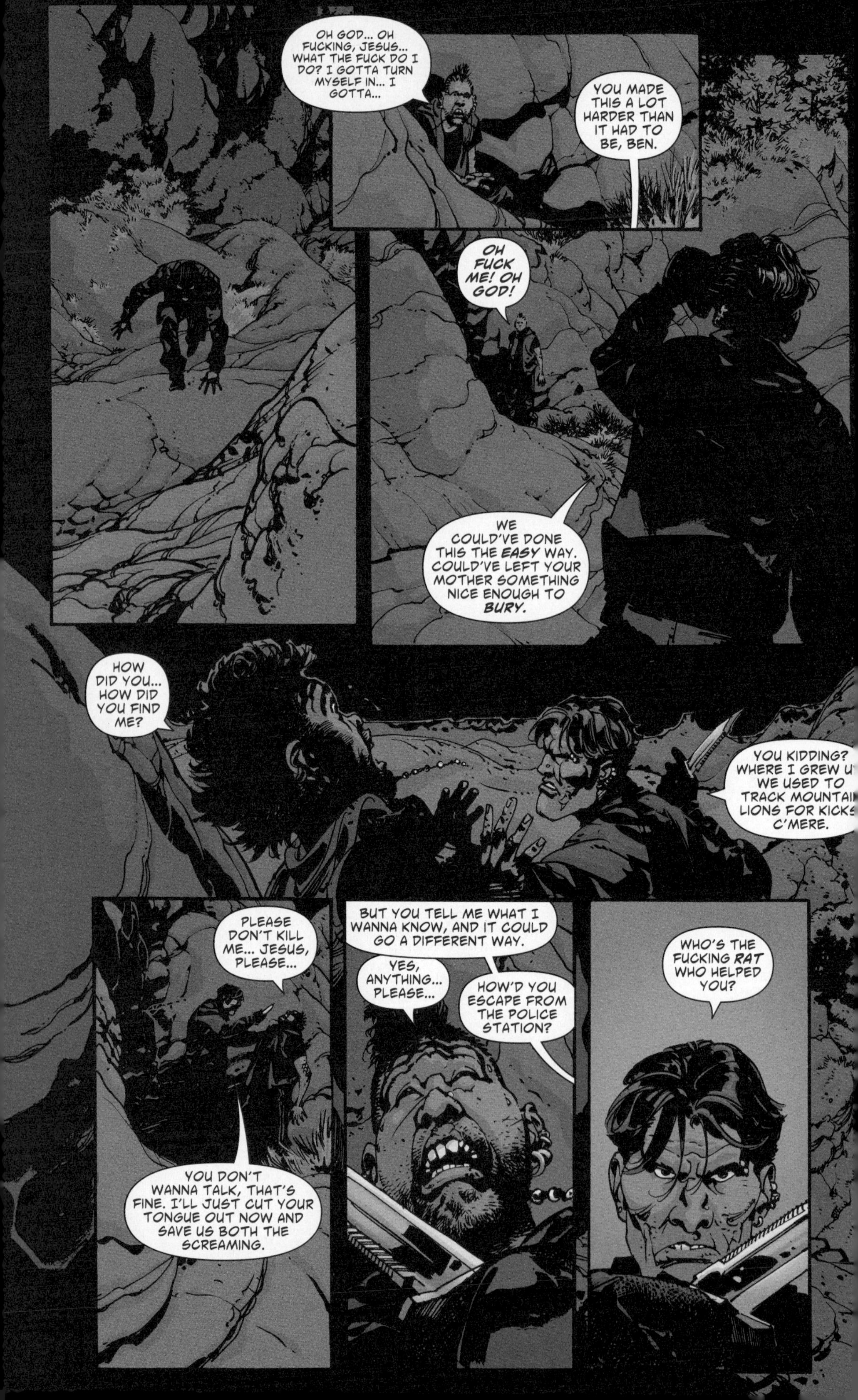
OH GOD... OH FUCKING, JESUS... WHAT THE FUCK DO I DO? I GOTTA TURN MYSELF IN... I GOTTA...
YOU MADE THIS A LOT HARDER THAN IT HAD TO BE, BEN.
OH FUCK ME! OH GOD!
WE COULD'VE DONE THIS THE EASY WAY. COULD'VE LEFT YOUR MOTHER SOMETHING NICE ENOUGH TO BURY.
HOW DID YOU... HOW DID YOU FIND ME?
YOU KIDDING? WHERE I GREW U WE USED TO TRACK MOUNTAI LIONS FOR KICKS C'MERE.
PLEASE DON'T KILL ME... JESUS, PLEASE...
YOU DON'T WANNA TALK, THAT'S FINE. I'LL JUST CUT YOUR TONGUE OUT NOW AND SAVE US BOTH THE SCREAMING.
BUT YOU TELL ME WHAT I WANNA KNOW, AND IT COULD GO A DIFFERENT WAY.
YES, ANYTHING... PLEASE...
HOW'D YOU ESCAPE FROM THE POLICE STATION?
WHO'S THE FUCKING RAT WHO HELPED YOU?

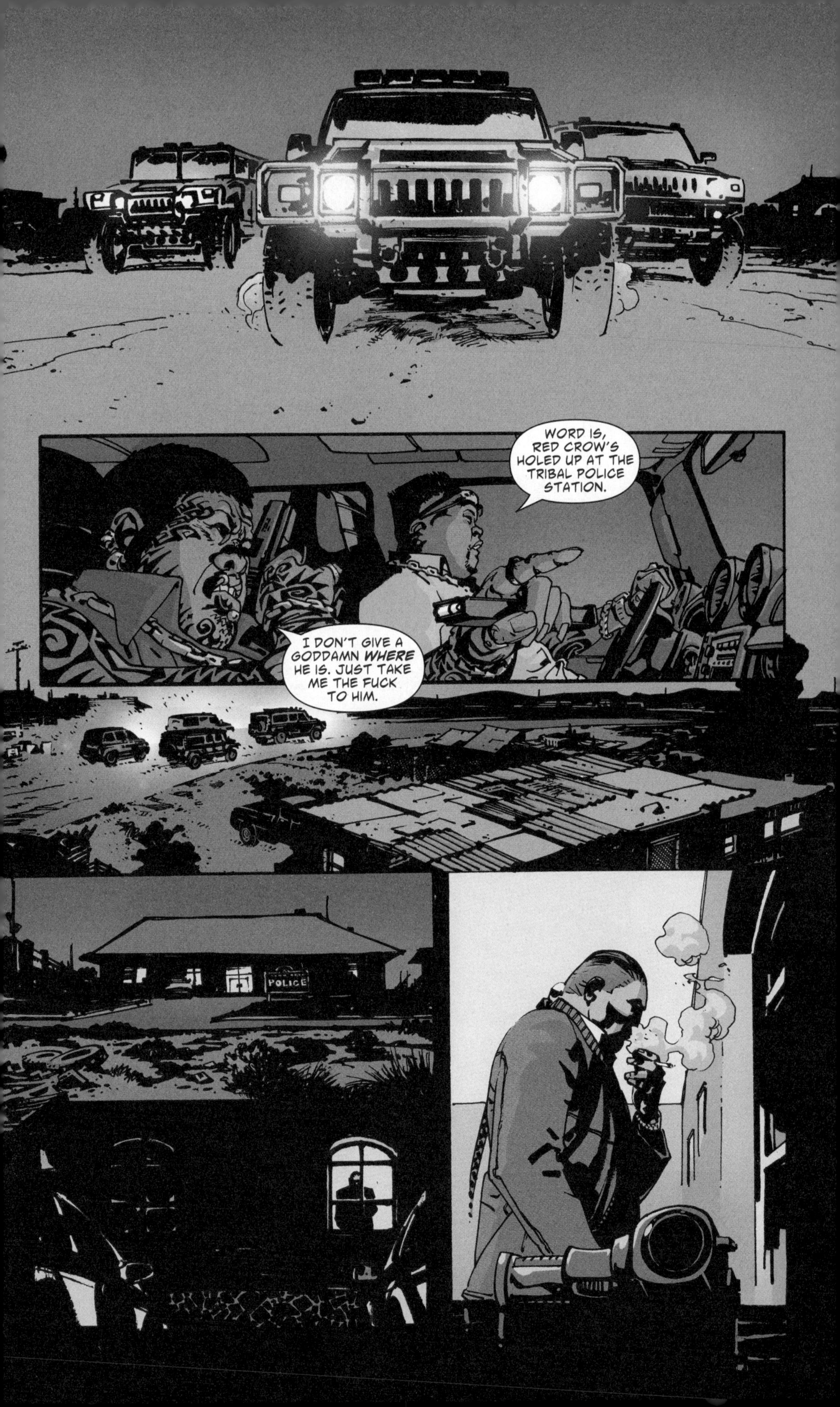
WORD IS, RED CROW'S HOLED UP AT THE TRIBAL POLICE STATION.
I DON'T GIVE A GODDAMN WHERE HE IS. JUST TAKE ME THE FUCK TO HIM.
POLICE

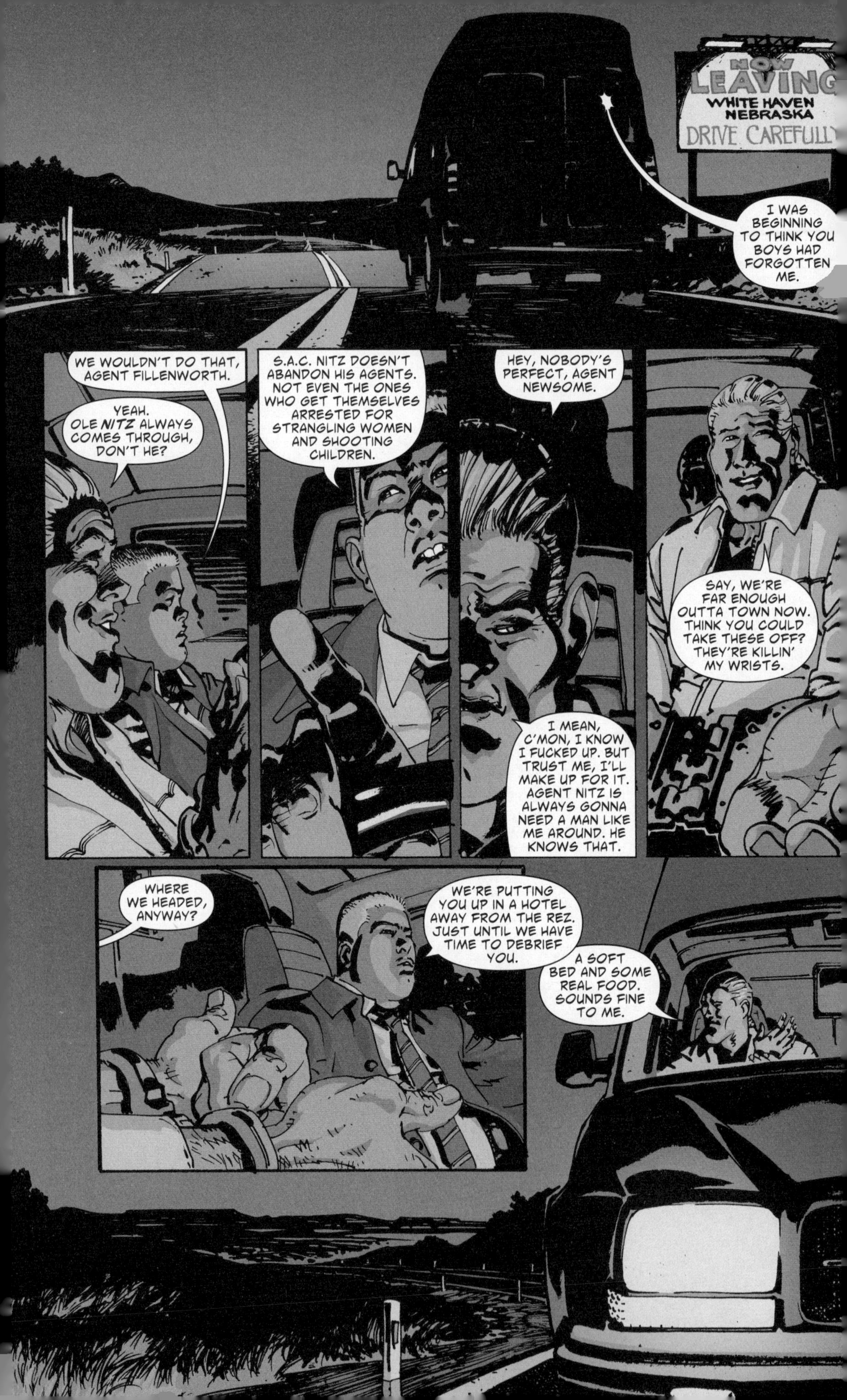
NOW LEAVING
WHITE HAVEN NEBRASKA
DRIVE CAREFULLY
I WAS BEGINNING TO THINK YOU BOYS HAD FORGOTTEN ME.
WE WOULDN'T DO THAT, AGENT FILLENWORTH.
YEAH. OLE NITZ ALWAYS COMES THROUGH, DON'T HE?
S.A.C. NITZ DOESN'T ABANDON HIS AGENTS. NOT EVEN THE ONES WHO GET THEMSELVES ARRESTED FOR STRANGLING WOMEN AND SHOOTING CHILDREN.
HEY, NOBODY'S PERFECT, AGENT NEWSOME.
I MEAN, C'MON, I KNOW I FUCKED UP. BUT TRUST ME, I'LL MAKE UP FOR IT. AGENT NITZ IS ALWAYS GONNA NEED A MAN LIKE ME AROUND. HE KNOWS THAT.
SAY, WE'RE FAR ENOUGH OUTTA TOWN NOW. THINK YOU COULD TAKE THESE OFF? THEY'RE KILLIN' MY WRISTS.
WHERE WE HEADED, ANYWAY?
WE'RE PUTTING YOU UP IN A HOTEL AWAY FROM THE REZ. JUST UNTIL WE HAVE TIME TO DEBRIEF YOU.
A SOFT BED AND SOME REAL FOOD. SOUNDS FINE TO ME.

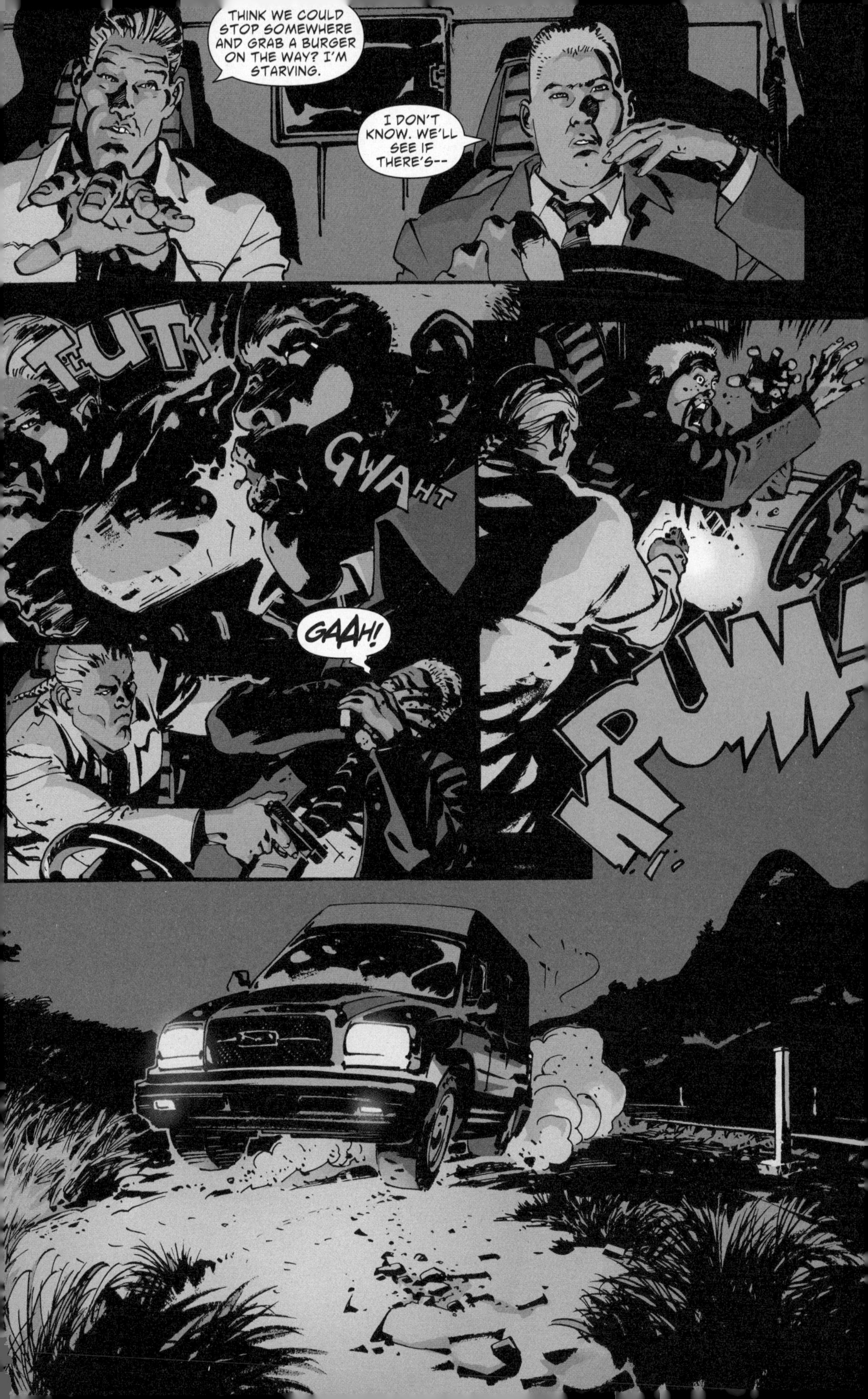
THINK WE COULD STOP SOMEWHERE AND GRAB A BURGER ON THE WAY? I'M STARVING.
I DON'T KNOW. WE'LL SEE IF THERE'S--
TUTK
GWAHT
GAAH!
KRUMP

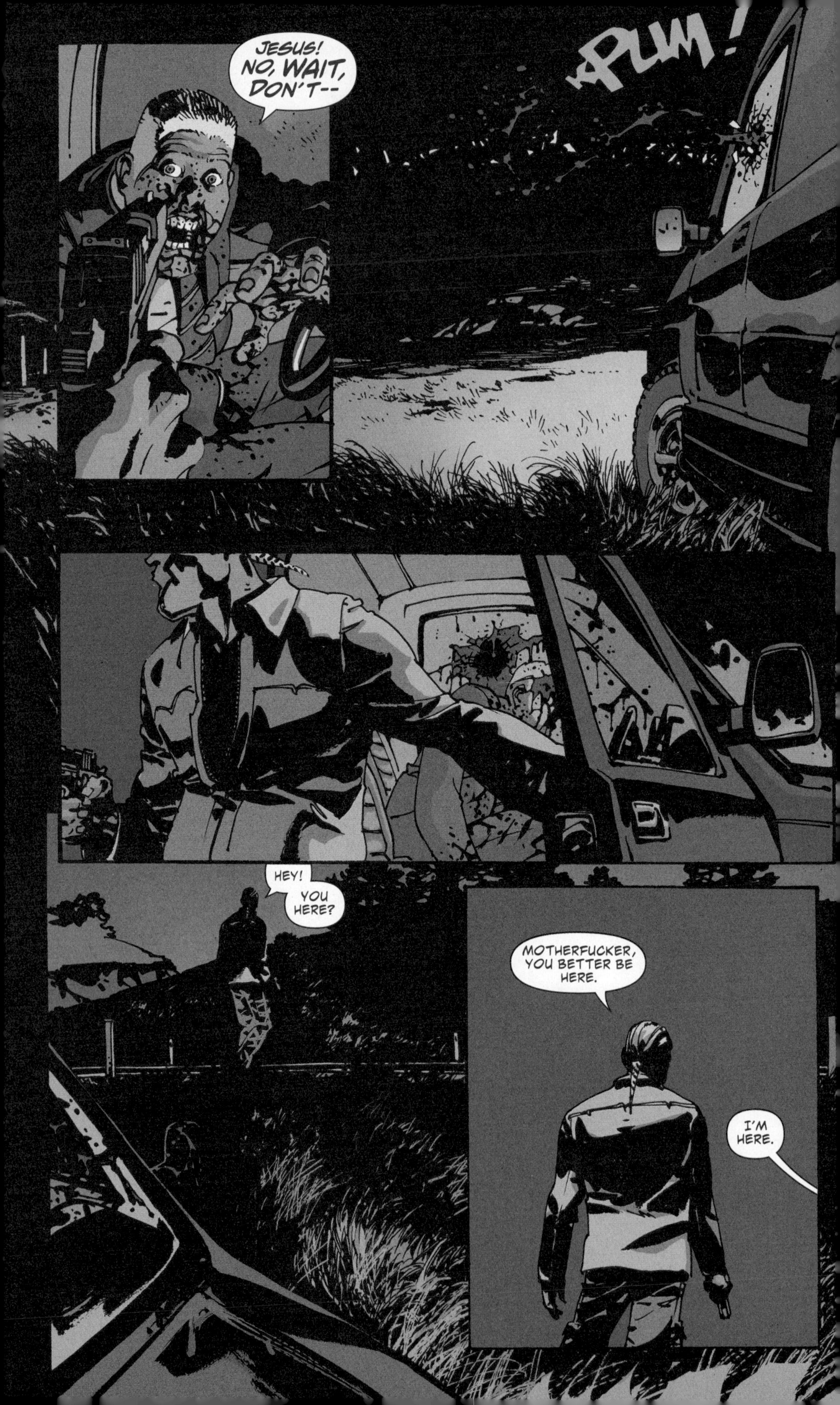

JESUS! NO, WAIT, DON'T--
KPUM!
HEY!
YOU HERE?
MOTHERFUCKER, YOU BETTER BE HERE.
I'M HERE.

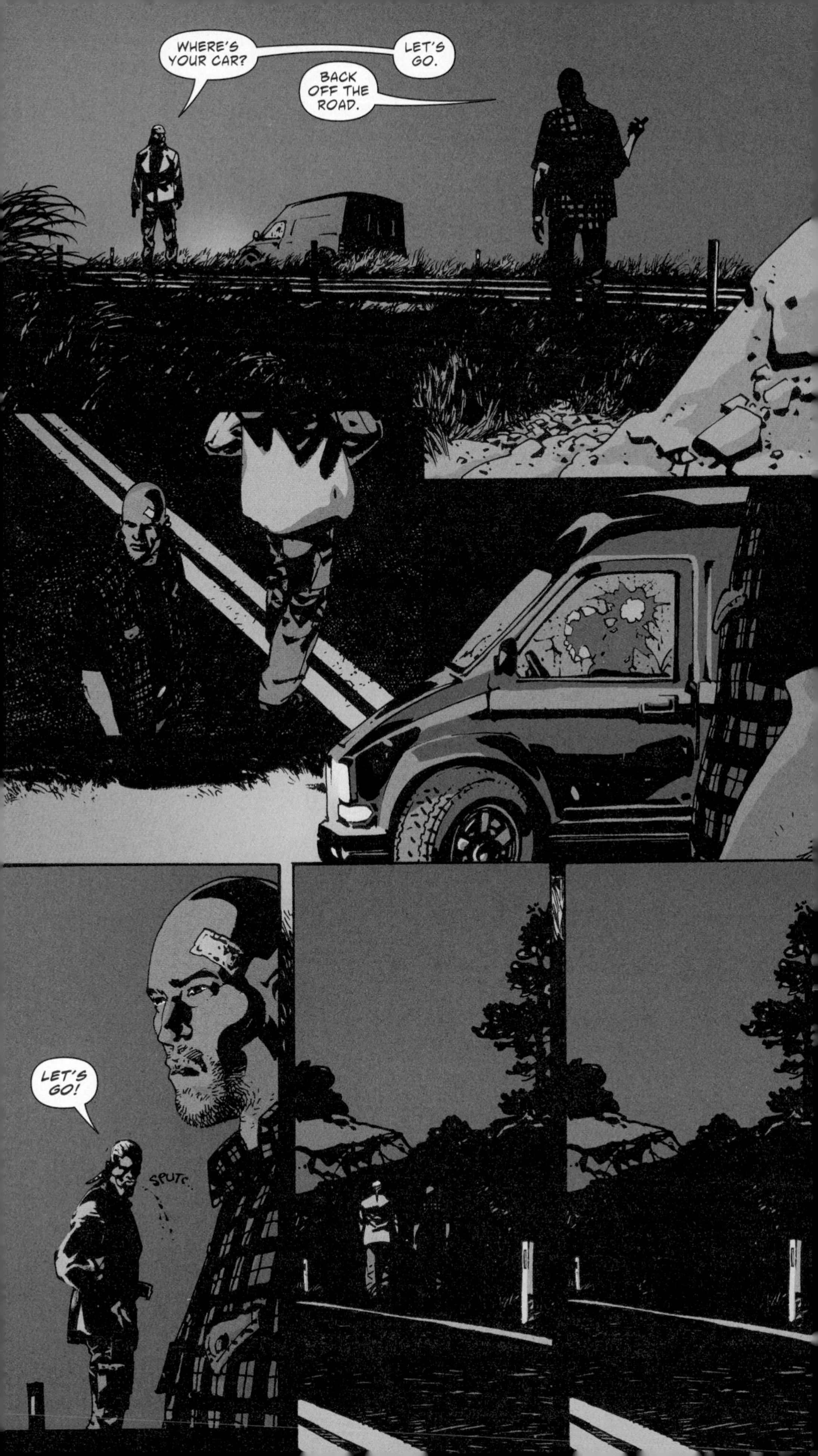
WHERE'S YOUR CAR?
LET'S GO.
BACK OFF THE ROAD.
LET'S GO!
SPUTC.

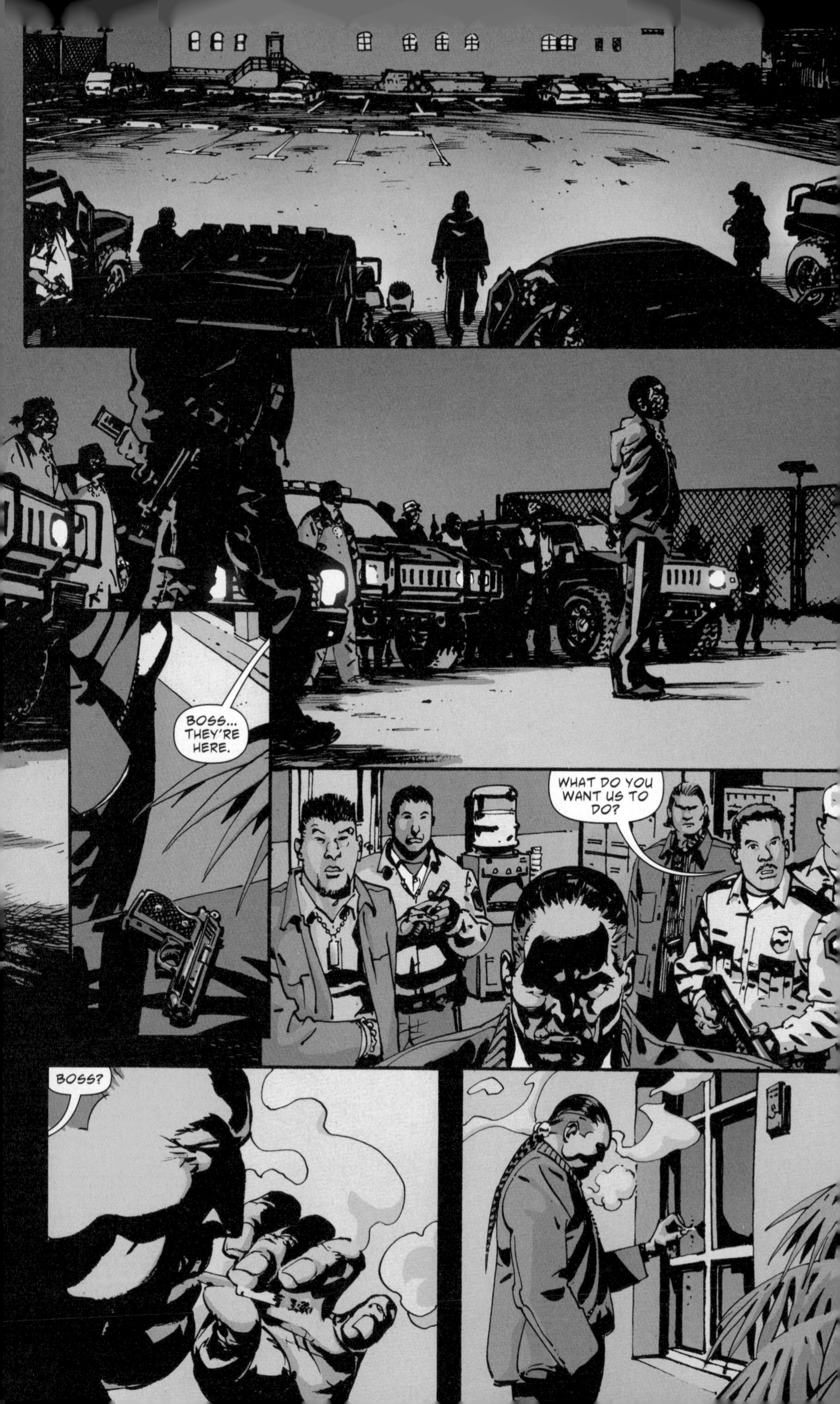
BOSS... THEY'RE HERE.
WHAT DO YOU WANT US TO DO?
BOSS?

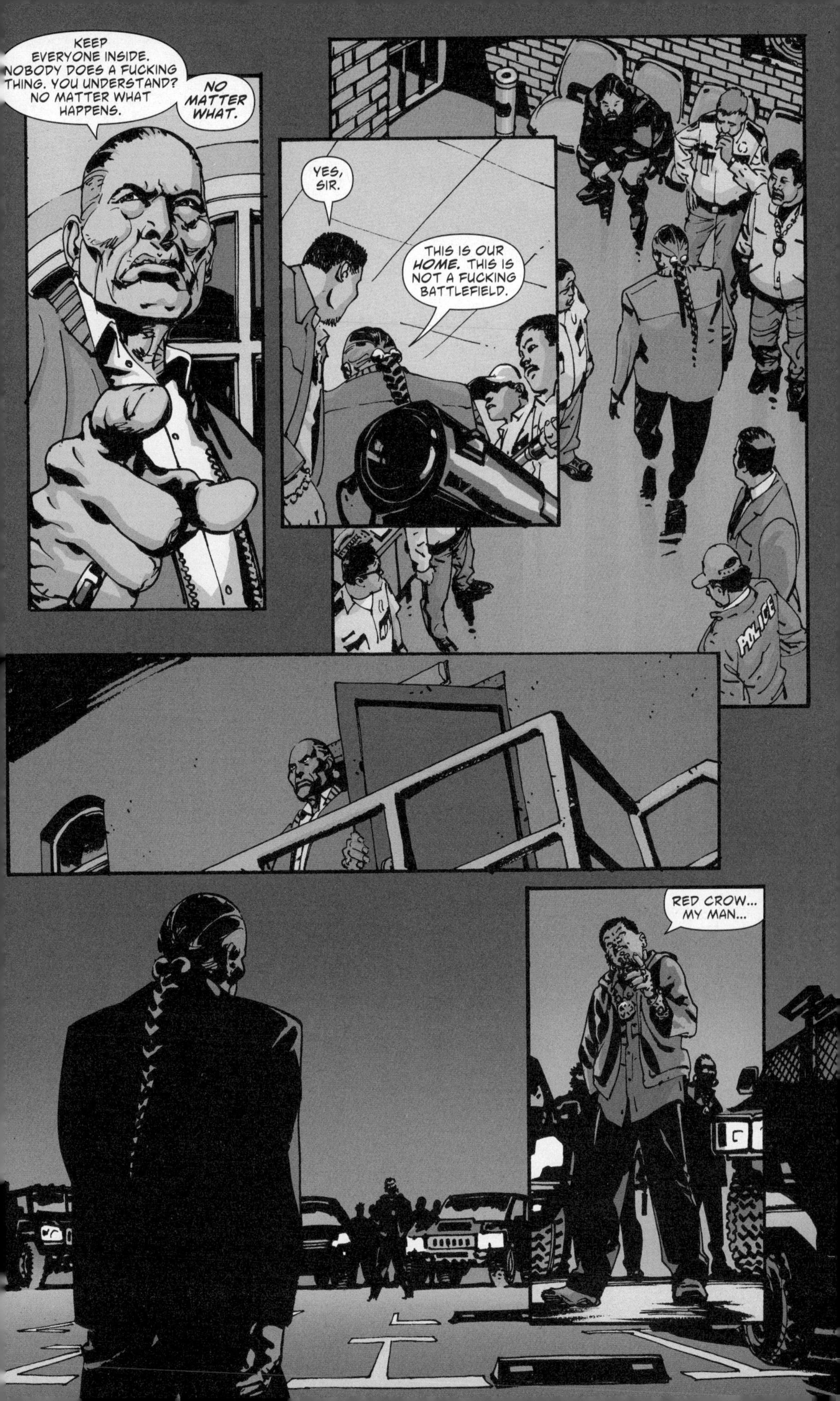
KEEP EVERYONE INSIDE. NOBODY DOES A FUCKING THING. YOU UNDERSTAND? NO MATTER WHAT HAPPENS.
NO MATTER WHAT.
YES, SIR.
THIS IS OUR HOME. THIS IS NOT A FUCKING BATTLEFIELD.
RED CROW... MY MAN...

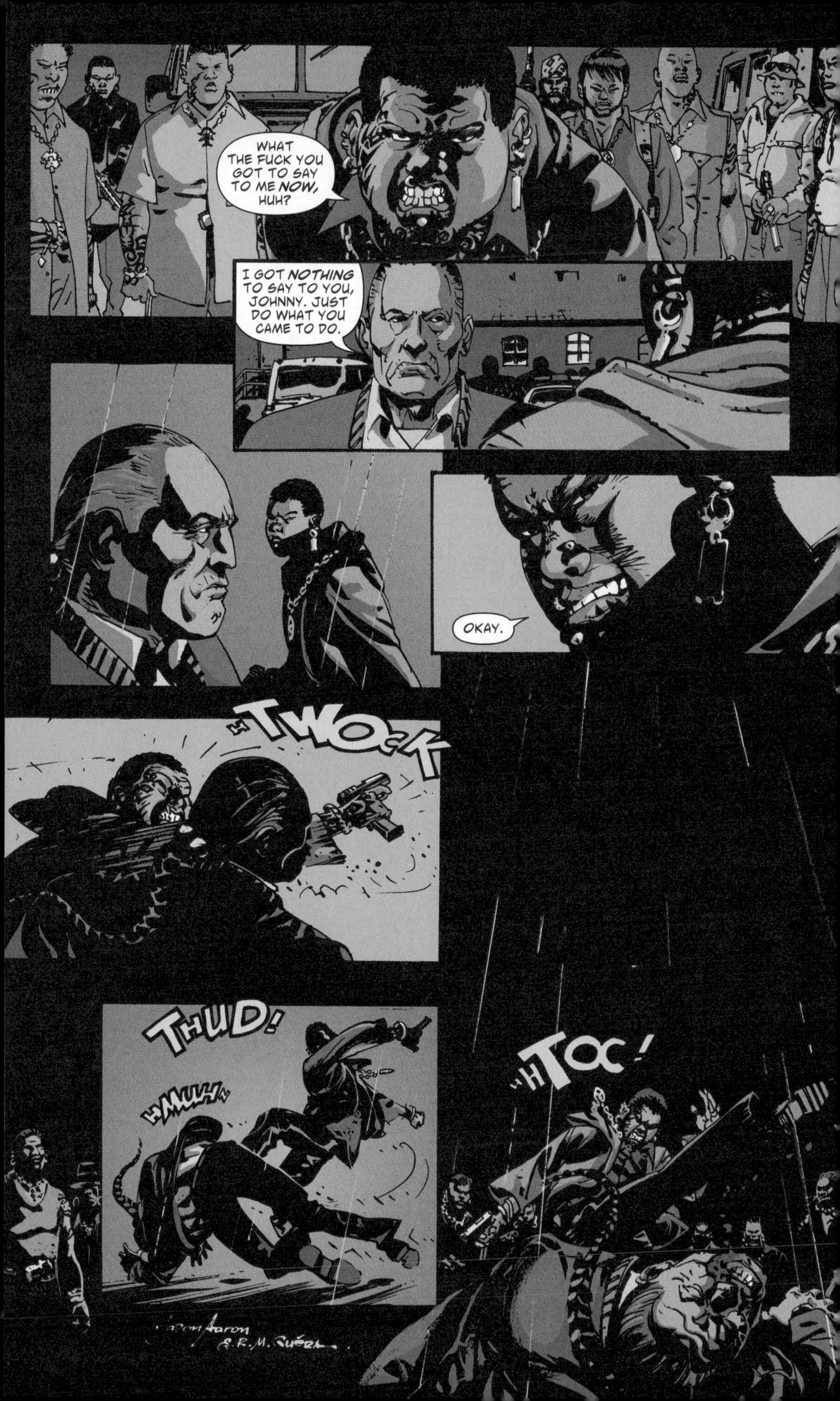
WHAT THE FUCK YOU GOT TO SAY TO ME NOW, HUH?
I GOT NOTHING TO SAY TO YOU, JOHNNY. JUST DO WHAT YOU CAME TO DO.
OKAY.
TWOCK
THUD!
WHUH
TOC!

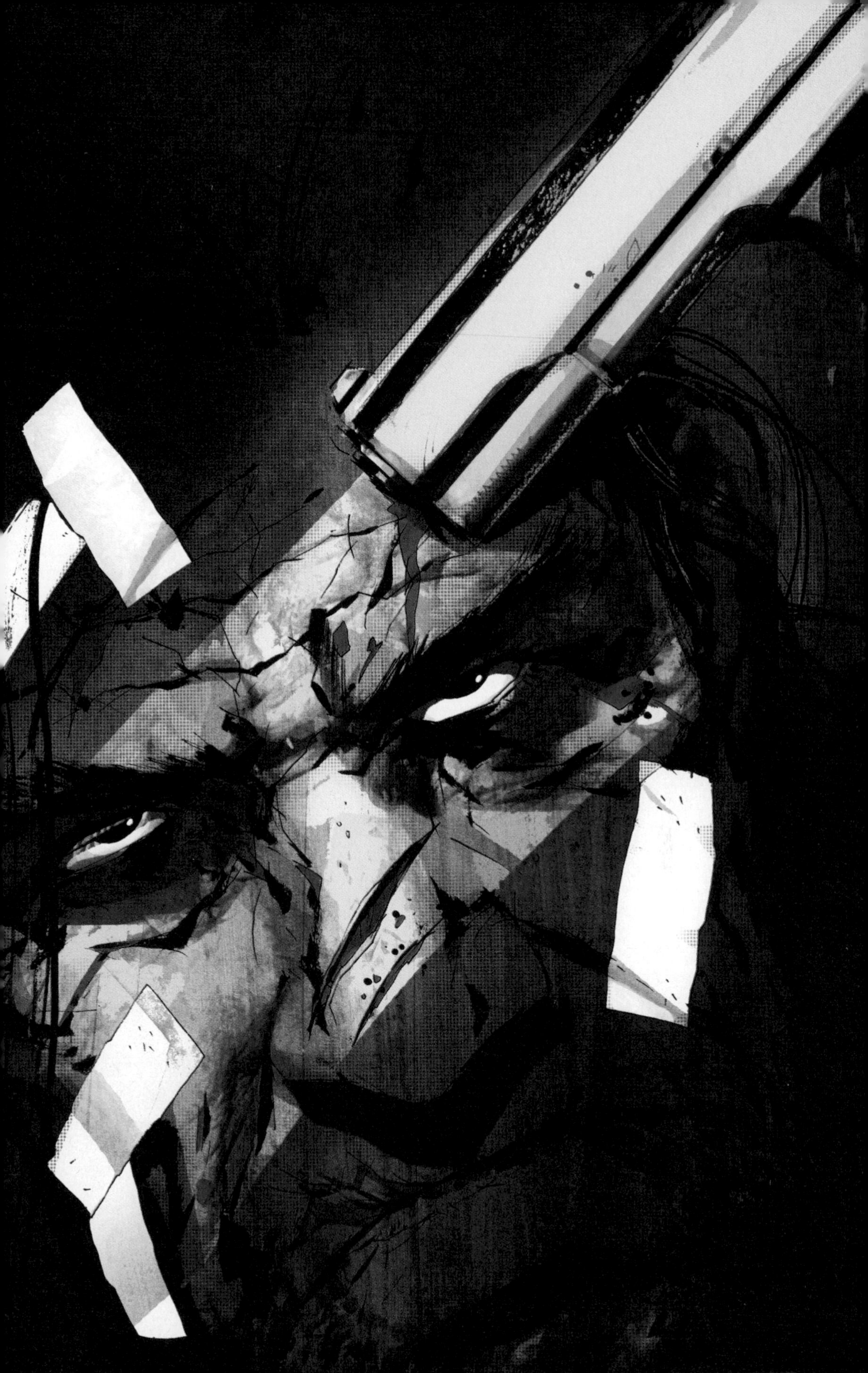

CHAPTER 5

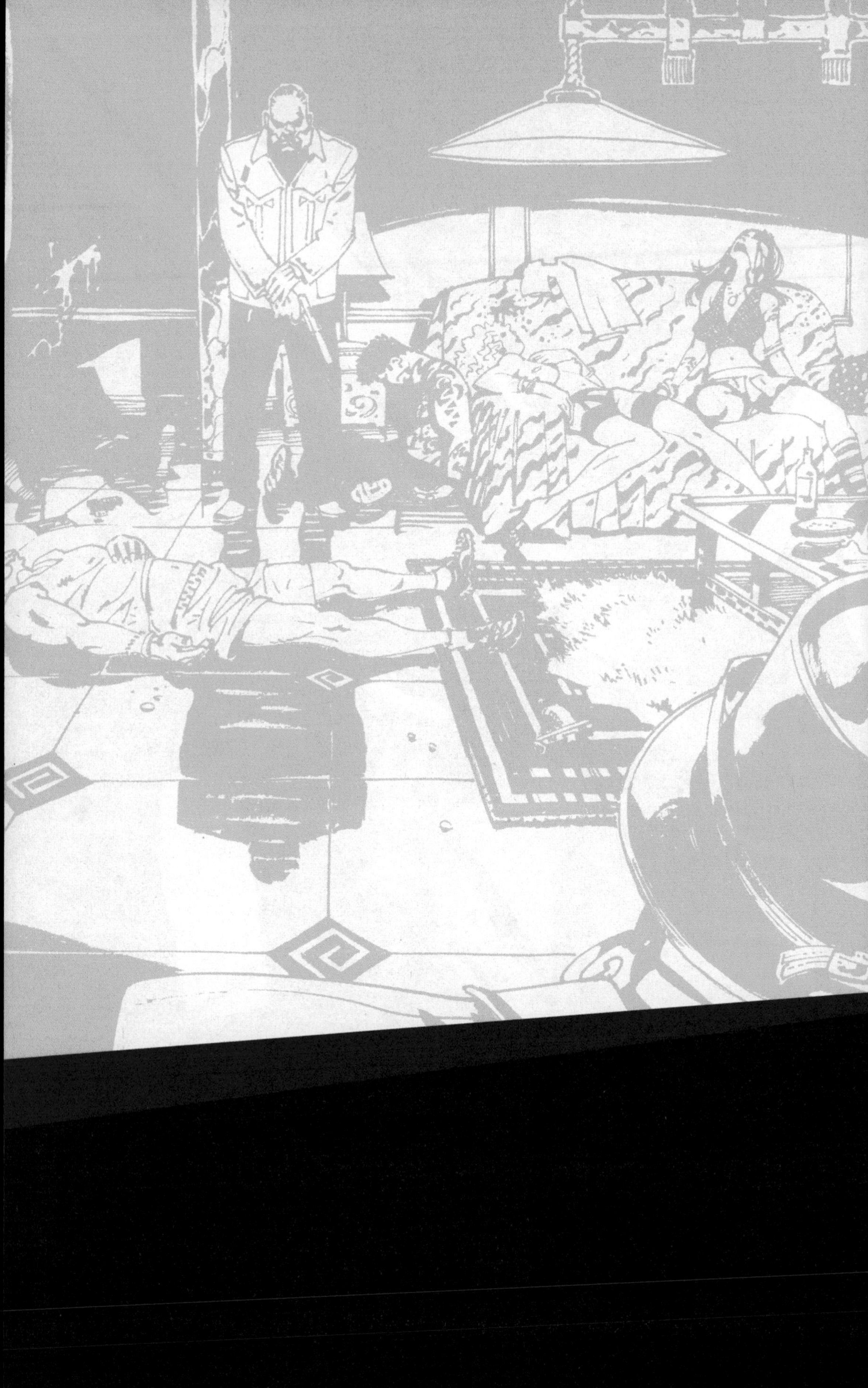

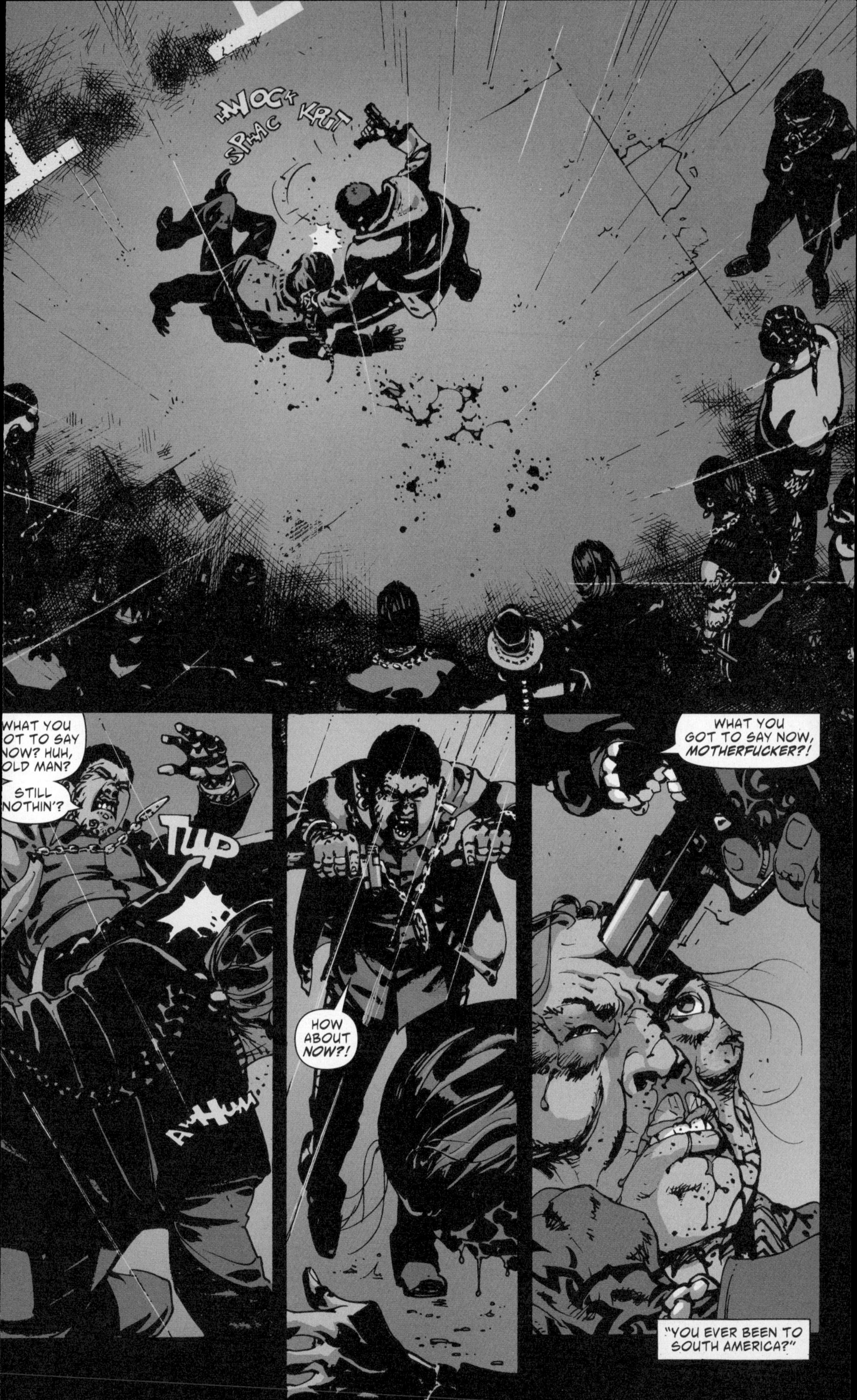
HWOCK
SPHAC
KRUT
WHAT YOU GOT TO SAY NOW? HUH, OLD MAN?
STILL NOTHIN'?
TUP
AHHUM
HOW ABOUT NOW?!
WHAT YOU GOT TO SAY NOW, MOTHERFUCKER?!
"YOU EVER BEEN TO SOUTH AMERICA?"

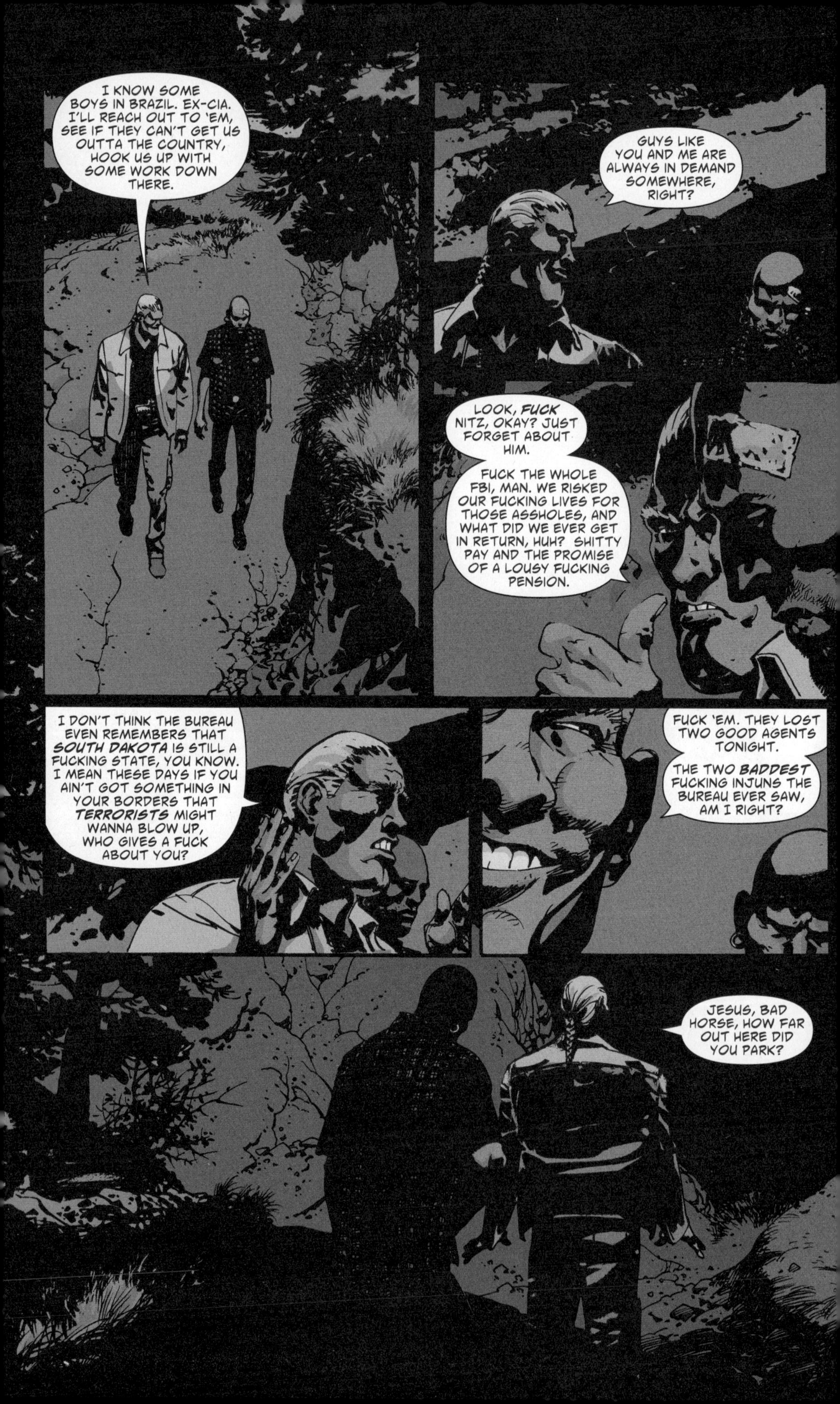
I KNOW SOME BOYS IN BRAZIL. EX-CIA. I'LL REACH OUT TO 'EM, SEE IF THEY CAN'T GET US OUTTA THE COUNTRY, HOOK US UP WITH SOME WORK DOWN THERE.
GUYS LIKE YOU AND ME ARE ALWAYS IN DEMAND SOMEWHERE, RIGHT?
LOOK, FUCK NITZ, OKAY? JUST FORGET ABOUT HIM.
FUCK THE WHOLE FBI, MAN. WE RISKED OUR FUCKING LIVES FOR THOSE ASSHOLES, AND WHAT DID WE EVER GET IN RETURN, HUH? SHITTY PAY AND THE PROMISE OF A LOUSY FUCKING PENSION.
I DON'T THINK THE BUREAU EVEN REMEMBERS THAT SOUTH DAKOTA IS STILL A FUCKING STATE, YOU KNOW. I MEAN THESE DAYS IF YOU AIN'T GOT SOMETHING IN YOUR BORDERS THAT TERRORISTS MIGHT WANNA BLOW UP, WHO GIVES A FUCK ABOUT YOU?
FUCK 'EM. THEY LOST TWO GOOD AGENTS TONIGHT.
THE TWO BADDEST FUCKING INJUNS THE BUREAU EVER SAW, AM I RIGHT?
JESUS, BAD HORSE, HOW FAR OUT HERE DID YOU PARK?

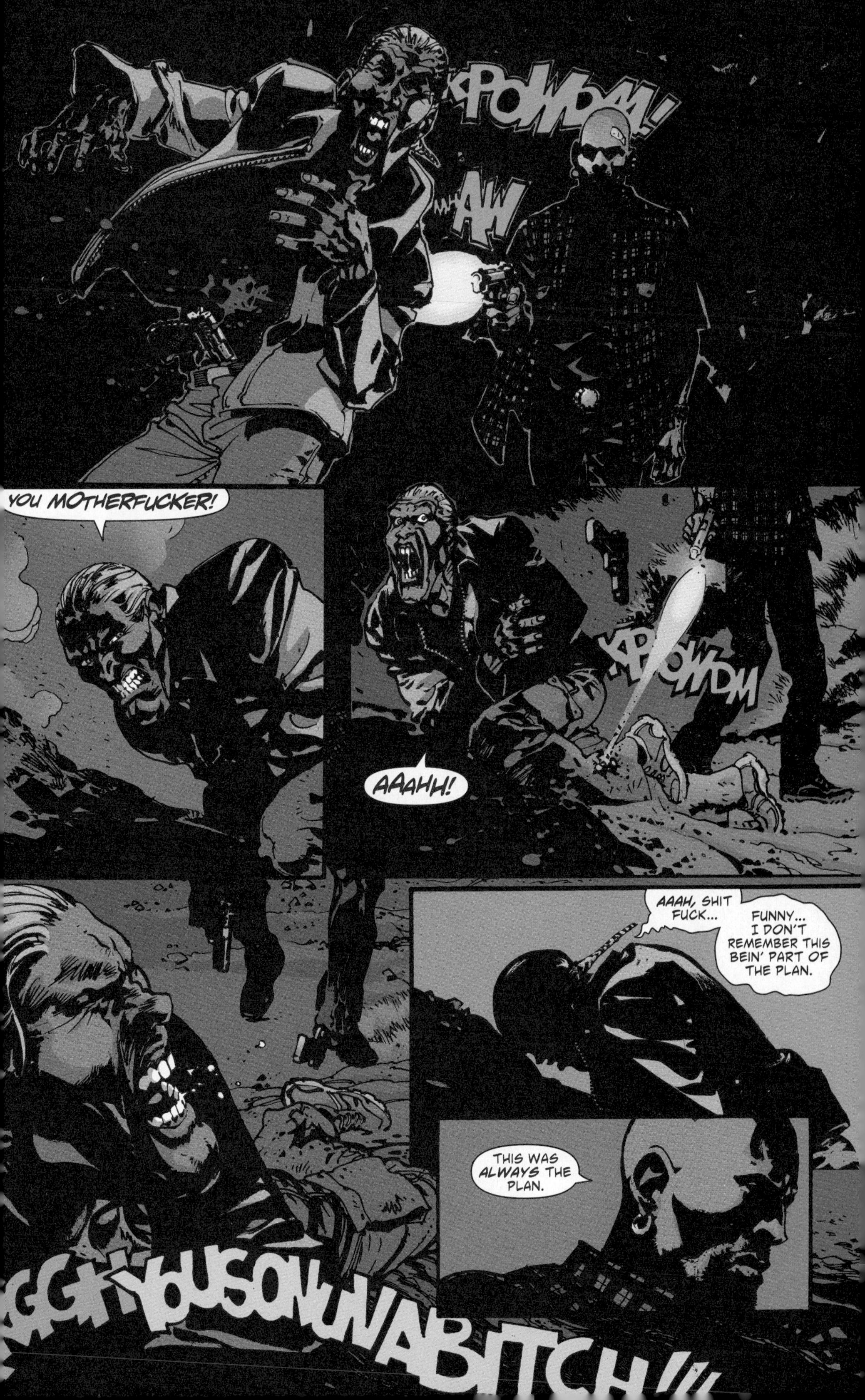
KPOWOM!
AW
YOU MOTHERFUCKER!
KPOWOM
AAAHH!
AAAH, SHIT FUCK...
FUNNY... I DON'T REMEMBER THIS BEIN' PART OF THE PLAN.
THIS WAS ALWAYS THE PLAN.
GGHYOUSONUVABITCH!!!

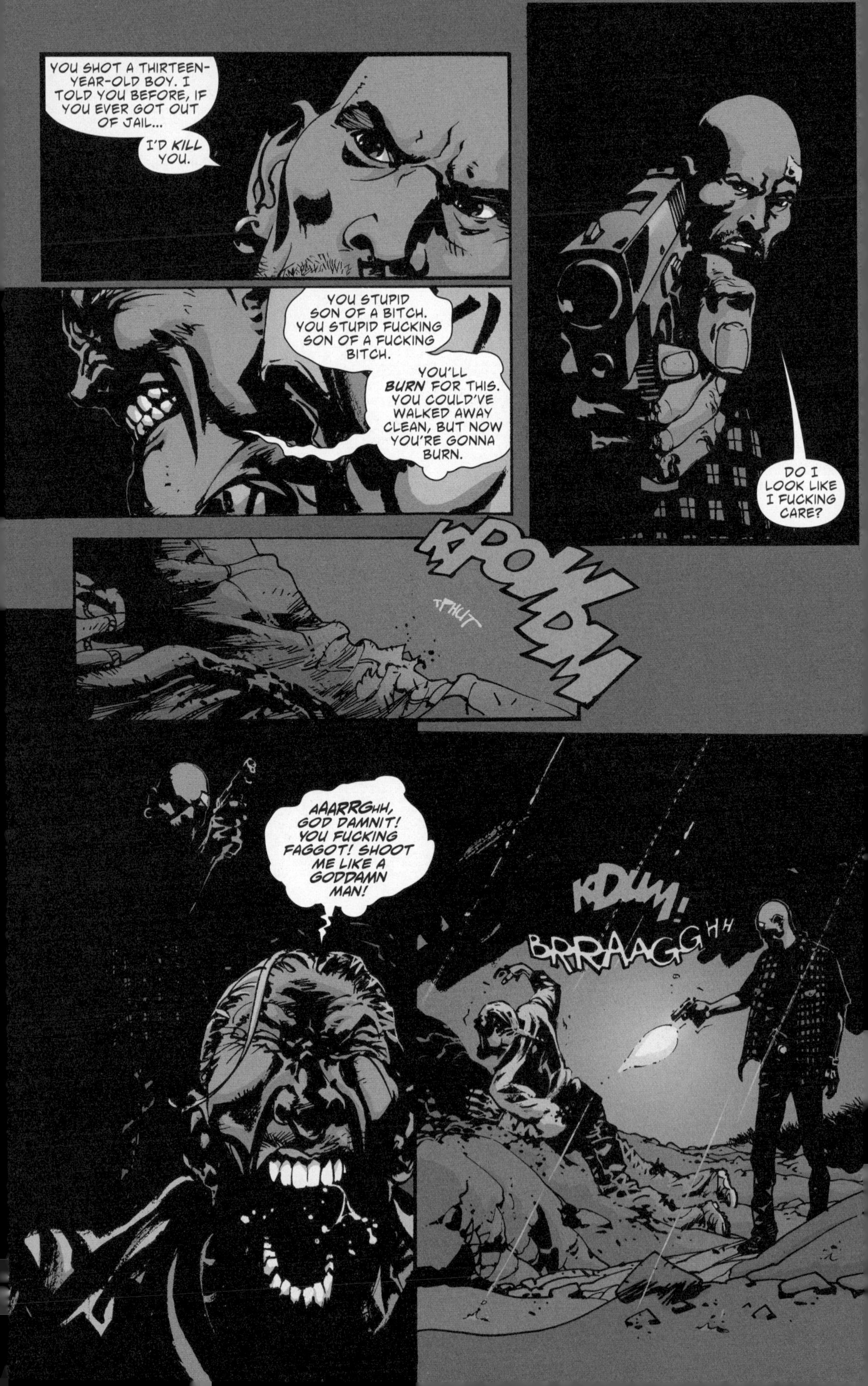
YOU SHOT A THIRTEEN-YEAR-OLD BOY. I TOLD YOU BEFORE, IF YOU EVER GOT OUT OF JAIL...
I'D KILL YOU.
YOU STUPID SON OF A BITCH. YOU STUPID FUCKING SON OF A FUCKING BITCH.
YOU'LL BURN FOR THIS. YOU COULD'VE WALKED AWAY CLEAN, BUT NOW YOU'RE GONNA BURN.
DO I LOOK LIKE I FUCKING CARE?
KPOW
TPHUT
AAARRGHH, GOD DAMNIT! YOU FUCKING FAGGOT! SHOOT ME LIKE A GODDAMN MAN!
KDUM!
BRRAAGGHH

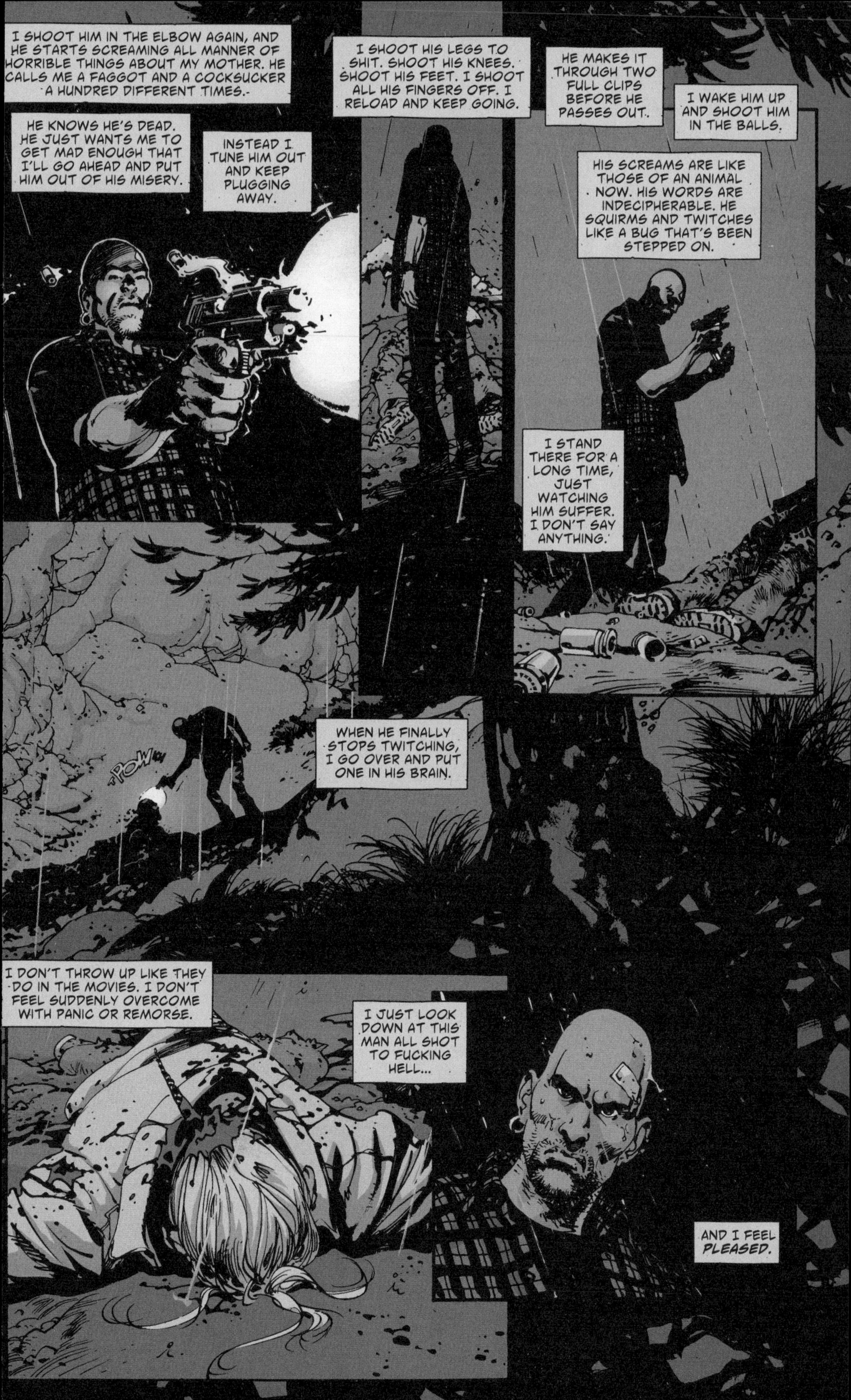
I SHOOT HIM IN THE ELBOW AGAIN, AND HE STARTS SCREAMING ALL MANNER OF HORRIBLE THINGS ABOUT MY MOTHER. HE CALLS ME A FAGGOT AND A COCKSUCKER A HUNDRED DIFFERENT TIMES.
HE KNOWS HE'S DEAD. HE JUST WANTS ME TO GET MAD ENOUGH THAT I'LL GO AHEAD AND PUT HIM OUT OF HIS MISERY.
INSTEAD I TUNE HIM OUT AND KEEP PLUGGING AWAY.
I SHOOT HIS LEGS TO SHIT. SHOOT HIS KNEES. SHOOT HIS FEET. I SHOOT ALL HIS FINGERS OFF. I RELOAD AND KEEP GOING.
HE MAKES IT THROUGH TWO FULL CLIPS BEFORE HE PASSES OUT.
I WAKE HIM UP AND SHOOT HIM IN THE BALLS.
HIS SCREAMS ARE LIKE THOSE OF AN ANIMAL NOW. HIS WORDS ARE INDECIPHERABLE. HE SQUIRMS AND TWITCHES LIKE A BUG THAT'S BEEN STEPPED ON.
I STAND THERE FOR A LONG TIME, JUST WATCHING HIM SUFFER. I DON'T SAY ANYTHING.
WHEN HE FINALLY STOPS TWITCHING, I GO OVER AND PUT ONE IN HIS BRAIN.
POW
I DON'T THROW UP LIKE THEY DO IN THE MOVIES. I DON'T FEEL SUDDENLY OVERCOME WITH PANIC OR REMORSE.
I JUST LOOK DOWN AT THIS MAN ALL SHOT TO FUCKING HELL...
AND I FEEL *PLEASED.*

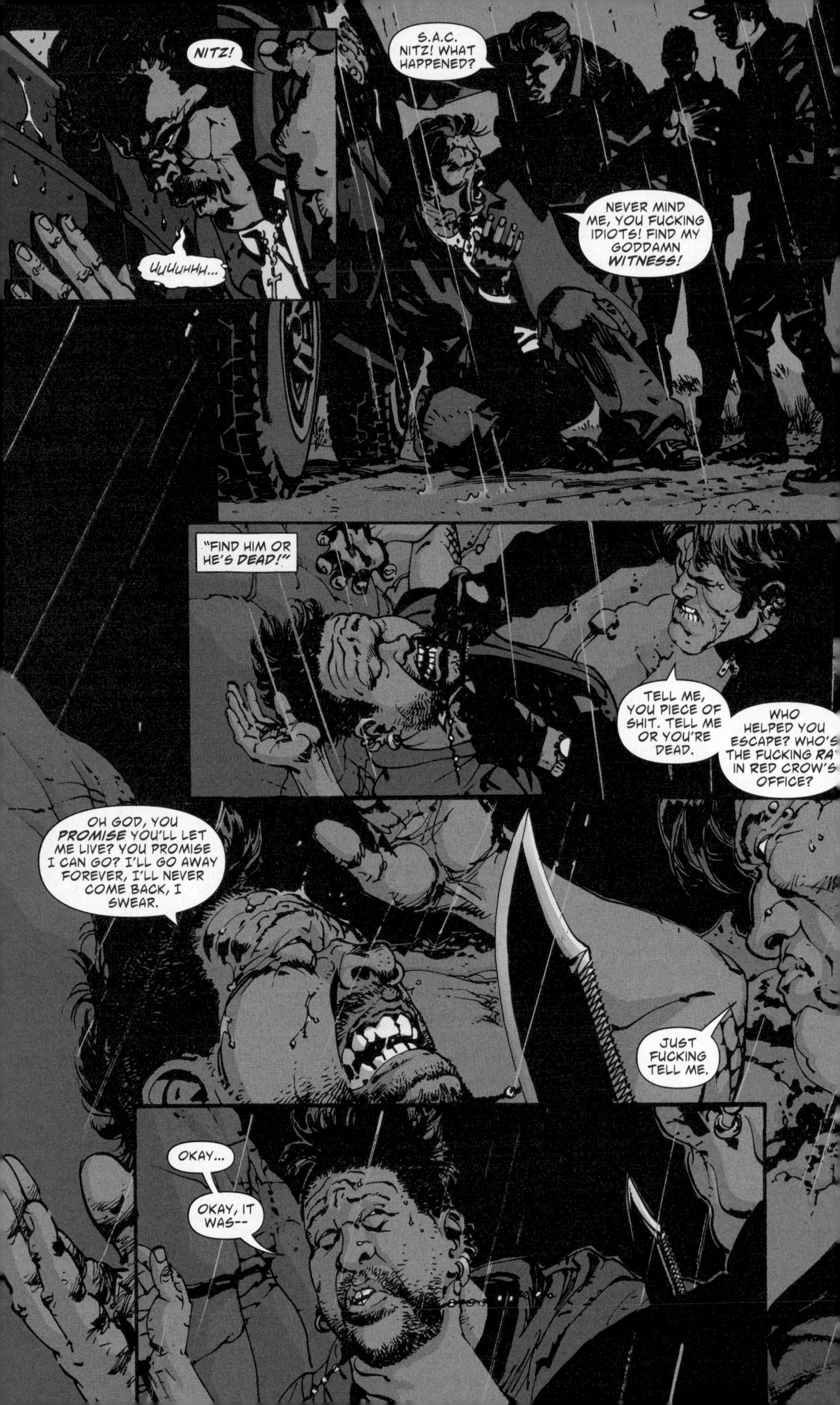
NITZ!
UUUUHHH...
S.A.C. NITZ! WHAT HAPPENED?
NEVER MIND ME, YOU FUCKING IDIOTS! FIND MY GODDAMN WITNESS!
"FIND HIM OR HE'S DEAD!"
TELL ME, YOU PIECE OF SHIT. TELL ME OR YOU'RE DEAD.
WHO HELPED YOU ESCAPE? WHO'S THE FUCKING RAT IN RED CROW'S OFFICE?
OH GOD, YOU PROMISE YOU'LL LET ME LIVE? YOU PROMISE I CAN GO? I'LL GO AWAY FOREVER, I'LL NEVER COME BACK, I SWEAR.
JUST FUCKING TELL ME.
OKAY...
OKAY, IT WAS--

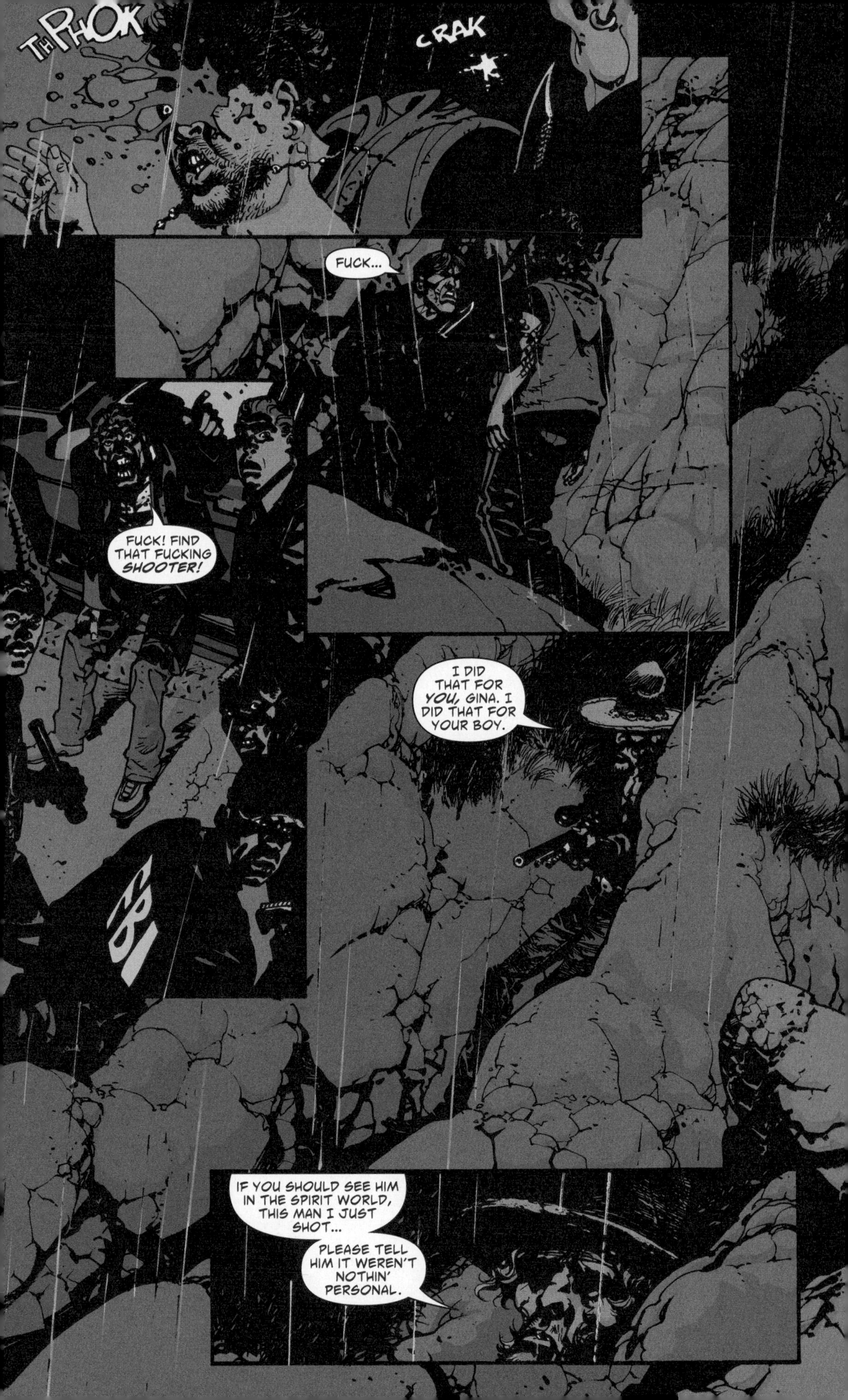
THPHOK
CRAK
FUCK...
FUCK! FIND THAT FUCKING SHOOTER!
I DID THAT FOR YOU, GINA. I DID THAT FOR YOUR BOY.
IF YOU SHOULD SEE HIM IN THE SPIRIT WORLD, THIS MAN I JUST SHOT...
PLEASE TELL HIM IT WEREN'T NOTHIN' PERSONAL.
FBI

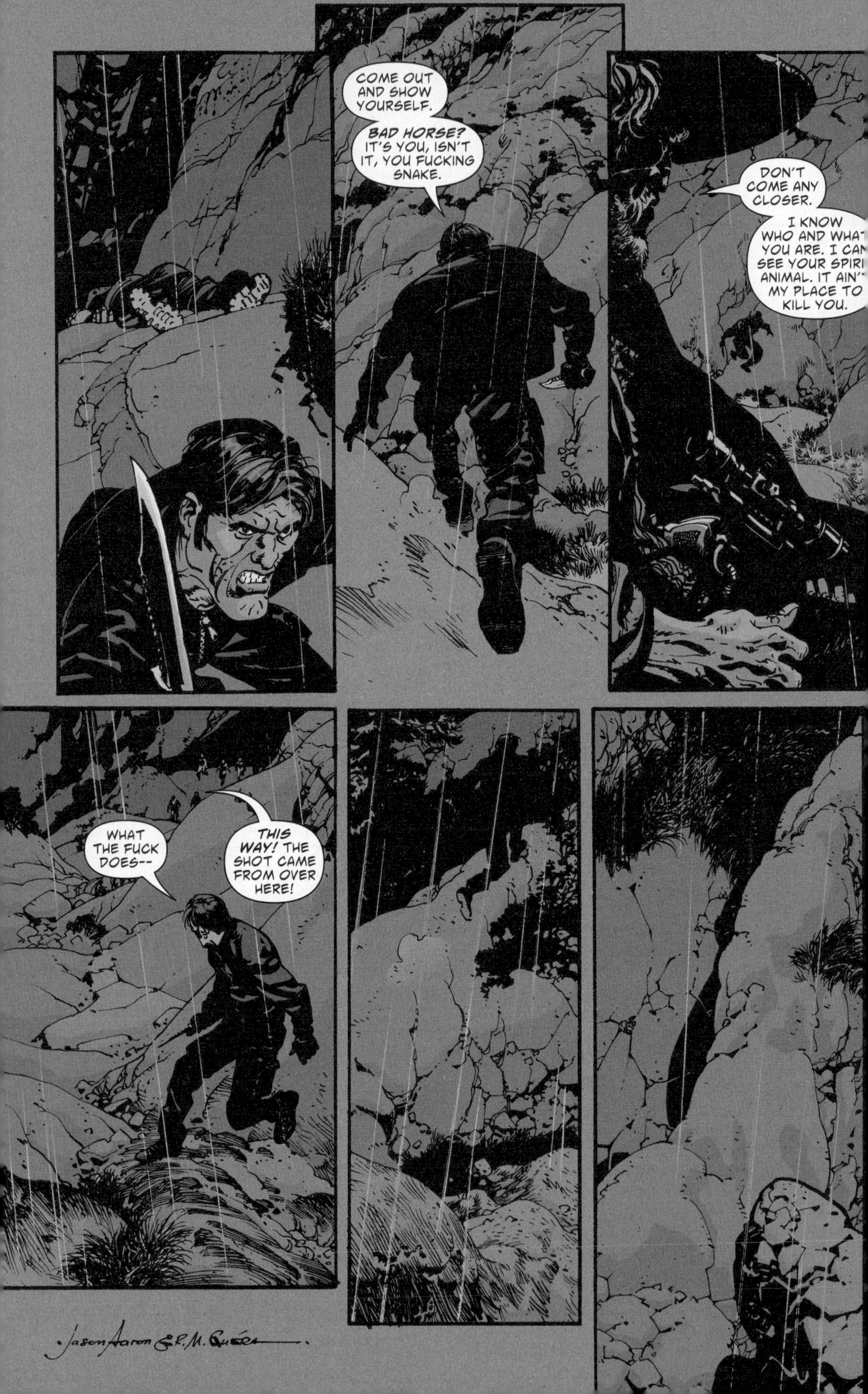
COME OUT AND SHOW YOURSELF.
BAD HORSE? IT'S YOU, ISN'T IT, YOU FUCKING SNAKE.
DON'T COME ANY CLOSER.
I KNOW WHO AND WHA YOU ARE. I CA SEE YOUR SPIRI ANIMAL. IT AIN' MY PLACE TO KILL YOU.
WHAT THE FUCK DOES--
THIS WAY! THE SHOT CAME FROM OVER HERE!

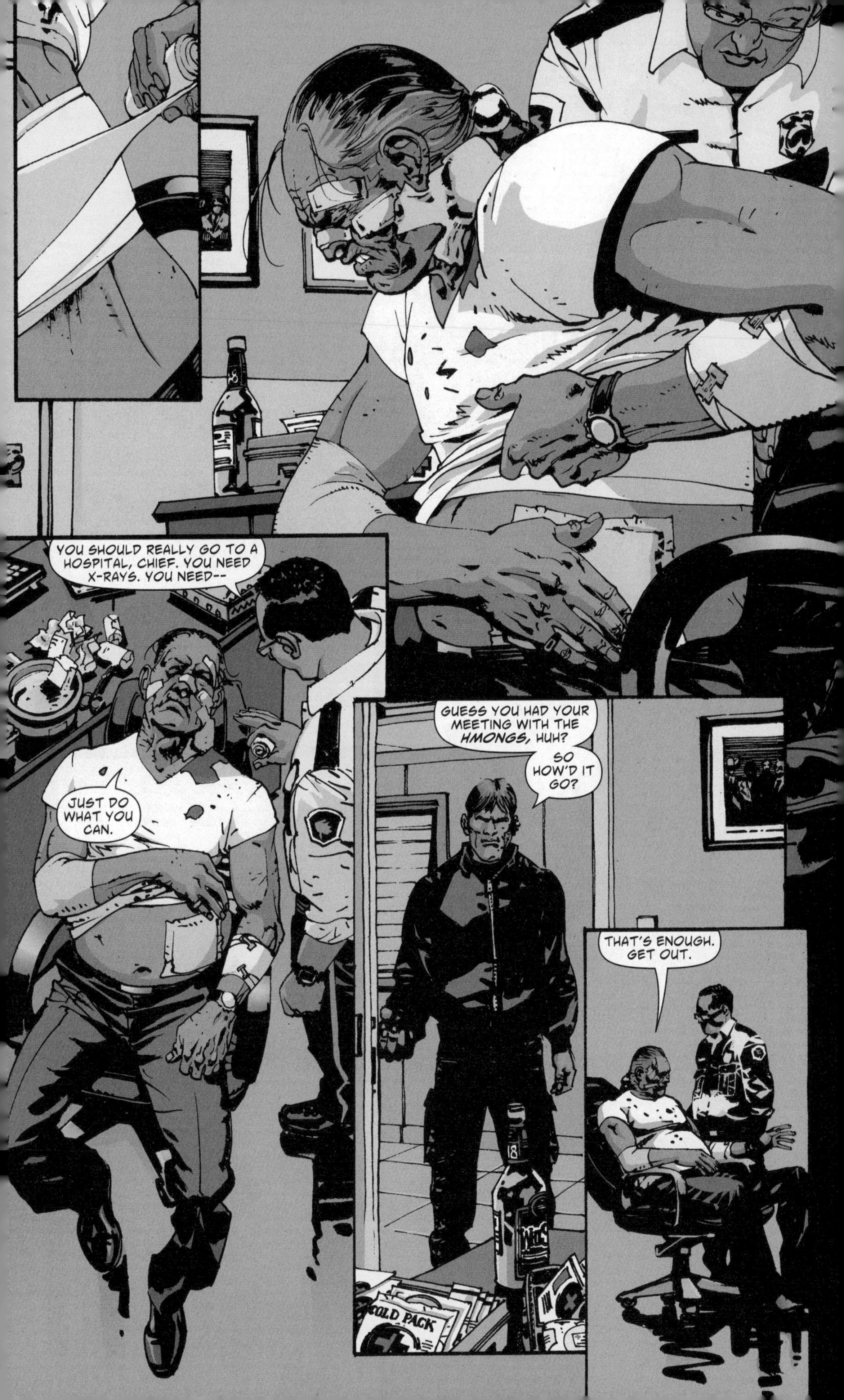
YOU SHOULD REALLY GO TO A HOSPITAL, CHIEF. YOU NEED X-RAYS. YOU NEED--
JUST DO WHAT YOU CAN.
GUESS YOU HAD YOUR MEETING WITH THE HMONGS, HUH?
SO HOW'D IT GO?
THAT'S ENOUGH. GET OUT.
COLD PACK

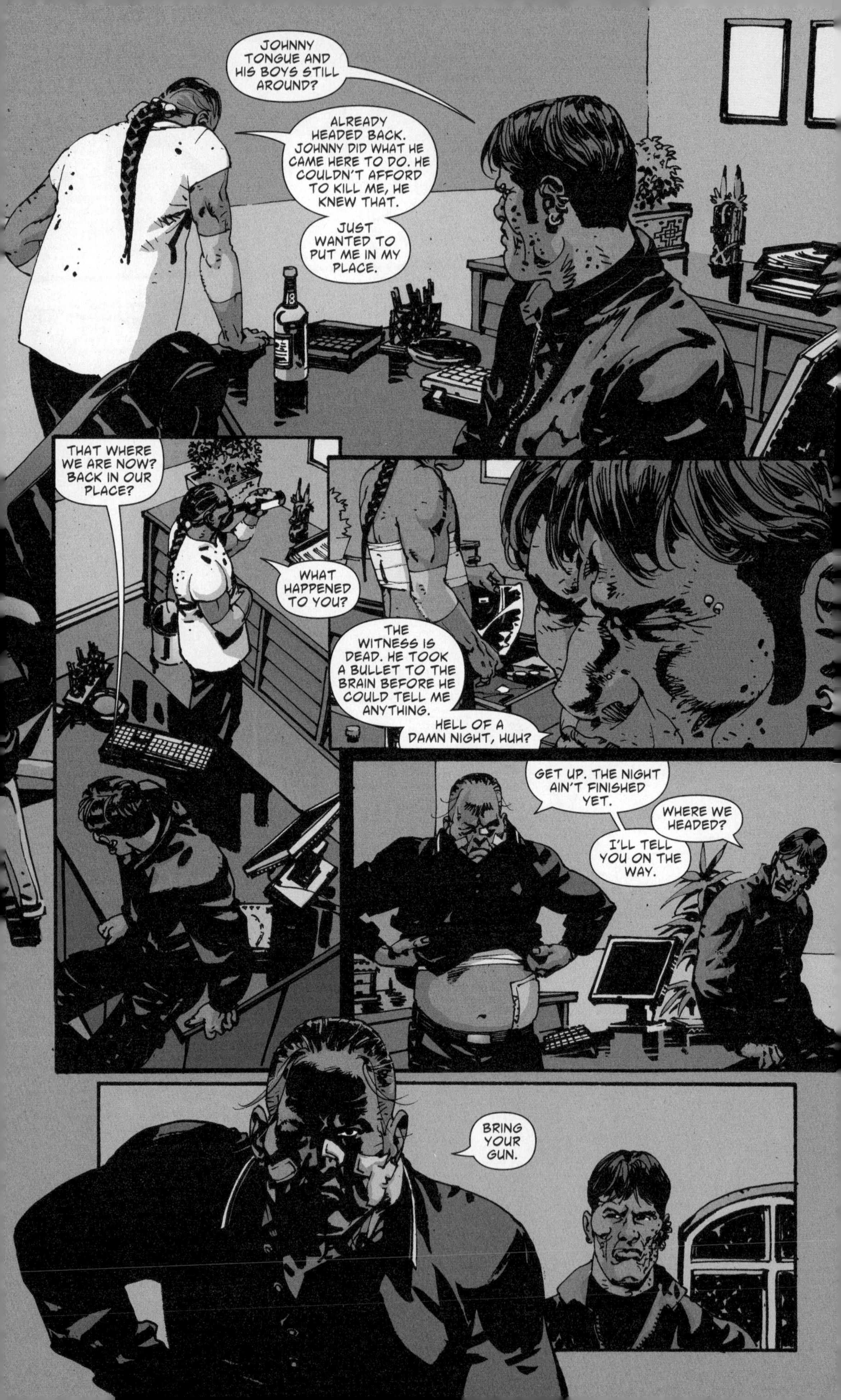
JOHNNY TONGUE AND HIS BOYS STILL AROUND?
ALREADY HEADED BACK. JOHNNY DID WHAT HE CAME HERE TO DO. HE COULDN'T AFFORD TO KILL ME, HE KNEW THAT.
JUST WANTED TO PUT ME IN MY PLACE.
THAT WHERE WE ARE NOW? BACK IN OUR PLACE?
WHAT HAPPENED TO YOU?
THE WITNESS IS DEAD. HE TOOK A BULLET TO THE BRAIN BEFORE HE COULD TELL ME ANYTHING.
HELL OF A DAMN NIGHT, HUH?
GET UP. THE NIGHT AIN'T FINISHED YET.
WHERE WE HEADED?
I'LL TELL YOU ON THE WAY.
BRING YOUR GUN.

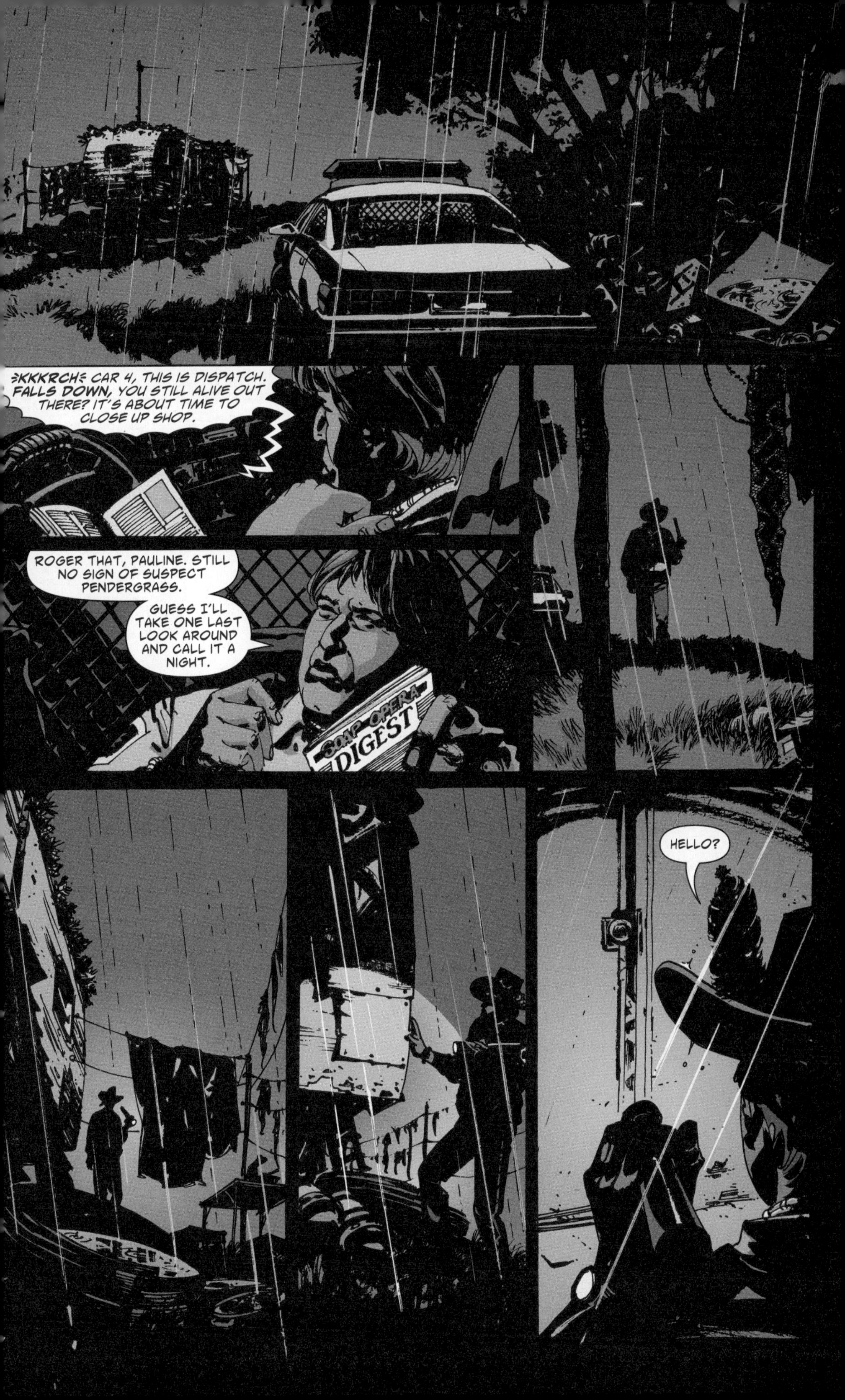
SKKKRCHS CAR 4, THIS IS DISPATCH. FALLS DOWN, YOU STILL ALIVE OUT THERE? IT'S ABOUT TIME TO CLOSE UP SHOP.
ROGER THAT, PAULINE. STILL NO SIGN OF SUSPECT PENDERGRASS.
GUESS I'LL TAKE ONE LAST LOOK AROUND AND CALL IT A NIGHT.
SOAP OPERA DIGEST
HELLO?

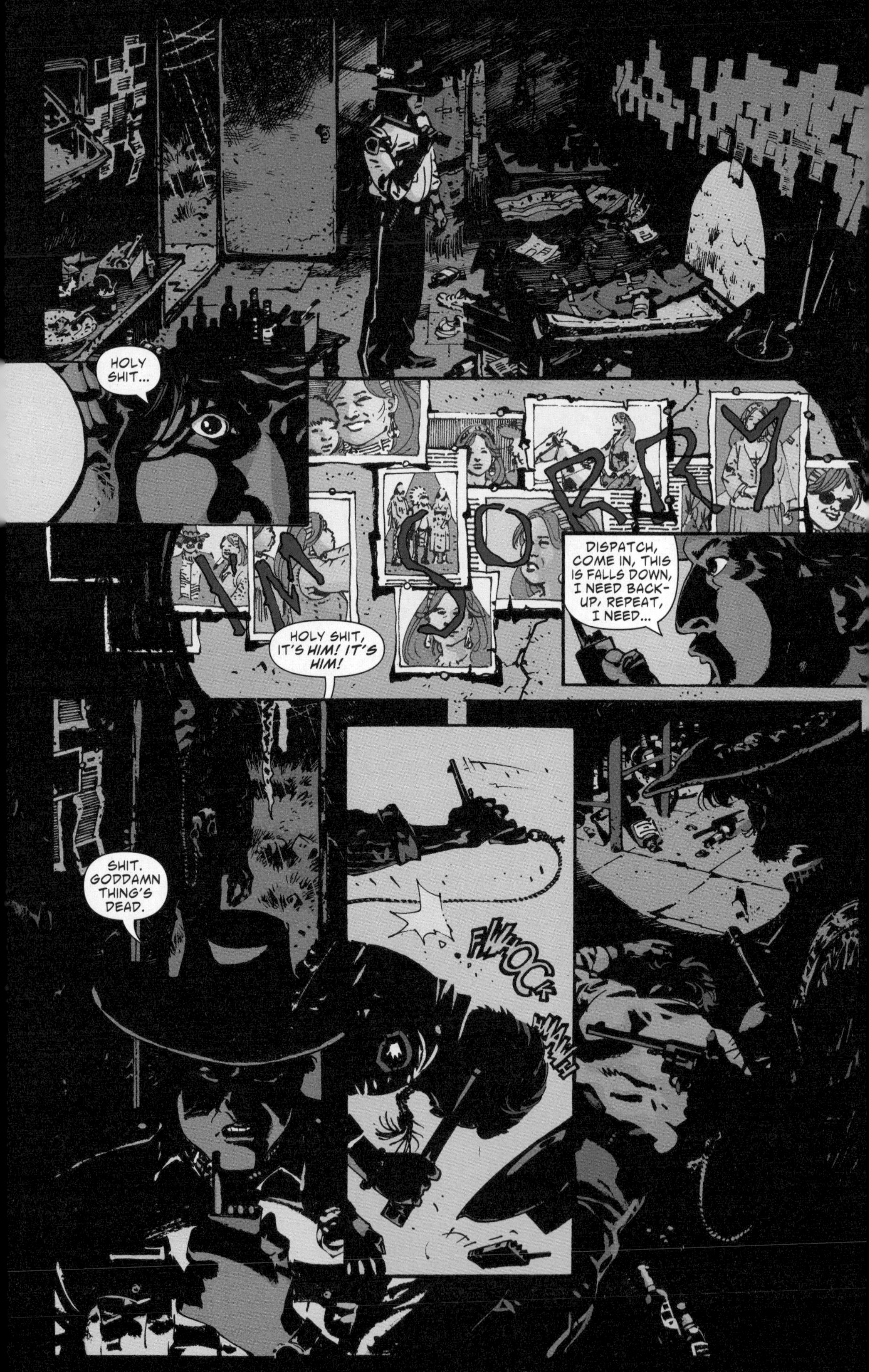
HOLY SHIT...
I'M SORRY
HOLY SHIT, IT'S *HIM!* IT'S *HIM!*
DISPATCH, COME IN, THIS IS FALLS DOWN, I NEED BACK-UP, REPEAT, I NEED...
SHIT. GODDAMN THING'S DEAD.
FWOCK

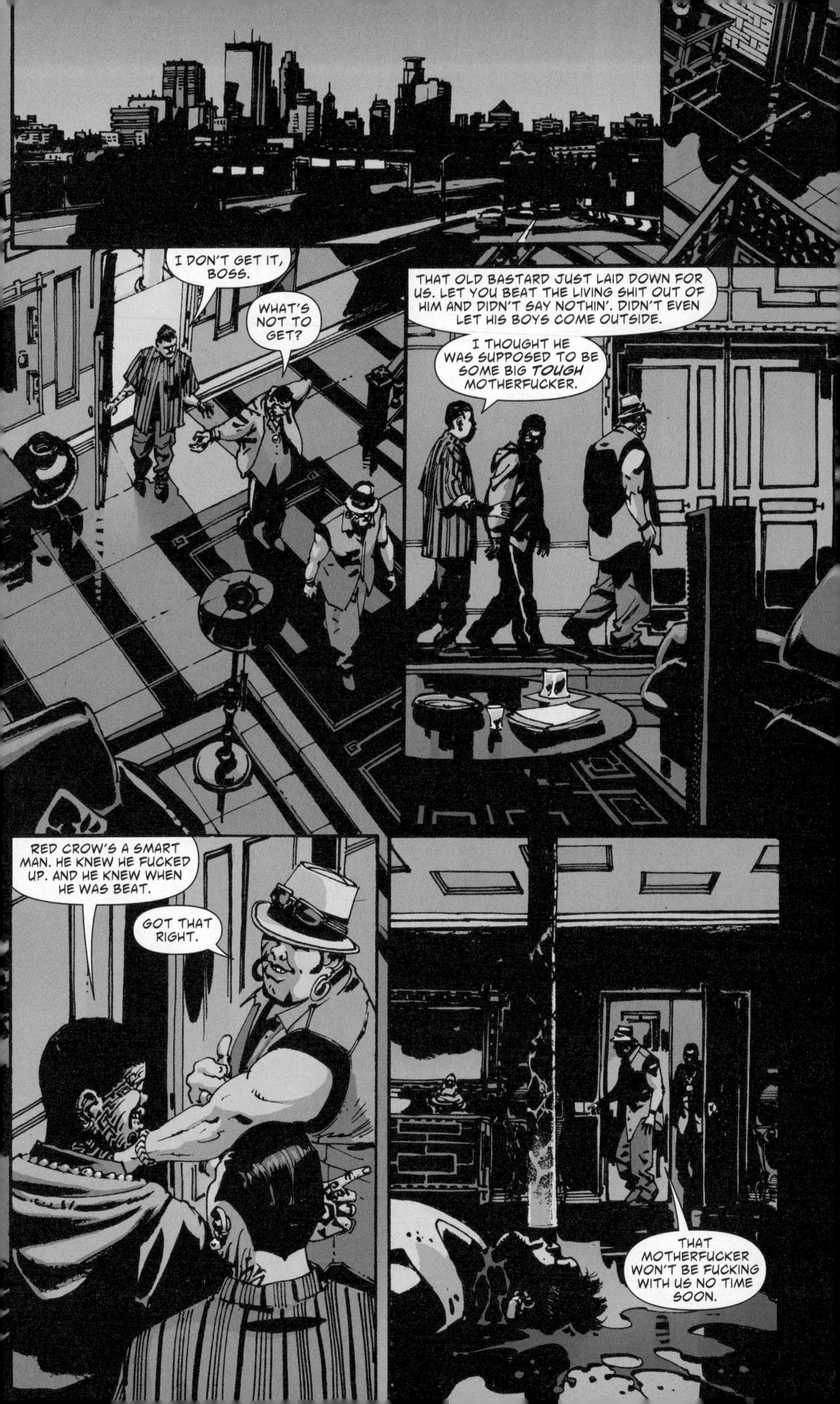
I DON'T GET IT, BOSS.
WHAT'S NOT TO GET?
THAT OLD BASTARD JUST LAID DOWN FOR US. LET YOU BEAT THE LIVING SHIT OUT OF HIM AND DIDN'T SAY NOTHIN'. DIDN'T EVEN LET HIS BOYS COME OUTSIDE.
I THOUGHT HE WAS SUPPOSED TO BE SOME BIG *TOUGH* MOTHERFUCKER.
RED CROW'S A SMART MAN. HE KNEW HE FUCKED UP. AND HE KNEW WHEN HE WAS BEAT.
GOT THAT RIGHT.
THAT MOTHERFUCKER WON'T BE FUCKING WITH US NO TIME SOON.

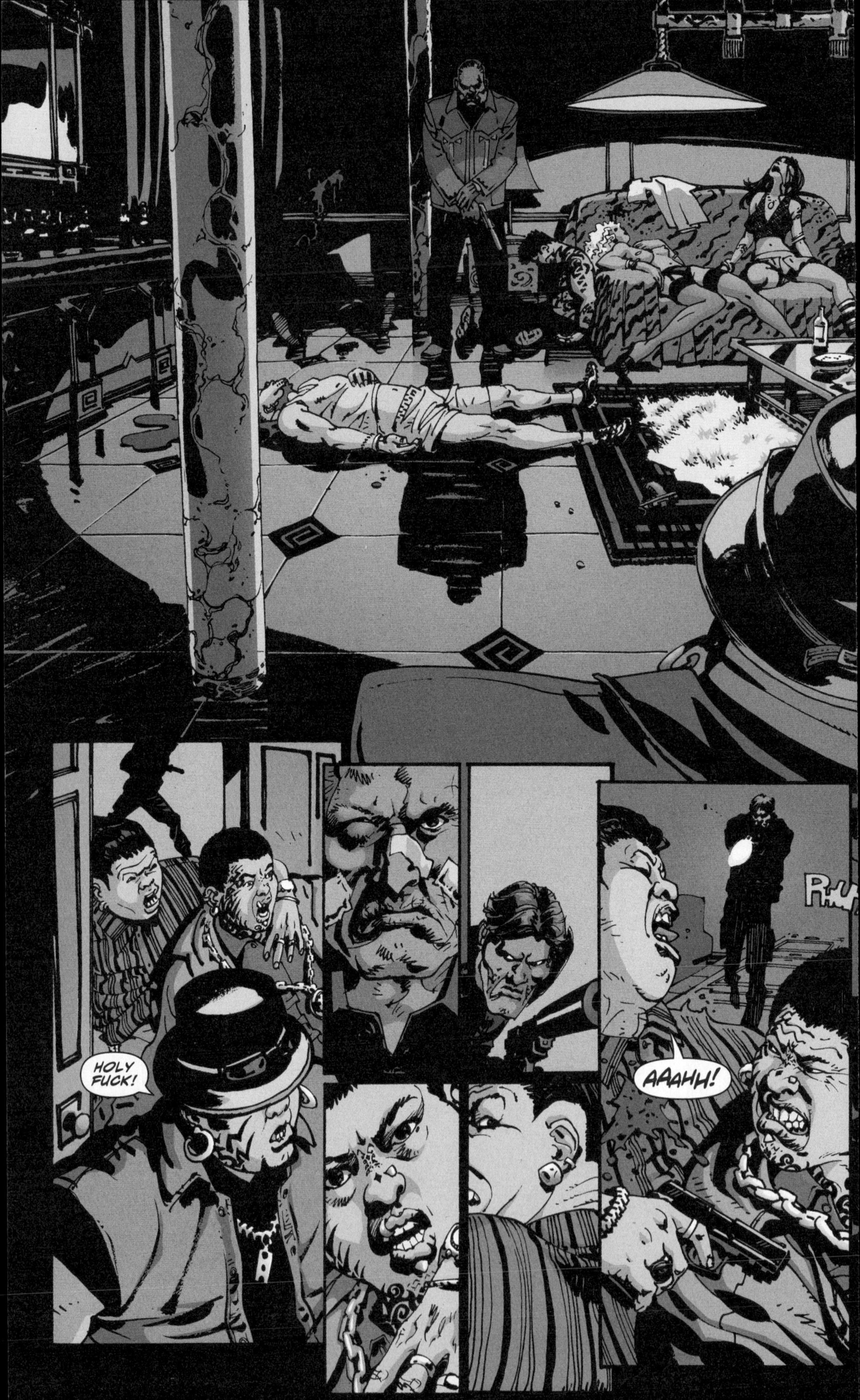
HOLY FUCK!
AAAHH!

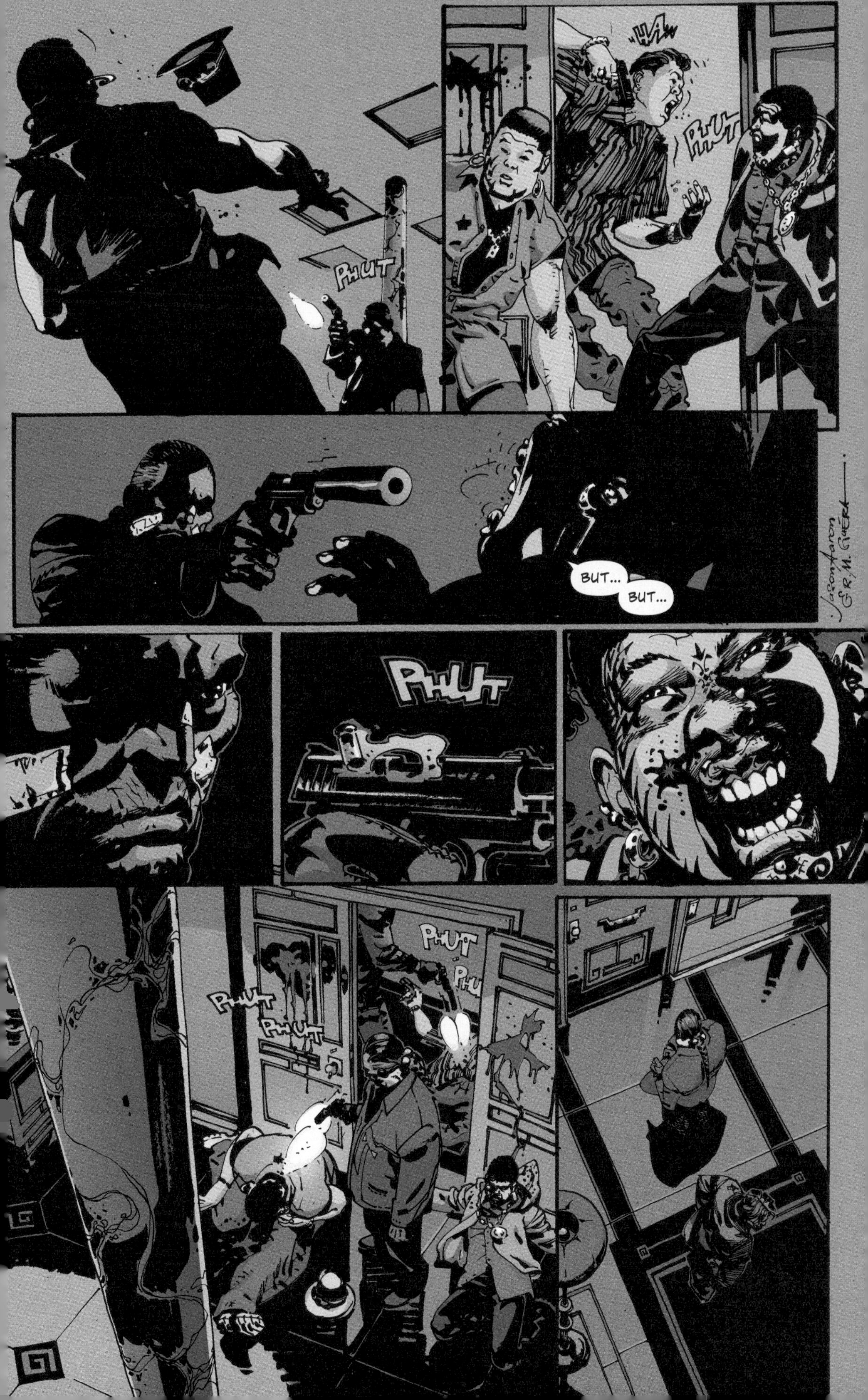
PHUT
WHA
PHUT
BUT...
BUT...
Jason Aaron & R.M. Guéra
PHUT
PHUT
PHUT
PHUT
PHU

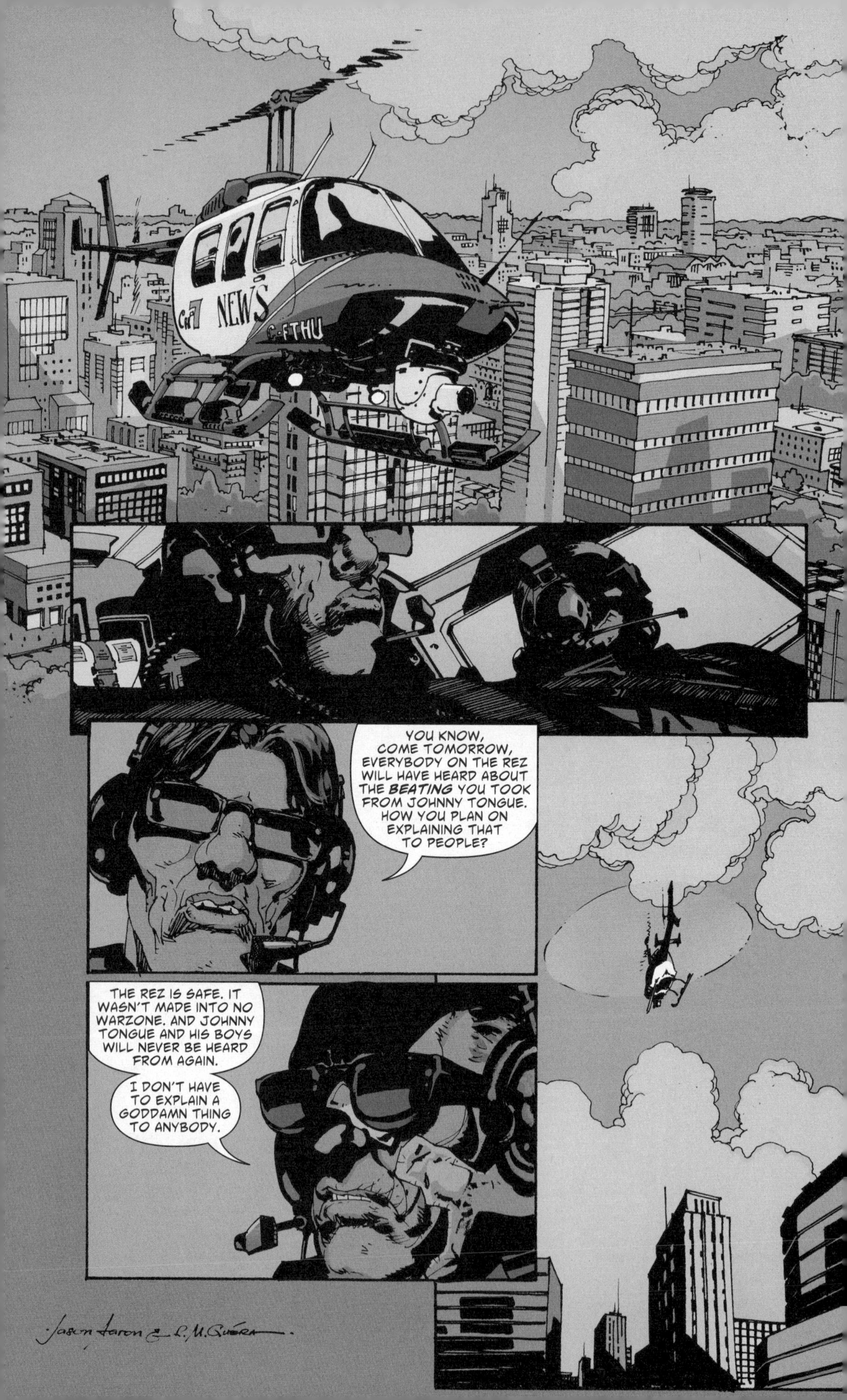
CH7 NEWS
C-FTHU
YOU KNOW, COME TOMORROW, EVERYBODY ON THE REZ WILL HAVE HEARD ABOUT THE BEATING YOU TOOK FROM JOHNNY TONGUE. HOW YOU PLAN ON EXPLAINING THAT TO PEOPLE?
THE REZ IS SAFE. IT WASN'T MADE INTO NO WARZONE. AND JOHNNY TONGUE AND HIS BOYS WILL NEVER BE HEARD FROM AGAIN.
I DON'T HAVE TO EXPLAIN A GODDAMN THING TO ANYBODY.

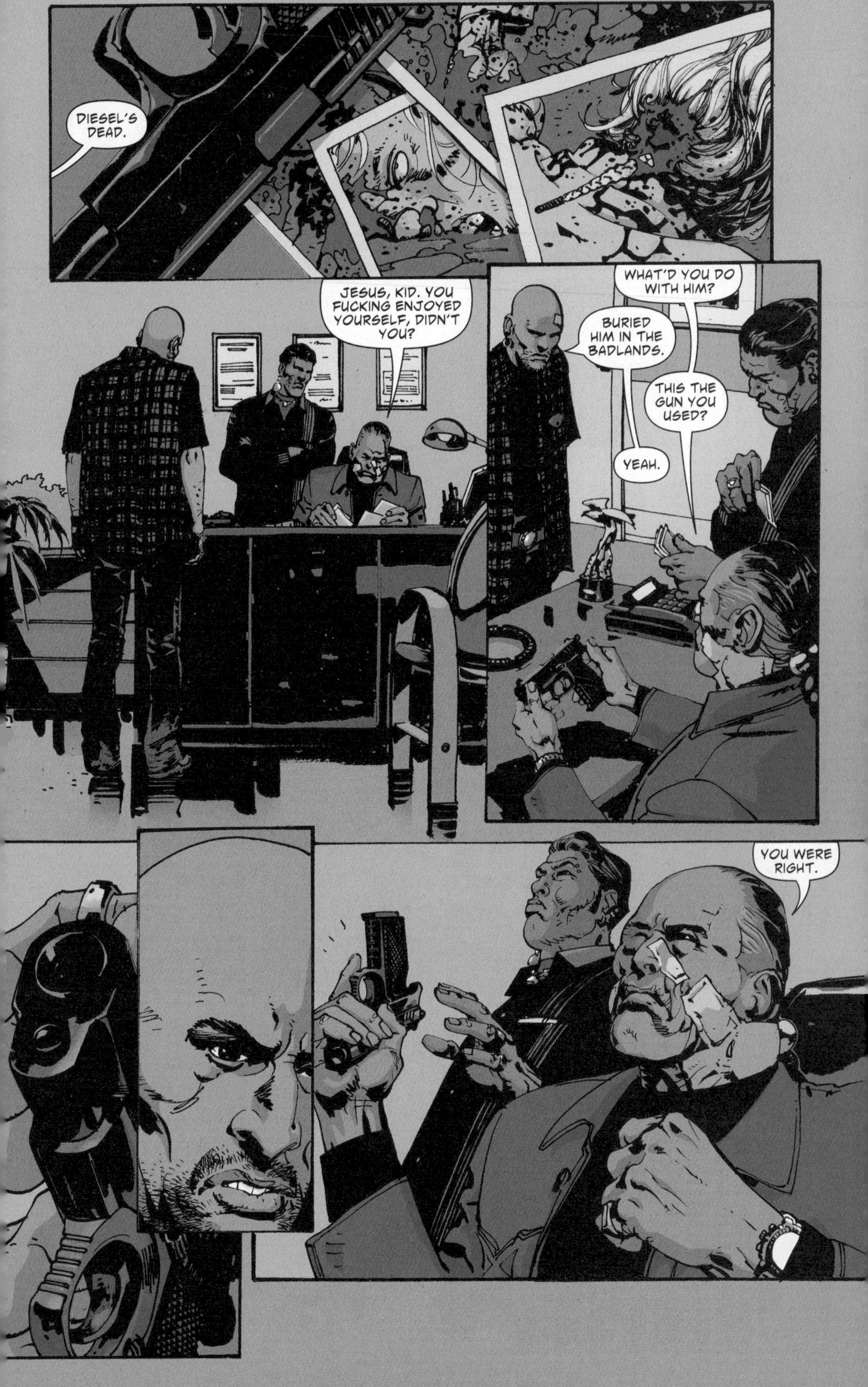
DIESEL'S DEAD.
JESUS, KID. YOU FUCKING ENJOYED YOURSELF, DIDN'T YOU?
WHAT'D YOU DO WITH HIM?
BURIED HIM IN THE BADLANDS.
THIS THE GUN YOU USED?
YEAH.
YOU WERE RIGHT.

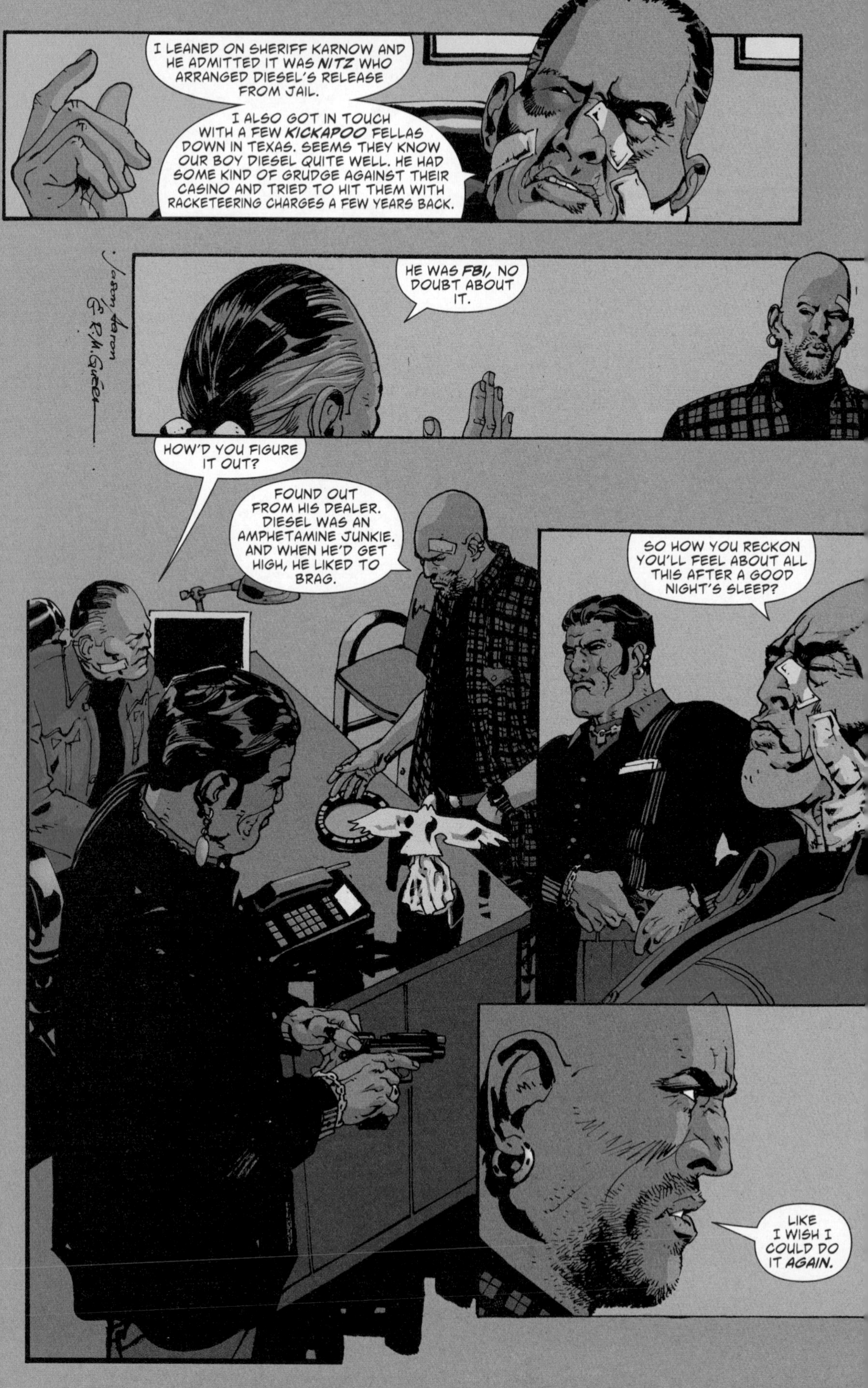
I LEANED ON SHERIFF KARNOW AND HE ADMITTED IT WAS *NITZ* WHO ARRANGED DIESEL'S RELEASE FROM JAIL.
I ALSO GOT IN TOUCH WITH A FEW *KICKAPOO* FELLAS DOWN IN TEXAS. SEEMS THEY KNOW OUR BOY DIESEL QUITE WELL. HE HAD SOME KIND OF GRUDGE AGAINST THEIR CASINO AND TRIED TO HIT THEM WITH RACKETEERING CHARGES A FEW YEARS BACK.
HE WAS *FBI,* NO DOUBT ABOUT IT.
HOW'D YOU FIGURE IT OUT?
FOUND OUT FROM HIS DEALER. DIESEL WAS AN AMPHETAMINE JUNKIE. AND WHEN HE'D GET HIGH, HE LIKED TO BRAG.
SO HOW YOU RECKON YOU'LL FEEL ABOUT ALL THIS AFTER A GOOD NIGHT'S SLEEP?
LIKE I WISH I COULD DO IT *AGAIN.*

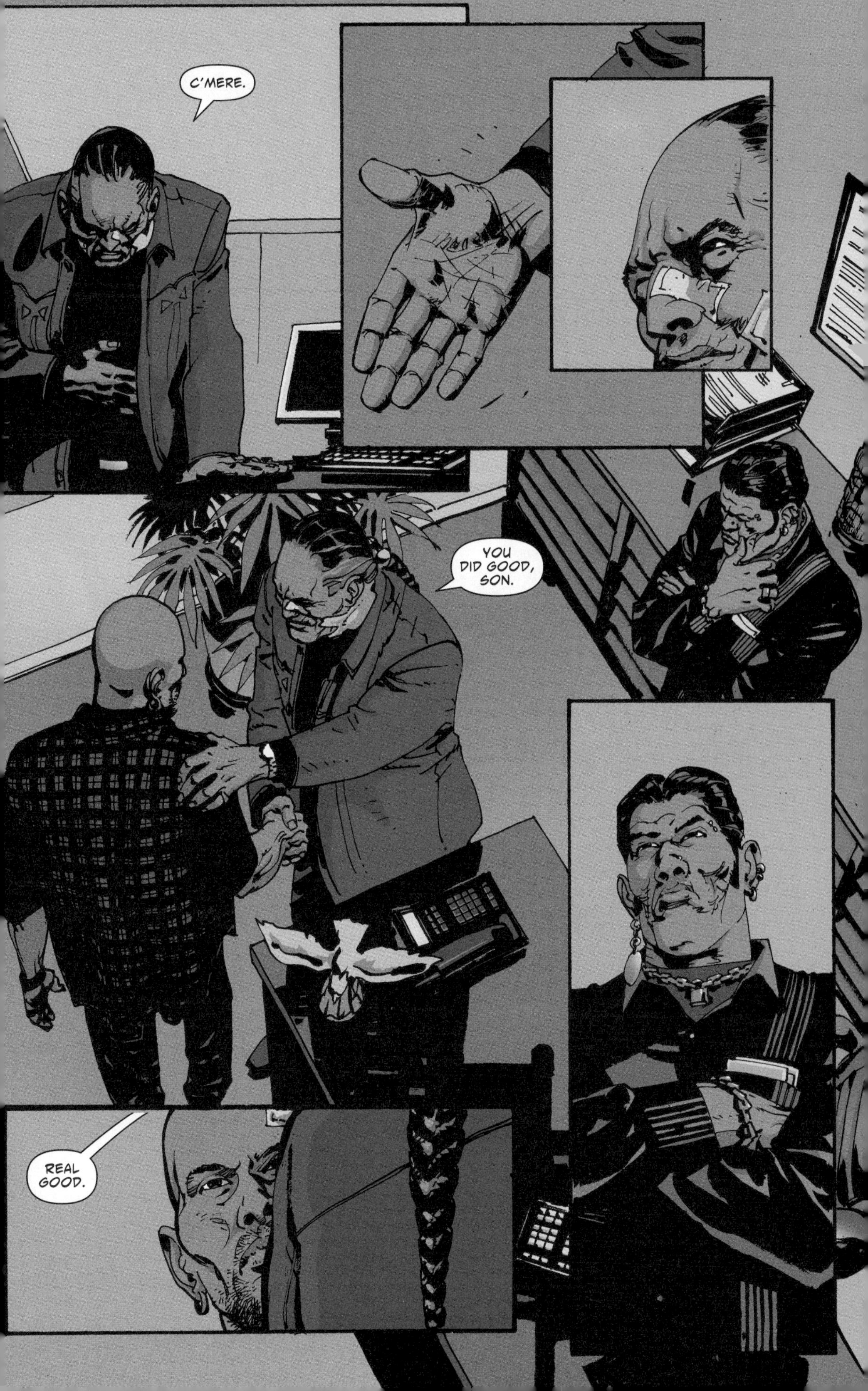
C'MERE.
YOU DID GOOD, SON.
REAL GOOD.

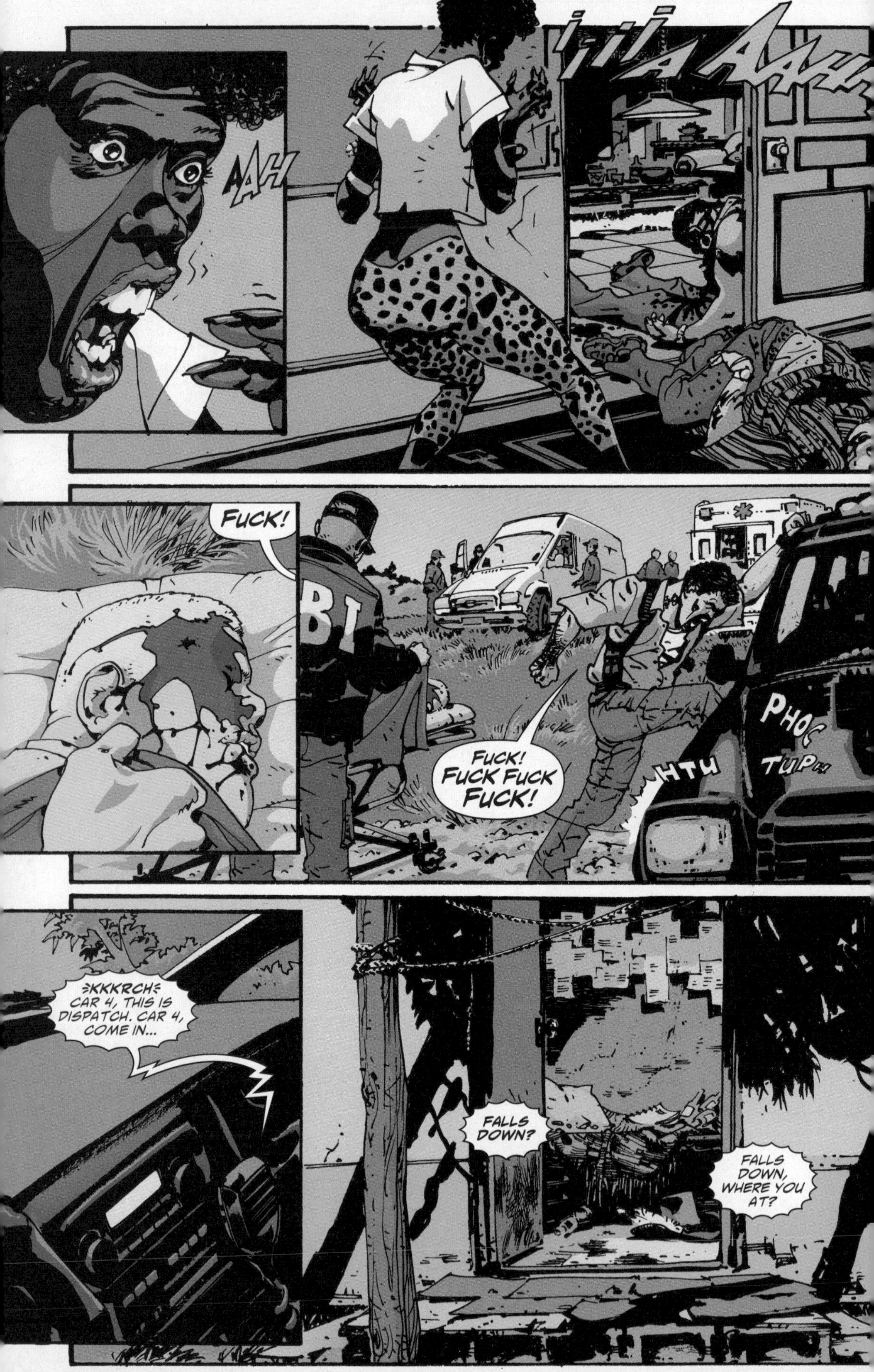

AAH
IIIAAAH
FUCK!
FUCK! FUCK FUCK FUCK!
PHOC
TUP!!
HTU
KKKRCH
CAR 4, THIS IS DISPATCH. CAR 4, COME IN...
FALLS DOWN?
FALLS DOWN, WHERE YOU AT?

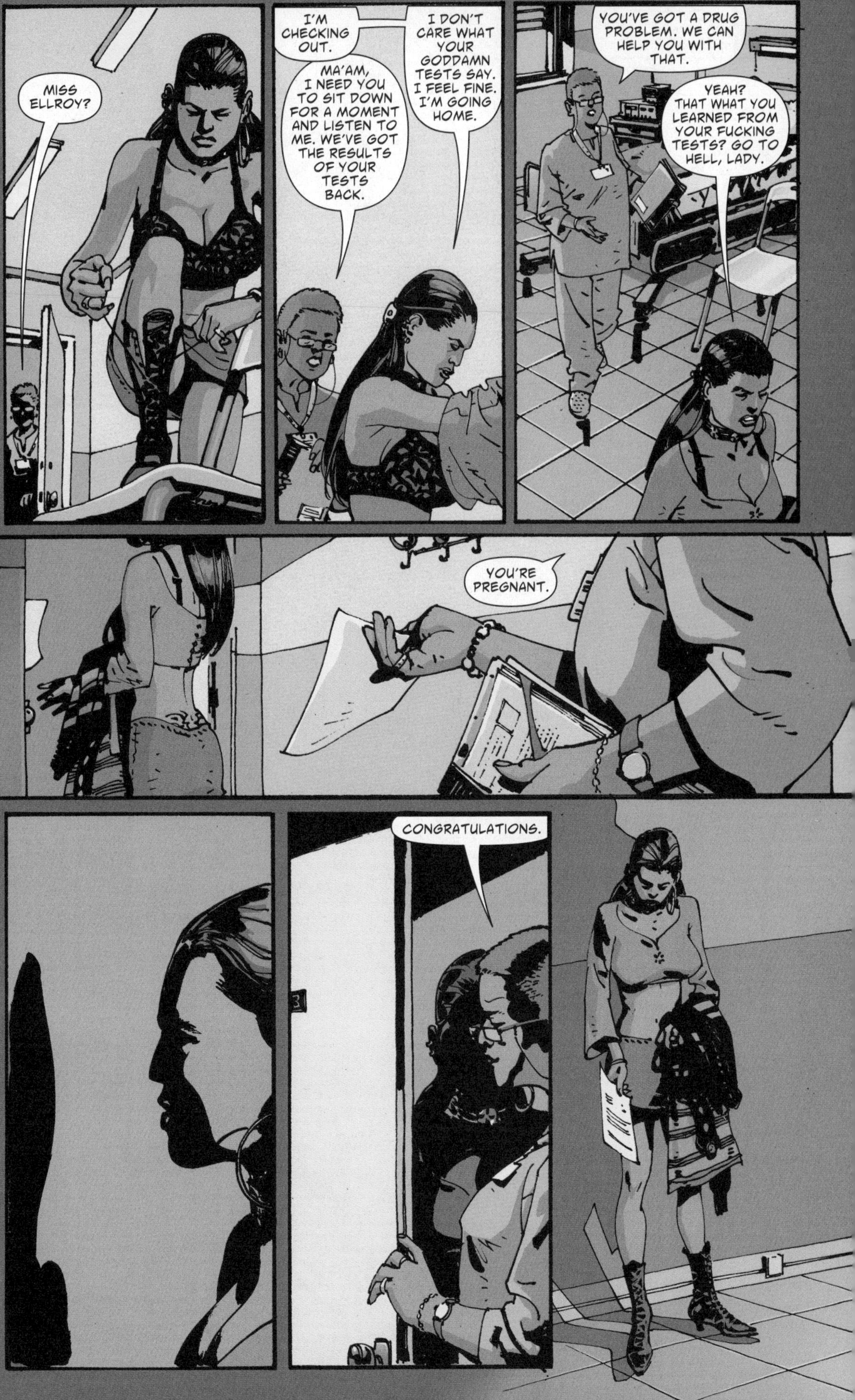
MISS ELLROY?
I'M CHECKING OUT.
MA'AM, I NEED YOU TO SIT DOWN FOR A MOMENT AND LISTEN TO ME. WE'VE GOT THE RESULTS OF YOUR TESTS BACK.
I DON'T CARE WHAT YOUR GODDAMN TESTS SAY. I FEEL FINE. I'M GOING HOME.
YOU'VE GOT A DRUG PROBLEM. WE CAN HELP YOU WITH THAT.
YEAH? THAT WHAT YOU LEARNED FROM YOUR FUCKING TESTS? GO TO HELL, LADY.
YOU'RE PREGNANT.
CONGRATULATIONS.

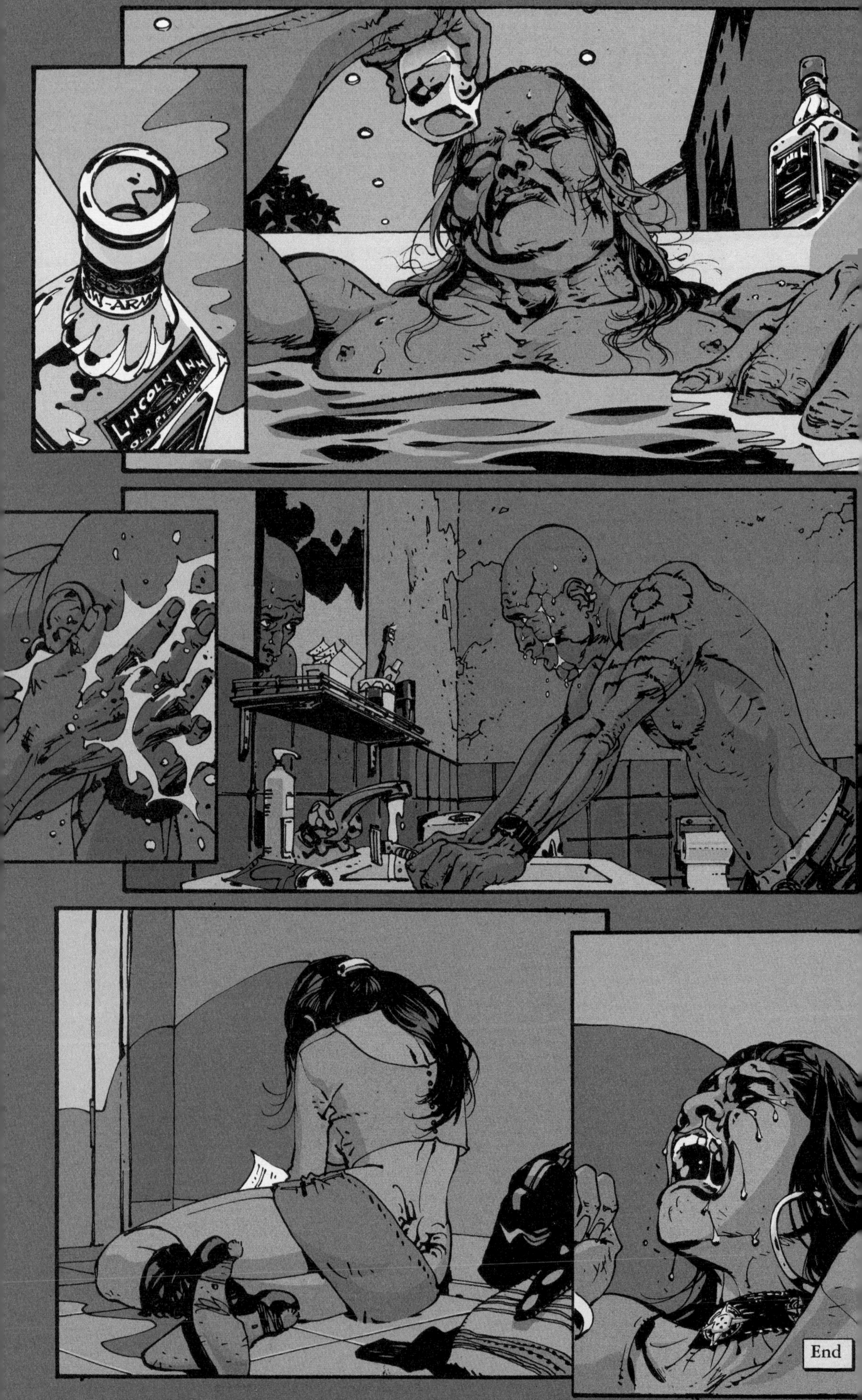
LINCOLN INN
OLD RYE WHISKEY
End